THE IMPOTENT IMAGE

To my mother and father, and those teachers of the social subjects who daily confront the problems of this book where it most matters.

THE
IMPOTENT IMAGE
Reflections of Ideology in the
Secondary School Curriculum

Rob Gilbert

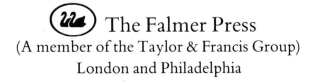 The Falmer Press
(A member of the Taylor & Francis Group)
London and Philadelphia

32403

UK   The Falmer Press, Falmer House, Barcombe, Lewes, East Sussex, BN8 5DL

USA   The Falmer Press, Taylor & Francis Inc., 242 Cherry Street, Philadelphia, PA 19106-1906

First published in 1984

Library of Congress Cataloging in Publication Data

Gilbert, Rob.
  The impotent image.

  Includes bibliographies and index.
  1. Social sciences—Study and teaching (Secondary)—
Great Britain. I. Title.
H62.5.G7G54 1984 300′.7′1241 84-13517
ISBN 1-85000-010-7
ISBN 1-85000-009-3 (pbk.)

Typeset in 11/13 Bembo by
Imago Publishing Ltd, Thame, Oxon

Jacket design by Leonard Williams

Printed in Great Britain by Taylor & Francis (Printers) Ltd, Basingstoke

Contents

Acknowledgements

For their advice, criticism and encouragement: John Eggleston, Pam Gilbert, Peter Gordon, Warren Hawkins, Ian Jackson, Alec McHoul, Geoff Whitty.

For their help with the manuscript: Lois Laivins, Lynne Mac-Lennan, Christine Royal, Maree Searston.

List of Tables and Figures

Introduction: The Impotent Image

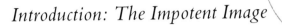

This book is an assessment of the ideas presented to adolescents in the social subjects in British secondary schools. Its importance is seen to lie in two central tenets.

First, the argument holds that in the quest to understand any society, nothing could be more revealing of its values, its central beliefs, its dominant ideologies, than the way the society explains itself to its initiates. If we are to understand the persistence of social problems, one requirement is to identify how people construe them, and how their conceptions of these problems are shaped. An important indicator of this lies in the society's formal attempts to explain these problems in schools.

Second, social understanding is the basis for human action, and the promotion of human welfare through education requires a form of social knowledge compatible with a general humanitarian interest. A social education motivated by this ideal must be clearly aware of the relationship between social knowledge and human action, both in explaining the current condition, and in providing the means for improving it.

Considerations of this kind may account for an increasing interest in the social content of the curriculum in the past decade or so, especially in analyses of current and past school books.[1] But such studies remain few, and the need persists for evaluations of the social subjects and their adequacy as a basis for confronting society's problems. Much of this work will inevitably be specific in its focus, addressing in detail issues of racism, sexism, class or national bias, often in particular discourses such as history or children's stories.

The present study takes a broader perspective; the context of its analysis is a selection of content across the range of the social subjects in the British secondary school. This case material offers the occasion

1

to ask to what extent the knowledge presented might augment the understanding and achievement of a general humanitarian interest, for the promotion of human welfare for all is quite simply the only valid warrant for a compulsory education.

Concepts of human interest are not easily formulated and less easily accepted, but in this work a number of elements of such a concept are taken for granted: that human interest requires a level of material welfare for all, such that people might participate in a normal range of the society's activities; that the expression and achievement of the range of human potentialities should not be arbitrarily prejudiced (say by one's class of origin, sex, race); and that the distribution of power in society should not sustain the interests of the privileged at the expense of those for whom the first two conditions do not apply. Questions of welfare, equality and power are important themes throughout this book.

Of course, all educational prescriptions are informed by some concept of human interest, most often a view of the needs of the individual or society. Social education, as later argument will show, is to a large extent imbued with a participatory and egalitarian ethos, but this seems at odds with the evidence that society is far from equal in the access it provides to welfare and power,[2] and that its power structures are not designed along participatory lines. This raises the interesting question of how curricular and text writers have dealt with this dilemma: the mismatch between curricular aims and the nature of the broader social context is the starting point for the following analysis.

The study proceeds by reviewing the relationships among social knowledge, social structures and schooling, both in the past and present, and argues that the theories on which any social knowledge is based will reflect aspects of the contemporary society. In social education, *a fortiori*, curricular content will be derived from prevailing conceptions of what problems and knowledge are thought most important, which in turn will rest on some view of what roles people will or should play in the social system, and of an appropriate set of social understandings. The important question is whether the theoretical conceptions which have most influenced the content of the social subjects are compatible with the humanitarian ethos of the curricular goals.

To see how this relationship operates in the content of the social subjects, an analytical device called an image is proposed, to represent how theories in the subjects identify and articulate important problems, what factors they deem relevant to explanations, in what terms and from what perspectives. The history of social thought can be viewed in this way, and exemplars are discussed to show how different images of individual human nature and society have operated in the past in conjunction with particular political and economic practices. Images of human nature and society then become the focus for the ideological critique of geography, economics, history and social science in the intermediate years of the British secondary school.

The approach might be termed a contemporary history of the curricular content. For each subject, the history of the discipline and of its teaching in schools is reviewed to establish important themes and issues, which are then investigated in a selection of school texts published or reprinted in the decade from 1969.[3] The analysis highlights ways in which the participatory and egalitarian concern for human welfare, expressed in general statements of the aims of social education, is in conflict with the subjects' images of the individual and society. In many, and on balance, overwhelming ways, the content of the texts is likely to discourage a constructive participation in the social process to promote a general human interest. The argument concludes with some suggestions which might remedy this anomaly.

The overall purpose is to suggest why the social subjects have so seldom been seen as central to the activities of schools, why they are not more highly valued, why they have so many detractors. For it might be expected that, of all areas of the curriculum, those subjects which purport to explain how society operates and how people might best conduct themselves in it would be of central importance. It is the author's hope that this will one day be so, and that the arguments here might contribute to this prospect.

Notes and References

1 See ANYON, J. (1979) 'Ideology and United States History Textbooks', in *Harvard Educational Review*, 43, pp. 361–85; CHANCELLOR, V. (1970) *History for Their Masters: Opinion in the English History Textbook: 1800–1914*, Bath, Adams and Dart; FITZGERALD, F. (1979) *America Revised*, Boston, Little Brown; GOLDSTROM, J. (1972) *The Social Content of Education 1808–1870: A Study of the Working Class School Reader in England and Ireland*, Shannon, Irish University Press; McCANN, P. (Ed.) (1977) *Popular Education and Socialization in the Nineteenth Century*, London, Methuen.

2 Inequality is obvious, but there are those who believe it is not marked, that it is disappearing, and that those who suffer it simply did not take the opportunities for advancement offered them. There is abundant evidence that these beliefs are wrong. Inequality of income and wealth is quite extreme, and has moderated only marginally in Britain in the first half of this century, and since 1950 barely at all. In some areas (of certain health measures, for instance), inequality has increased. Opportunity for mobility is far from equally distributed; for men beginning life in the working class, chances of later improvement have actually declined. Recent history can as fairly be viewed in terms of persisting inequality as egalitarian progress. For evidence of these and other instances of the degree of inequality, see CARTER, C. and PEEL, J. (Eds.) (1976) *Equalities and Inequalities in Health*, London, Academic Press; GEORGE, V. and LAWSON, R. (Eds.) (1980) *Poverty and Inequality in Common Market Countries*, London, Routledge and Kegan Paul; GOLDTHORPE, J. (1980) *Social Mobility and Class Structure in Modern Britain*, Oxford, Clarendon; HALSEY, A., HEATH, A., and RIDGE, J. (1980) *Origins and Destinations: Family, Class, and Education in Modern Britain*, Oxford, Clarendon; TOWNSEND, P. (1979) *Poverty in the United Kingdom*, Harmondsworth, Penguin; WESTERGAARD, J. and RESLER, H. (1976) *Class in a Capitalist Society: A Study of Contemporary Britain*, Harmondsworth, Penguin.

3 Texts were analyzed if they dealt with British rather than overseas topics, were written for the age group indicated, and in the period from 1969. The main source was the University of London Institute of Education's National Textbook Reference Library, though schools, Education Authority Resource Centres and bookshops were also surveyed. In all, 180 books were analyzed. For more details see GILBERT, R. (1982) *Images of Human Nature and Society in the Social Subjects: An Analysis of Ideas in the Secondary School Curriculum*, unpublished PhD thesis, University of London.

1   *Aspiration and Failure in the Social Subjects*

Official bodies are understandably reluctant to specify the intended results of social education[1], for education is meant to change people, and any clear statement of such an intention will provoke accusations of state indoctrination, totalitarianism or conformism. Some people prefer to see education as an unfolding of human nature or the development of the individual's inherent capacities.

Forty years ago such a view was taken when the Spens Committee reported on the curriculum of grammar and technical high schools. In stating its faith in school autonomy of curriculum decision, the report rejected the state control it had noted in the Dominions and on the Continent:

> For where the schools lose their freedom, the freedom of the individual citizen is in peril. The State may through its schools offer much which the young will accept, even with enthusiasm; nevertheless, though they may not know it, their minds are in prison. We find it impossible to believe that a community will not, in the long run, suffer by such a drastic limitation of intellectual autonomy, and that, on the other hand, it has not everything to gain from the free growth of individuality among its potential citizens. *In our view a school fulfils its proper purposes in so far as it fosters that growth, helping every boy and girl to achieve the highest degree of individual development of which he or she is capable....*[2]

But liberalism is never unconditional, and often the most interesting aspect of individualist prescriptions is the nature and source of the limitations they deem necessary. In this case, the Committee saw individual development proceeding within the tradition of 'English character at its best'.[3] Presumably what was best about English character was common knowledge at the time, and quite uncontroversial, for the Committee saw no need to discuss it further. It is significant that this peremptory treatment of social and political questions was in contrast to the report's conscientious review of the individual psychology of intelligence and learning: if the social goals of schooling were unquestioned, education became a technical problem. Modern educators must look enviously on a period when the social implications of curricular specifications could be so glibly dealt with, and relations between the individual and society so simply accepted.

For times have changed, and educators in the last quarter of the twentieth century seem more sensitive to the political implications of educational decisions. A recent statement by Her Majesty's Inspectorate illustrates the problem. In advocating a common curriculum for the schools of England and Wales, they try to avoid a naive individual-society dichotomy, and acknowledge that 'in any curriculum the selection of subjects and skills that are taught and of the attitudes and activities that are encouraged implies certain political and social assumptions and values, however unconscious'.[4] But despite this awareness of the difficulties, the non-commital balancing of contradictory views (so typical of official documents) prevents any solution: neither society nor the schools should arbitrate on what is taught; though education should not give direct ideological support to every aspect of the existing political system, it has to be sensitive to public opinion; schools are accountable to society but do not owe allegiance to particular social philosophies; socialization is justified, but schools must deploy all their resources to help each individual pupil to fulfil her or himself as a person. Such equivocation is common in discussions of social education, a sensitive and controversial topic.

Social Education: The Aspiration ...

The potential for controversy derives from the central position of social knowledge in human experience. How people define, interpret and evaluate day to day events are its very contents. For the social disciplines explicitly or implicitly present a view of human nature. They tell us what people are like, what can be expected of them, how they are motivated, what is important in them to be understood, what unimportant to be ignored. In presenting an image of society they define one's place in it, they proclaim what is possible and what necessary, they explain how things came to be. This is both a service and a monumental arrogance. People need to make sense of their relations with others, to rationalize events, to predict the results of action, and the social disciplines are one source of such knowledge. On the other hand, people are understandably wary of moves to impose definitions on them, to tell them how they should and should not interpret events, what and what not to question. The tension derives from the dual possibilities of social knowledge as 'a potential instrument of the expansion of *rational autonomy of action*, but equally as a potential *instrument of domination*'.[5]

Consider the problems posed by the following statements about the purposes of social education:

> The curricular justification of social subjects lies in ... considerations affecting the whole educational well-being and development of the individual as regards both intellect and personality.[6]

> The problem is to give every man (*sic*) some access to a complex cultural inheritance, some hold on his personal life and on his relationships with the various communities to which he belongs, some extension of his understanding, discrimination and judgment in the human field....[7]

When such hopes are made concrete in stated aims, they are typically of the following form:

> The following cognitive aims apply to the Social Subjects generally:
> 1 to extend the student's knowledge and understanding of his own society and his relationship to it;
> 2 to increase his knowledge and understanding of the world in which he lives;
> 3 to promote a knowledge and understanding of the dynamics of social and environmental change;
> 4 to develop learning skills, problem-solving skills and methods of study.

> In the affective domain the Social Subjects aim to foster the following qualities in the student:
> 1 an enquiring attitude;

2   a willingness to consider differing viewpoints and ways
    of life;
3   an appreciation of human values;
4   a concern for the needs of society and of the environment;
5   a respect for evidence as a basis for forming judgments
    and drawing conclusions.[8]

We are shown here a part of the education system widely
accepted as essential, which attempts to influence in all its clients the
most fundamental aspects of human thought and experience, touch-
ing on the identities of the learners themselves; and which must
assume positions on the most complex questions of the nature of the
individual and society and the relations between the two.

The problems treated so briefly by the Spens Committee are still
with us. Social education aims to change people for the better, and
assumes that this improvement can be beneficial to all, without
favour or distinction. In placing its faith in increased social understanding and sensitivity, it assumes that it can present images of
human nature and society which are accurate and therefore helpful
to people coming to terms with social experience. But accurate
conceptions of social relations are hard to come by, for in studying
people the scholars and teachers are studying themselves, and they
will bring to the task pre-conceived images of what they are trying to
understand. The preconceptions will be difficult to identify; some
may be visible only to future observers.[9] The only sure thing is that
any attempt to describe and explain social experience must contain
assumptions of political and social theory, and that these may be
simply incorrect, leading to misjudgment and failure in social action,
or incomplete, masking possibilities for solving problems. The first
requirement of a successful social education is constant criticism of
these assumptions, testing their limits, challenging their conclusions.

. . . And The Failure

While there are those for whom education is an end in itself, the aims
of the social subjects are most often justified as a preparation for life.
Life needs have been a major source of curricular specification,
challenged only by the structure of knowledge as a determinant of
curriculum planning, both far outstripping the consideration of
student interest. Civic or social competence,[10] political literacy,[11]
and varied interpretations of citizenship[12] have been prescribed as

desirable end products of social education, and the extent to which students exhibit these qualities used as the major yardstick of success in the social subjects. Political education has attempted to develop informed participation in the political process;[13] economics courses have sought more knowledgeable decisions by citizens in their economic roles;[14] and courses in the humanities, history and related subjects have made similar attempts.[15]

It is very difficult to ascertain the success of these curricula, since the problems of identifying effects, attributing causes to them, and establishing with confidence the contribution of schooling, have proved insurmountable. There is, however, little cause for optimism in this uncertainty: research provides few grounds for believing that at present the overt curriculum makes more than a slight and diffuse contribution to people's judgments and actions in the ways aimed at in the social subjects.[16] Researchers and curriculum developers continually lament their failure to produce active, informed partici-pating and effective citizens who will contribute constructively to their society. On the one hand, they complain of the difficulties of changing the curriculum to comply more effectively with the demands of society as they see them: on the other, they bemoan the failure of their graduates to display in action the qualities so fervently proclaimed as the benefits of schooling. The most damning state-ment of this is to be found in a major cross-national study of civic education. Having studied over 30,000 students in ten countries, the authors succinctly reported: 'The widely-held objective of producing loyal, informed, critical, and active participating democratic citizens was *not* successfully attained in any of the countries of this study'.[17] One fault claimed of existing provision is its lack of relevance.

Though the term 'relevance' as generally used is ambiguous and inadequate as a criterion for judging schooling,[18] there can be no escaping the widespread feeling that schooling does not provide the skills, knowledge and dispositions valued by much of the com-munity, and many of the students themselves. Grace's observation of teachers illustrates this problem:

> In particular, many teachers appeared to be convinced that the curriculum was not sufficiently relevant, without being very explicit as to what being more relevant would involve. They appeared to register an *intuitive sense of disjuncture* between the curriculum and their pupils' present and future lives, a sense which they encapsulated as 'not relevant'.[19]

Telling evidence of the disparity between the knowledge valued by educators, parents and students was provided by the Schools Council study of preferred school objectives. Teachers valued such things as personality and character, drama and poetry, much more highly than the other groups, while consistently devaluing, in comparison with parents and students, aspects of education connected directly with careers and everyday life.[20] Studies elsewhere suggest that such disparities are widespread,[21] and that in general the social subjects are not highly valued.[22]

The picture then is of a widespread claim by the education system to develop in pupils an active and informed role in the social process, but a discouraging result of an apparent lack of success and a dearth of interest. In seeking an explanation, it seems necessary to look beyond the immediate possibilities of educational strategy and provision, for the failure is too general to admit of such localized solutions. One possible explanation is proffered by the group of analysts and critics who have argued that schooling is so conducted that, rather than being a force for individual liberation of the kind aspired to in the programmes just discussed, it is in fact an instrument of domination, of social control.

Social Control and Nineteenth-Century Social Education

The argument from the concept of social control is, put bluntly, that schools operate to maintain the existing order by imposing the views of dominant social groups. For instance, Tapper and Salter[23] argue that political education has always aimed at producing stability, involving, in a society such as ours, the legitimation of inequality. Though tensions occur and forces for liberation and change are active, the ultimate condition of stability in a hierarchical society prevents a concerted and radical approach to political education. In accepting this limit, as they must if they are to work within the education system, reformers negate any chance of success, and in the end become, albeit reluctantly, a part of the legitimating process. Tapper and Salter's scepticism reaffirms the futility of a liberating education which does not challenge traditional social relations and control. The result is that, '... political education is in danger of being labelled as an attempt to place ... class control on a firmer and more subtle basis'.[24]

The extent to which this control ideology dominates the present curriculum must for the moment be left open. The historical record however seems clear in its support for this case.

The last 150 years have seen a development in English society from an elitist oligarchy whose power was vested in property and heredity, to a more democratic (or less oligarchic) one where power is more widely distributed on meritocratic and economic lines. Educational change has reflected this shift, its social goals having proceeded from maintaining the power of the natural rulers to accommodating the problems of increased pluralism. While the substance of these political and educational ideas has changed noticeably, the connection inevitably remains, and to grasp its present nature it is useful to analyze earlier conceptions of the proper study of humankind.

The most striking feature of social education seen with the hindsight of a century and a half is the open espousal of the belief that the masses should be educated to accept the contemporary state of society, marked as it was by gross inequalities in power and wealth, and largely bereft of the opportunity for advancement. Social education was clearly viewed by some as the means by which this state of affairs would be continued.

Early nineteenth-century social education was effected through religious instruction, a major goal being that children should 'learn through their readers about the demarcations between rich and poor, and the mutual dependence of each in a harmonious society'.[25] McCann quotes a contemporary explanation of this process by an Evangelical preacher when, speaking on behalf of the new Spitalfields National School in 1819, he said:

> In every country, but especially in this free state, the mass of your Poor, like the base of cone, if it be unsteady and insecure, will quickly endanger every superincumbent part. Religious education, then, is the spring of public tranquility. It not only cherishes the interior principle of conscience; but by infusing the higher sentiments of penitence and faith and gratitude and the love of God communicates the elements of a cheerful and uniform subjection to all lawful authority.[26]

The use of religion in schools as described in these and other educational histories,[27] with its catechistic pedagogy, its premise that society was divinely inspired and not to be questioned, and its rigidly hierarchical view of social structure, was to dominate the first third of the century. Similarly, school history in the first half of the century depended for its existence on highly moralistic elementary readers, the most well known being those written by Mrs Sarah Trimmer and used by the National Society's schools. History was the source of evidence for the infallibility of Christianity, the superiority of the ruling class and the dangers of questioning one's station in life. Even in the public and grammar schools history teaching was desultory, and of poor quality, being seen as a largely profitless distraction from classical studies.[28]

The secularization of schooling in mid-century saw little change in these aspects of social education; catechistic instruction of political economy explained the necessity of social inequality by resort to natural rather than divine law, but these 'ascertained truths' and '*correct* political information', as Kay (later Sir James Kay-Shuttleworth) called them[29] were no less infallible for their changed origin.

The history of political economy in schools is an interesting one,[30] but its influence declined with the religious societies and the general dissipation of the dominance of the curriculum by their set textbooks.[31] However, the tone and substance of the message of political economy for nearly half a century are well illustrated by the British and Foreign School Society's text of 1864:

> Nothing is more certain than that, taking the working classes in the entire mass, they get a fair share of the proceeds of the national industry.[32]

The effects of the Revised Code of 1861, the decline of the influence of the religious societies and their associated publishing enterprises, and the Education Acts of 1870 and 1902 provide something of a hiatus in the development of this theme in the last quarter of the nineteenth century. Goldstrom[33] notes 'a shift in emphasis away from the school-book and towards the training college manual'; and the expansion of schooling and the concomitant decentralization of control renders more difficult broad generalizations about the social content of English education.

However the earlier period just reviewed throws into stark relief the ways in which social education has been used as an instrument of subordination of the masses to the *status quo*. It is important to note however that such a brief review as this ignores the complexity of the matter. While on the one hand there was a clear intention behind the activities of the like of Kay-Shuttleworth and Mrs Trimmer that the masses should know their place and stay in it, they were by no means devoid of philanthropy, and in some respects contributed to their own defeat. The history of nineteenth century England, while lacking the more stormy events of Europe, did see a dilution of the power of the privileged classes, associated with the spread of school knowledge which, while in some ways aimed at ensuring subjection, carried with it at least the seeds of liberation.

The texts were not wholly uncritical of the ruling classes or even the monarchy, which was equally subject to the laws of God and morality, and whose reputations fluctuated with the spirit of the times.[34] Also, as education became institutionalized it developed its own values, which did not always comply with those of its patrons. Tapper and Salter[35] have elaborated on this discrepancy between the expectations or fears of those who see schooling as a conservative force, and the actuality of education's potential for both individual liberty and social control. The National and BFSS schools themselves were using secular books before their respective societies officially condoned them, and the increasing tendency for school books to be written by teachers and academics introduced values of professional 'objectivity' which were to become strong by the turn of the century. Moreover, the middle and later the lower classes made their own demands of the curriculum, and to some extent took from it what they wanted, resisting much of the propaganda.[36]

The Twentieth Century: Ideology or Independence?

Social education since 1900 has been seen as a fluctuating contest between conservative and reformist forces, the former seeing the traditional study of history and geography as adequate preparation for participation in society, the latter advocating various alternatives such as moral instruction, citizenship education, social studies and the newer social sciences.[37] Goldstrom identifies in the nineteenth century the tendency for curriculum development in social education to quicken its otherwise gradual pace in response to fears of social tension and turmoil associated with the French Revolution, the political agitation of the 1830s, and the mass education of future masters towards the end of the century. Similar fluctuation can be identified in the twentieth century, though for different reasons. While the overall trend was towards increasingly scientific history and geography as the standard study of society, the early part of the century saw the continued discussion of the problem of socialization.[38]

A conference on history teaching in 1911 reflects the tension between these two aims, for while lamenting the moralism and propaganda which distorted history in the English past and the contemporary Europe, the conference could not neglect the social purpose of history teaching, with all its attendant moral and political dilemmas:

> ... it is by instilling the historical habit of thought, by re-garding the present in the light of the past, that we can hope best to conserve the good and reform the evil in political and social organizations.[39]

In fact, the debates of the Historical Association conferences of 1906–20 illustrate the range of issues and controversies which have featured in social education curricular discussion in this century, and while some of the positions may have moderated with time, they are quite familiar to the student of the 1980s.[40] At this time, history was the predominant vehicle for social education, and discussion of the need for civic instruction was conducted within the context of history teaching. An illustration is the urgent call by Showan in 1923 for a study of citizenship through history 'with the least possible modification of existing syllabuses'.[41]

Rogers[42] sees 1925 as the turning point in the development of history teaching from a servant of patriotism and citizenship to its own master as an intellectual discipline. It is interesting to note also that 1931 has been nominated as the point when trained professional geographers established their dominance over their subject, and amateurs came to be called 'non-geographers'.[43] And there is evidence that economics became the province of a professional group of academics, as distinct from laymen or generalists or those without specific training, in the 1920s.[44] This growing professionalism is one reason why the social purposes of the social subjects, while still acknowledged, became less direct in their statement and implementation.

The particular academic traditions which had produced this situation no doubt also prevented the overt curriculum from espousing direct political goals. An American observer, Merriam, in reviewing the uses of schooling for political socialization in Europe in 1931, was able, in the case of England, to point to 'a general denial of any conscious attempt to engender national sentiment through the agency of education'.[45] In comparison with the rest of Europe, the English curriculum of the 1920s was not an overt means for national propaganda, though Merriam notes both the stirring fears of developments in the USSR, and the highly effective indirect teaching of civic values and allegiance through the class structure of the English school system. 'On the direct teaching of government as such they lay little emphasis, and are inclined to challenge its value'.[46]

This may in part account for the development in the 1930s of the Association for Education in Citizenship, a broadly based association whose approach to the curriculum was comprehensive, moving beyond the content of the traditional subjects to direct education for citizenship. The Association was an active advocate of strengthening the democratic base of British society in the face of authoritarian challenges abroad. Its rhetoric was alarmist, citing the 'decay of democracy' and the 'crisis of civilization'[47] and its remedies were traditional and elitist, reflecting its origins and chief support in the educational and academic establishment.[48] While its ideals were nobly presented, some of its programmes were strange for their elitist tone and their admiration for the strength and single-mindedness of Fascist and Communist youth education, a sympathy ironically reminiscent of the regimes they wished to combat.[49] The dominant theme was for a strong, 'responsible' citizenry, united in its opposition to attacks on the social democracy that was developing in Britain. The search for a liberal consensus was a search for consensus nonetheless.

Though the influence of the Association for Education in Citizenship carried over to the post-war period, attempts to implement programmes of this kind as social studies were not successful,[50] and more recent variations on the social education curriculum have had similar results. While there is now a greater variety of school subjects related to social education than ever before, this very variety has seemed at times an obstacle to the concerted and substantial change advocated by the reformers,[51] and even the more successful innovations such as economics and sociology have become so by following the example of the traditional subjects, presenting themselves as intellectual disciplines rather than the 'education for life' which the perennial reformers continue to seek.[52] 'In this area of the curriculum schools have shown themselves to be highly resistant to change throughout the century'.[53]

The history of the social education curriculum of the last 150 years, and especially the last fifty, has yet to be written, but this brief review suggests some interesting contrasts between this century and the last. A major preoccupation of social education for most of the nineteenth century was the socialization of the masses in the face of fears of internal disorder and shifts in the distribution of power. This pre-occupation is by no means as prominent in the twentieth century. The growth of professional academic disciplines and the valuing of a scientific objectivity supported the advocates of learning for learning's sake, to whom extraneous purposes seemed corrupting.

Also, while the educational guardians of the nineteenth century genuinely feared internal insurrection, twentieth century fears were provoked more by external affairs, and the literature of the social education curriculum reflects this. The need for knowledge of Empire early in the century, the internationalism which followed two world wars, and the patriotism that preceded them, and most recently the progress to European union have to some extent swung the focus from internal to international considerations. Certainly the implications of nineteenth-century social education content for social relations have received much more critical attention than have those of the twentieth, where until very recently nationalism has apparently been thought a more likely betrayer of objectivity than has social control or class interest.[54]

Eggleston has noted a general dearth of radical discussion over curriculum content in the 1920s and 1930s, when the British left wing debate 'was largely focused on the conflict over distribution under the persistent leadership of Tawney ... a preoccupation that continued at least into the 1960s'.[55] This is borne out by Barker's detailed study of the Labour Party's education policies in the first half of this century, in which he notes that curriculum content was not generally thought the main cause of the social and political effects of education,[56] and that there was little disagreement between Labour and Conservative spokesmen on the nature of citizenship education.[57] Those critics claiming anti-Labour bias and calling for a more radical political education were ignored by the party, or, in the case of the Teachers' Labour League, expelled.[58] Barker holds that after the second war, 'Philistinism and commercialism were to replace capitalism as the leading bogies whose influence it was thought the schools must combat ...'.[59] He concludes of the Labour Party's policies:

The only political organization which could reasonably claim to be the representative of the British working class remained stolidly committed to the value and ethos of the existing order.[60]

No doubt such developments reflect political goals and policies of powerful groups, but incidents like the expulsion of the Teachers' Labour League were, after all, rare. The more pervasive factors in the apparent submergence of overt political propaganda were changes in the disciplines which increasingly provided the basis for the definitions of subjects and the selection of their content. In the early part of this century, a powerful aspect of the approach to social knowledge was the belief in science as the means to enlightenment and social improvement.

In sociology, Comte, Spencer and Durkheim laid the foundations. The geographers Mackinder and Herbertson sought to apply scientific knowledge of the physical environment to explanation of human activities. In history, Ranke was a forerunner to and Comte also an influence on, the traditions of the likes of Bury, and Acton, with his desire to 'meet the scientific demand for completeness and certainty'.[61] Running through this range were a common thread and a number of differences. Common to them was a belief in value-free observations which could establish the facts of a situation. Facts were independent of the enquirer and the enquiry, and the guarantee of truth or accuracy was the rigorous search for more factual information from which more reliable theories or interpretations could be drawn. There were however wide differences among the writers, one important distinction being between those who sought grand theories, such as Toynbee, or Huntington,[62] and those who preferred a close description of individual cases, such as the local studies movement in geography or the historians' emphasis on the uniqueness of individual events.

The faith in science, objectivity and facts as the only valid, and also the most useful form of knowledge, was fitting in a period dominated by the impact of scientific world schemes as neat, universal and certain as Darwin's evolution and Newtonian physics. Such a solid basis for belief and planning was very attractive to social reformers of the day, and T.H. Huxley was one of many who sought 'the reconstruction of society on a scientific basis'.[63] There can be no better and few more important examples than Beatrice Webb's reaction to her reading of Comte and her discussions with Spencer: 'From the flight of emotion away from the service of God to the service of man, and from the current faith in the scientific method, I drew the inference that the most hopeful form of social service was the craft of social investigator'.[64]

The impact of such views on education can not be simply gauged. While the emphasis on facts as the base of knowledge was evident in the calls for more objective content in history and geography, the progressive movement was a counter to the goal of rigorous factual description; the trend was for the elementary school to become more progressive, the secondary school more scientific.[65] On the choice between grand theory and idiographic description the latter won out, probably because the theory of knowledge regarded it as more reliable, it fitted the tradition of memorization and examination in schools, and it was felt that pupils were not capable of abstract theorizing. It was also politically safer.

But the development was for educationists a solution and a dilemma. For those concerned about the dangers of opinion, radical ideas, or indoctrination of the *status quo*, the concentration on fact was thought to offer a way of distributing valuable knowledge, free of political constraint and controversy. On the other hand, for those concerned with the moral ends of education, it created the difficulty of relating objective and value-free knowledge to the inculcation of moral values. To complicate things further, many, perhaps most, were in both camps. Reformers sought objectivity as a means of breaking down traditional prejudices, but also wanted to develop moral ideals such as compassion and social justice. Conservatives saw facts as a way of avoiding radical theories, but found it difficult to ensure the continuance of traditional virtues and values. The belief that only facts could be demonstrated meant that values could only be asserted.[66]

With periodic exceptions, this approach through 'scientific' understanding has this century been a dominant ethos in the social disciplines; but the traditional value-laden role of education as a vehicle for social progress and individual improvement remains. This ambiguity is an interesting entry point for the search for answers to the questions of aspiration, failure and social control. For in understanding how social education has sought to resolve this dilemma, we can discover how it has defined social progress and individual improvement, how it has sought to implement these conceptions in practice, and how compatible the definitions and practices are with the espoused ideal that the needs of students and society are best realized by an active, informed and discriminating citizenry.

Conclusion

Stated aims of social education are imbued with an ideal that schooling will operate in the best interests of students and society at large. The public response to many of the subjects indicates that this ideal is not often realized. Critics have in fact argued that the ideal is, if not hypocritical, at least naive, and that the social subjects are for the most part vehicles of social control.

Clearly the social control argument has much to support it in the educational record of the nineteenth century, but the social content of the curriculum has in more recent times been dominated by claims of objectivity. Overt moralizing has become less apparent, and emphases on disciplined enquiry have lauded critical thought, problem solving and the acquisition of concepts. Social control, if it exists, is not what it used to be.

The argument of the following analysis is that, by design or otherwise, social control is an inevitable outcome of much of the social content of the contemporary curriculum. Armed with an understanding of the kind of knowledge which would best promote the student interest in the present society, we must conclude that the social subjects have not only not provided, but have ignored and even contradicted it. But such an argument is based on particular views of human interest, the present social order, and the social knowledge which constitutes them. These perspectives must first be established.

Notes and References

1 Precision requires some clarification of terms. *Social education* refers to the process of curriculum development and teaching about society, and is based on the recognized *social disciplines* such as history, geography, law, and the *social sciences*, here used in the narrow sense to include sociology, anthropology, psychology and political science. Social education is carried out through the overt school curriculum in subjects referred to here as the *social subjects*, which include, as well as the disciplines above; *social studies* (a subject whose long history has made it

a familiar and widely if inconsistently used label), *social science* (a relatively recent development based largely on sociology and political science), and other activities like moral education, liberal studies, integrated studies, where these are scheduled parts of the school curriculum.

2 GREAT BRITAIN BOARD OF EDUCATION (1938) *Report of the Consultative Committee on Secondary Education with Special Reference to Grammar Schools and Technical High Schools*, London, HMSO, p. 151.
3 *Ibid.* p. 153.
4 GREAT BRITAIN DEPARTMENT OF EDUCATION AND SCIENCE (1977) *Curriculum 11–16. Working Papers by H.M. Inspectorate: A Contribution to Current Debate*, London, HMSO, p. 10.
5 GIDDENS, A. (1976) *New Rules for Sociological Method: A Positive Critique of Interpretative Sociologies*, London, Hutchinson, p. 159.
6 SCOTTISH EDUCATION DEPARTMENT CONSULTATIVE COMMITTEE ON THE CURRICULUM (1973) *Bulletin No. 1. Social Subjects for Young School Leavers*, Edinburgh, HMSO, p. 3.
7 SCHOOLS COUNCIL (1965) *Raising the School Leaving Age. A Cooperative Programme of Research and Development*, Working Paper No. 2, London, HMSO, p. 14.
8 SCOTTISH EDUCATION DEPARTMENT (1976) *Curriculum paper No. 15: the Social Subjects in Secondary Schools*, Edinburgh, HMSO, p. 26.
9 As Pocock notes: 'It is part of normal experience to find our thought conditioned by assumptions and paradigms so deep-seated that we did not know they were there until something brought them to the surface; we suspect, if we are historians, that there are others present and operative of which we shall never be aware because they will only be visible from the vantage-points provided by historical moments in the future'. POCOCK, J. (1971) *Politics, Language and Time. Essays on Political Thought and History*, London, Methuen, p. 32.
10 PIPER, K. (1977) *Essential Learning About Society*, Hawthorn, Australian Council for Educational Research.
11 CRICK, B. and PORTER, A. (Eds.) (1978) *Political Education and Political Literacy*, London, Longman.
12 SHAVER, J. (1977) *Building Rationales for Citizenship Education*, Arlington, National Council for the Social Studies.
13 CRICK, B. and PORTER, A. (Eds.) (1978) *op. cit.*
14 DUNNING, K. (1975) 'Aims in economic education', in LEE, N. (Ed.) *Teaching Economics*, London, Heinemann Educational; JOINT COMMITTEE OF THE ROYAL ECONOMIC SOCIETY, ASSOCIATION OF UNIVERSITY TEACHERS OF ECONOMICS, and ECONOMICS ASSOCIATION (1973) *The Teaching of Economics in Schools*, London, Macmillan.
15 SCHOOLS COUNCIL (1967) *Society and the Young School Leaver: A Humanities Programme in Preparation for the Raising of the School Leaving Age*, London, HMSO; COLTHAM, J. and FINES, J. (1972) *Educational Objectives for the Study of History: A Suggested Framework*, London, Historical Association.
16 SHAVER, J. and LARKINS, A. (1973) 'Research on Teaching Social

Studies', in TRAVERS, R. (Ed.) *Second Handbook of Research on Teaching*, Chicago, Rand McNally; HEATER, D. (1977) 'International studies at school level: the findings of recent British research', in CRICK, B. and HEATER, D. (Eds.) *Essays in Political Education*, Lewes, Falmer Press.

17 TORNEY, J., OPPENHEIM, A. and FARNEN, R. (1975) *Civic Education in Ten Countries*, New York, Wiley, p. 18.

18 See HAYDON, G. (1973) 'Educational relevance: a slogan examined', in *Proceedings of the Philosophy of Education Society of Great Britain*, 7, 2, pp. 223–38; MADGIC, R. (1973) *Relevance and the Social Studies: A Conceptual Analysis*, Belmont, Fearon.

19 GRACE, G. (1978) *Teachers, Ideology and Control: A Study in Urban Education*, London, Routledge and Kegan Paul, p. 195.

20 SCHOOLS COUNCIL (1968) *Enquiry 1. Young School Leavers. Part 2.* London, HMSO.

21 PIPER, K. (1977) *op. cit.*

22 EHMAN, L. (1977) 'Research on social studies curriculum and instruction: values' in HUNKINS, F. *Review of Research in Social Studies Education: 1970–1975*, Boulder, ERIC Clearinghouse for Social Studies/Social Science Education Consortium.

23 TAPPER, T. and SALTER, B. (1978) *Education and the Political Order: Changing Patterns of Class Control*, London, Macmillan.

24 *Ibid.* p. 20.

25 GOLDSTROM, J. (1977) 'The content of education and the socialization of the working-class child, 1830–1860', in McCANN, P. (Ed.) *Popular Education and Socialization in the Nineteenth Century*, London, Methuen, p. 98.

26 McCANN, P. (1977) 'Popular education, socialization and social control: Spitalfields 1812–1824' in McCANN, P. (Ed.) *op. cit.* p. 1.

27 CHANCELLOR, V. (1970) *History for their Masters: Opinion in the English History Textbook: 1800–1914*, Bath, Adams and Dart; GOLDSTROM, J. (1972) *The Social Content of Education 1808–1870: A Study of the Working Class School Reader in England and Ireland*, Shannon, Irish University Press.

28 DOBSON, J. (1957) 'The teaching of history in English grammar schools and private schools: 1830–1870' in *The Durham Research Review*, 8, pp. 129–41; HOLWELL, E. (1967) 'The teaching of history in public and endowed schools in the middle of the nineteenth century', in *The Durham Research Review*, V, 9, 179–188.

29 JONES, D. (1977) 'Socialization and social science: Manchester Model Secular School 1854–1861', in McCANN, P. (Ed.) *op. cit.*

30 GILMOUR, R. (1967) 'The Gradgrind school: political economy in the classroom', *Victorian Studies*, 11, pp. 205–24; GOLDSTROM, J. (1966–7) 'Richard Whately and political economy in school books, 1833–80', in *Irish Historical Studies*, 15, 131–46; MARSH, J. (1977) 'Economics education in schools in the nineteenth century: social control' in *Economics*, 13, pp. 116–18.

31 GOLDSTROM, J. (1972) *op. cit.*

32 From the British and Foreign School Society Lesson Book for Standard

3, 1864, p. 50. Quoted in GOLDSTROM, J. (1972) *op. cit.*, p. 170.

33 GOLDSTROM, J. (1972) *op. cit.*, p. 175.

34 CHANCELLOR, V. (1970) *op. cit.*

35 TAPPER, T. and SALTER, B. (1978) *op. cit.*

36 McCANN, P. (1977) *op. cit.*; RUBINSTEIN, D. (1977) 'Socialization and the London School Board 1870–1904: aims, methods and public opinion' in McCANN, P. (Ed.) *op. cit.*; JONES, D. (1977) *op. cit.*

37 CANNON, C. (1964) 'Social studies in secondary schools', in *Educational Review*, 17, pp. 18–30; BERNBAUM, G. (1969) 'Sociology and general studies', in *Education and Social Science*, 1, pp. 21–30; GORDON, P. and LAWTON, D. (1978) *Curriculum Change in the Nineteenth and Twentieth Centuries*, London, Hodder and Stoughton.

38 BRAMWELL, R. (1961) *Elementary School Work 1900–1925*, Institute of Education, University of Durham.

39 LONDON COUNTY COUNCIL EDUCATION COMMITTEE (1911) *Report of a Conference on the Teaching of History in London Elementary Schools*, London County Council Education Office.

40 ROGERS, A. (1961–2) 'Why teach history? The answer of fifty years, 1', in *Educational Review*, 14, 10–20.

41 SHOWAN, P. (1923) *Citizenship and School*, Cambridge, Cambridge University Press, p. 1.

42 ROGERS, A. (1961–2) *op. cit.*

43 GILBERT, E. (1972) *British Pioneers in Geography*, Newton Abbot, David and Charles, p. 27.

44 COATS, A. (1967) 'Sociological aspects of British economic thought (ca. 1880–1930)', in *Journal of Political Economy*, 75, p. 723.

45 MERRIAM, C. (1931) *The Making of Citizens*, Chicago, University of Chicago Press, p. 96.

46 *Ibid.*

47 ASSOCIATION FOR EDUCATION IN CITIZENSHIP (1935) *Education for Citizenship in Secondary Schools*, London, Oxford University Press, p. v.

48 For details of the Association's members and its basically conservative goals, see WHITMARSH, G. (1974) 'The politics of political education: an episode', in *Journal of Curriculum Studies*, 6, pp. 133–42.

49 HAPPOLD, F. *et. al.* (1937) *Experiments in Practical Training for Citizenship*, London, Association for Education in Citizenship.

50 CANNON, C. (1964) *op. cit.*

51 Newmann has noted this result in the United States. NEWMANN, F. (1977) 'Building a rationale for civic education', in SHAVER, J. (Ed.) *op. cit.*

52 GLEESON, D. and WHITTY, G. (1976) *Developments in Social Studies Teaching*, London, Open Books; EGGLESTON, J. (1977) *The Sociology of the School Curriculum*, London, Routledge and Kegan Paul.

53 GORDON, P. and LAWTON, D. (1978) *op. cit.* p. 120.

54 DANCE, E. (1960) *History the Betrayer: A Study in Bias*, London, Hutchinson; HALES, E. (1970) 'History in Europe's secondary schools', *Trends in Education*, 17, 16–20.

55 EGGLESTON, J. (1977) *op. cit.* p. 41.

56 BARKER, R. (1972) *Education and Politics: 1900–1951: A Study of the Labour Party*, Oxford, Oxford University Press, p. 137.
57 *Ibid.*, p. 140. Whitmarsh's study shows the relative ease with which Liberal, Labour and Conservative sympathies joined forces in the Association for Education in Citizenship. WHITMARSH, G. (1974) *op. cit.* pp. 137–8.
58 BARKER, R. (1972) *op. cit.* p. 152. An exception was a 1926 Conference resolution calling for a report on the eradication of class bias in school methods and materials, and for the cultivation of a proletarian attitude to life. The motion was subsequently revised in committee and its radical import emasculated. *Ibid.* pp. 149ff.
59 *Ibid.* p. 154.
60 *Ibid.* p. 158.
61 Quoted in MARWICK, A. (1970) *The Nature of History*, London, Macmillan, p. 54.
62 On Huntington's environmental determinism, see FREEMAN, T. (1961) *A Hundred Years of Geography*, London, Duckworth, p. 314.
63 Quoted in HOUGHTON, W. (1957) *The Victorian Frame of Mind*, New Haven, Yale University Press, p. 35.
64 Quoted in MACKENZIE, N. and MACKENZIE, J. (1979) *The First Fabians*, London, Quartet Books, p. 124.
65 The Spens Report noted this distinction between activity and experiential approaches to learning in primary schools, and the emphasis on acquisition and storage of factual knowledge in secondary school. GREAT BRITAIN BOARD OF EDUCATION (1938) *op. cit.*
66 However, while the fact-value dichotomy led to moral relativism in some, the more common response was to argue moral imperatives from a base of religion, idealism, or tradition. Citing Acton as an example, Watson argues: 'The morality of the age is objectivist, and contemptuous of the view that moral choices are merely matters of personal opinion'. WATSON, G. (1973) *The English Ideology: Studies in the Language of Victorian Politics*, London, Allen Lane, p. 52.

2 Order, Action and Social Knowledge: The Ideological Role of Images of the Individual and Society

The preceding discussion questioned the extent to which school curricula reflect the goals of the social subjects with their emphasis on a willing and effective application to and participation in the process of individual and social betterment. Part of the problem as expressed by pupils and their parents, as well as the critics of the left (if for different reasons), has been the mismatch between the practice and ideals of the social subjects and the demands of life outside school.

An obvious element of this mismatch is the apparent conflict between egalitarian curricular aims and the inequality of the society to which they are intended to contribute. Inequality is, *prima facie*, an important aspect of the difficulties in social education which prompt this study. It is, however, also a fundamentally important social problem in its own right. Gross inequality in material resources prevents the poor from participating in the normal activities of their society. Lack of power in its various forms can prevent individuals and groups from fulfilling their legitimate interests. To the extent that inequality limits human expression and achievement, it is an evil to be overcome. To the extent that it can be exposed and criticized in schools, it is an important issue in the curricula of the social subjects.

It has been shown that the social content of the nineteenth century curriculum aimed at promoting social harmony. In the grossly unequal social relations of the time this harmony could be rationalized only by showing how the more favoured groups were deserving of their position (through moral desert, divine blessing or natural law), and how the existence of society was dependent on this arrangement.

However, after World War 1 the professionalism of the disciplines was gaining ascendance, with its values of objectivity and its tradition of defending the integrity of the academic pursuit. This coincided with a period in which advocates of the direct social purpose of the curriculum were prompted by international events to seek to develop ideals of patriotism, community service and leadership, rather than the nineteenth century ideals of contented submission. Also, critics of the curriculum's content were moved more by international and cultural ideas than by egalitarian resistance to hierarchical ideology. For most of the twentieth century, there has been a general lack of concern for connections between social inequality and curriculum content.[1]

This allows a number of explanations. The most obvious is the claim that inequality no longer exists, and that the curriculum need not, indeed cannot, say anything about it. However, evidence exists of high degrees of inequality in important elements of welfare, and in the opportunity for individual advancement.[2] In many of them change in the degree of inequality has not been great for much of this century; in some respects it has grown worse. Large parts of the population are deprived of welfare and benefits they might under different social arrangements have.[3] The system favours some over others, and the lack of ideological debate over curriculum content cannot be attributed to the eradication of inequality.

Another view might be that professional objectivity created a curriculum which was either impartial or benign on issues of inequality of power and welfare. The first alternative can be associated with Bell's famous 'end of ideology' thesis, that the welfare state, decentralized power, the mixed economy and political pluralism produced 'a rough consensus among intellectuals on political issues'.[4] The second alternative of a wholly benign account of society would be possible only if all people's interests could equally be served by a single set of policies, for then a wholly benign social content would be the values, knowledge and skills which would best advance these policies.

While such beliefs may well account for the relative lack of critique of curricular ideology in earlier decades, neither option is viable. Impartiality is impossible in the study of a society which creates unjust inequality through its structure and rules of operation (though, unfortunately, indifference is not). And since in an unequal situation moves to equality cannot benefit all, no set of policies and related ideas and skills can be universally beneficial in all respects.[5] Thus social studies are always potentially controversial, since they will either ignore or comment on aspects of society which reveal and produce inequality, the differential access to resources, welfare and power which favours some people and handicaps others.

But the curriculum in the social subjects has rarely been controversial in this way; it has not drawn critical attention to the inequalities, their causes, and remedies. Here lies a clue to the problem posed earlier, for no social subject can promote a questioning participation in an unequal society without either provoking controversy and criticism, or disguising or legitimating the inequality. In the latter case, the subject will clearly be open to accusations of irrelevance and insincerity, and will not address the problems of people trying to overcome inequality in their attempts to promote their own and others' welfare.[6]

There are grounds then to believe that the curriculum justifies inequality and legitimates the system which sustains it. Since the critical factors in the defence and legitimation of inequality are power and the idea of authority, the argument so far directs attention to the political system and how it is explained, the connection between social order and social knowledge.

The Political System, Social Order, and Political Knowledge

There is widespread agreement among political analysts that the dominant political system in the western world can be described as a 'pluralist elitist equilibrium model' of democracy.[7]

Pluralism has been the modern attempt to establish harmony amongst diverse interests and to prevent any single group from dominating. Its main features have been listed as an acknowledgement of the necessity of diverse interests; acceptance of the right of all legitimate groups to be heard and protected; the assumption that human attachment is to group rather than general interests; a conciliatory and accommodating role for state intervention; and the recognition of the need for some diffusion of power among groups so they can effectively press their interests.[8]

By emphasizing groups rather than individuals, and representation rather than participation, by recognizing only some groups as 'legitimate' voices for individual interests, and by permitting inequality of access and influence among groups, modern democracy has been described as elitist, usually, though by no means always, pejoratively. Twentieth century political elitism includes the advocacy of elites of experts, and the meritocratic ethos provides a justification for this.[9] Democracy is then a mechanism consisting of 'a competition between two or more self-chosen sets of politicians (elites), arrayed in political parties, for the votes which will entitle them to rule until the next election. The voters' role is not to decide political issues and then choose representatives who will carry out these decisions: it is rather to choose the men who will do the deciding'.[10]

Some supporters of greater citizen participation government deny that this can be called democracy, much less an ideal form of it. They prefer such labels as 'elective autocracy'.[11] Other writers have argued its merits. Speaking of its American performance, Dahl concludes 'it appears to be a relatively efficient system for reinforcing agreement, encouraging moderation, and maintaining social peace in a restless and immoderate people operating a gigantic, powerful, diversified, and incredibly complex society'.[12] English commentators have similarly praised the efficiency of the system. Plamenatz[13] sees the process as a rational way of conducting affairs, since the voter places confidence and authority in the hands of the political leader, subject to the constant influence of pressure group politics and the ultimate control of the next election. Oakeshott[14] has been similarly sanguine about the scheme, seeing no need for greater participation in any but its present form. These views hold that, far from indicating apathy, the present level of citizen participation is adequate for the operation of the system, and that people are right in being satisfied with it. The implications of these views will be important considerations in deciding appropriate types of social education.

A third major feature of present democracy is the notion that it provides an equilibrium between the demand and supply of political goods. The popularity of the economic analogy is related to the more general rise of the input–output model of systems analysis, and its provision of a modern counterpart to the idea of harmony and Adam Smith's 'invisible hand'. It found widespread acceptance among major theorists of this form of democracy.

> They all see the citizens as political consumers, with very diverse wants and demands. They all see competition between politicians for the citizens' votes as the motor of the system. They all find that this mechanism does produce a stable equilibrium.[15]

This third element not only explains the operation of the system and its persistence, but is also a measure of its success, and becomes a justification. The implication that the system is neutral, even natural, in its operation, masks many of its much criticized features, raising again the problem of the way this feature of the model will be incorporated into teaching about society.

Two related aspects of the elitist and pluralist nature of modern democracy are the importance to the system of bureaucratic and professional functionaries. Developed by applying the ideas of specialization and division of labour to knowledge of how the system works, bureaucracy and professionalism relieve the citizens of the need, and in so doing deprive them of the ability, to become directly involved in decision making. Birnbaum shows how theorists have related this development to the widespread apathy of western political publics, and concludes:

> In the models of Parsons, Easton and Dahl, an empirically established political apathy is explained by the survival of primary groups and of communal or organic forms of social organization. This depoliticization, contrary to classical models of democracy, is then accepted and justified by the assertion of the inevitable character of the division of labour which requires entrusting the regulation of the social system to professionals who will exercise this power in a neutral and legitimate fashion. The political apathy of citizens devoted to their private life, the professionalization of elites accepting as their duty the organization of the social system, these should be the bases of a new consensus which is quite compatible with the absence of citizen participation.[16]

These arrangements must be viewed critically in any assessment of how they are to influence curriculum planning, but for the moment it can be noted that such a system presents a view of knowledge as instrumental, specialized and neutral, and will function best not on a high degree of citizen participation but on the practice of 'reasoned deference'.[17] For instance, in Plamenatz' view,

> ... only a minority should be founders and managers of associations having a considerable influence on the government or on the people generally, or should be able to publish their opinions widely....[18]

This is so mainly for pragmatic reasons, that leaders 'must not have more information or more advice thrust upon them than they can take in and act upon'.[19] The only condition is that the 'associations' mentioned 'must cover all sections of the people, and there must be freedom to compete for popular support between them and sometimes even inside them'.[20] Plamenatz does not explain just how it is that the number of associations is small enough not to strain the leaders' ability to take in information. Nor does he elaborate on how 'freedom to compete' should be defined, especially whether groups are free irrespective of their relative power to influence government decisions or publicize their activities.

The elitist, pluralist model is strong here, but the educational significance of these analyses of liberal democracy lies in its influence on the world of ideas, the way the political system becomes a political culture – how it is described and evaluated, the symbols it creates, and the issues it raises or disguises. The most obvious implication is the knowledge required by the citizen in such a system.

One extreme view is that illustrated in the following criticism of the Hansard Society's programme for Political Education. Inspired largely by Bernard Crick, the programme aims to create 'a proclivity to action' in people 'able to devise strategies for influencing and achieving change'.[21] In questioning this goal, one political historian has observed:

> All political science suggests the need for a great mass of passivity as ballast. Professor Crick gives no serious answer to the question of what a society of politically literate people all taking part in making arrangements would involve ... but the real objection is that it is impossible. He does not propose to repeal the iron law of oligarchy; yet the elite, acting in the name of equality, are to coerce those, who by position, habit, and probably inclination are and must be outside the political nation, into adopting the vocabulary and responses of an elite which they cannot in principle join.[22]

More commonly, advocates of pluralism argue that citizens must be informed of the possibilities of the solution to problems, their likely consequences (though Plamenatz questions even this),[23] and who might best be entrusted with them, but they do not need to know how to solve them themselves, nor can they contribute to decisions about the solutions.

It is not a condition of political responsibility that all or most electors should understand the policies of the candidates or parties competing for their votes.[24]

Similarly conservative views on the relation between knowledge and politics are argued by Hayek and Oakeshott, though like Plamenatz in the liberal tradition. Hayek[25] and Oakeshott[26] argue that rationalism in politics and social planning are misplaced, for the political culture has been developed through evolution, not design. Since it is impossible to know all the facts of a situation, and to predict the consequences of an action, scientific planning and a rationalist approach to social problems are dangerous. Again the main point is that this approach to politics leads to the conclusion that citizens should not seek major social change through the application of reason. A school subject aimed at developing a rationalist approach to political problems and planning would be seen as folly.[27]

But there are other characteristics of the pluralist, elitist equilibrium model which, while having less overt relevance for the form and goals of social education, clearly influence its content. For if such a model is accepted as the closest approximation to present social reality, it predisposes us to focus attention on those aspects of society which are most important to it, and can disguise alternative possibilities which its adherents have chosen, or found necessary, to ignore.

As the ideology of pluralism was developed to accommodate divergent group interests, and the belief in expertise and competence as a way of achieving them, the political culture became preoccupied with the means of satisfying diverse ends, rather than of assessing the ends themselves. Political problems became technical problems, and were therefore to be dealt with not by citizens or even politicians, but by technical and professional experts. 'The further the competence of the latter spread, the more oligarchy replaced democracy; the more broad political discussion was replaced by particular and technical discussion, the more fragmented and inaccessible the action of the state became'.[28]

Barker has traced in twentieth century British political thought, and Howell[29] in the deliberations of its largest reformist party, how political debate contracted from ideas of ideology or interpretations of national interest, to problems of making the system work, a process as Oakeshott put it, in which there is 'neither starting-place nor appointed destination. The enterprise is to keep afloat on an even keel'.[30] Oakeshott's metaphor of the ship of state is more plainly put by Enoch Powell:

So far as I have ideals, which is an inappropriate word – I prefer to say political objects – they are much more concerned with the removal of blemishes or the avoidance of dangers than with the idea of a democracy which pre-exists in the mind.[31]

This political empiricism was echoed in academic political thought,[32] for the shift of the study of politics to the behaviourist school and fuctionalist ideology had produced a similar separation of means and ends, and in doing so provided arguments of justification for the system,[33] and a compatible view of political education which emphasized its socializing role.[34] Ironically, a clear and most authoritative testimony to this comes from Zbigniew Brzerzinski:

A profound change in the intellectual community itself is inherent in this development. The largely humanist-oriented, occasionally ideologically-minded intellectual dissenter, who saw his role largely in terms of proferring (*sic*) social critiques, is rapidly being displaced either by experts and specialists, who become involved in special government undertakings, or by the generalist-integrators, who become house-ideologues for those in power, providing overall intellectual integration for disparate actions.[35]

Wolin[36] and Hayek[37] link the decline of political philosophy and its concern for ends, and the rise of empiricism, especially in economics, as the terms in which social thought is conducted, to the liberal tradition developed by pluralists and the advocates of efficient organization. By deeming impossible the problems of the questions of ends and ideas of general interest, liberal theory was left only to provide a framework which would accommodate what divergence it could, bending to its framework those interests which did not easily adjust to it, ignoring those interests which it could not satisfy. 'Contrary to what modern interpretations of liberalism have led us to suppose, we find later liberals devoting a surprising amount of emphasis to justifying the necessity and desirability of social conformity'.[38]

Similarly, by seeing the political system as a framework within which social and economic relations could proceed unimpeded, the liberal conception of politics created for itself an impossible dilemma. It has been argued that equal political power has never been a goal of liberal political democracy (certainly the nineteenth-century founders of modern democracy saw no contradiction in giving some citizens more votes than others), but the modern myth of one vote, one value must certainly assume equality as its moral base. Yet it is pointless to claim political equality in a situation of gross social and economic inequality, not to mention the great discrepancy between citizens in political influence beyond the level of voting. The dilemma of liberalism is how to reconcile a *laissez faire* philosophy with the need to eradicate oppressive social inequality.

The idea of a dominant social theory related to politics and policy needs much qualification, and its unity and hegemonic nature should not be put too simply. But the rise of bureaucracy and professionalism has institutionalized orthodoxies into dominant roles in social policy. Keynesian economics, organization theory and the welfare state are examples of social theory which have rapidly gained widespread acceptance and application through bureaucratic admin-istration. In an unprecedented way, the centralized hierarchies of modern government and corporations have called on social know-ledge to aid them in making and executing decisions, and have available administrative organizations which can swiftly implement new ideas. In this context the relation between social knowledge and social practice is clearly a strong one.

The role of the schools in this set of relations is less clear. While institutes of higher education are central to the process of developing and applying knowledge in the ways described above by Brzerzinski, it is hardly feasible that schools play a part in establishing the official orthodoxy of particular ideas in social policy. It is generally acknow-ledged that a substantial time lag ensues between the acceptance of new ideas and their appearance in the curriculum.[39] Schools will then tend to be conservative in the ideas they present, especially at the level of official policy, but they may also be sources of radical thinking, for teaching and its professional preparation provide some independence of other institutions, as well as intellectual resources which can be applied critically to dominant practices.

Schools then are in a position to respond as well as imitate, and while the response will be partly critical as the orthodoxies are placed alongside alternatives which have existed in the past, or which are found elsewhere, the balance will be confirmatory. Teachers and schools in general are conservative,[40] and the knowledge from which curricula are constructed characterized by the limitations described above. The built-in limits to debate in modern liberal democratic social theory are likely to be even more powerful at school level, where simplification is thought necessary, and the relativism of qualified and tentative discussion is thought to confuse. Even those in the schools who seek a more critical and reformist approach to social education will be limited by the nature of the knowledge on which their courses are based.

Liberal democratic social theory restricts social thought to issues and terms of debate which will ultimately justify it, by placing beyond discussion its major failings. If schools succumb to this particular version of social knowledge, they are clearly instruments of the prevailing social order, conservative, and unworthy of the optimistic hopes of those who see education as a means of social improvement for all.

But it is inadequate if not tautologous to say that modern social theory is related to prevailing social relations. To show how modern thought has been related to the nature of society is not to say that such thought is deficient, for such judgments rest not only on the history of ideas, but also on issues of epistemology.

Theories, Action and Social Knowledge

While it might be accepted that social knowledge is related to institutions and practices in mutually sustaining ways, this can have a variety of educational implications. First, it could be argued from some functionalist view that this is inevitable and necessary, and that there is no point in trying to change it, or that change could occur only through revolution of the material base. This exaggerates the strength of the dominant ideology and the unity of prevailing beliefs, ignoring the complexity and conflict which characterize society, ideology and schooling. A second position, therefore, and the one to be progressively developed in this study, is that there is cause for change, and some as yet unfathomed potential for achieving it, or at least helping to create enabling conditions for its achievement, through schooling.

A third view, however, is that both these positions, the resigned functionalist and the critical reformer, are irrelevant, that knowledge is its own rationale, with its own criteria for selection and validation. This argument springs from idealist and objectivist epistemologies, and the view that the important content of education can be identified by analyzing the structure of knowledge itself, rather than its instrumental connections with particular forms of social practice or utopian schemes. In arguing that social knowledge is the product of inductive empirical science, of irreducible concepts derived from a transcendental form of knowledge, or of the application of a set of disciplinary methods, philosophers and educationists have diverted attention away from the connections between their theories, procedures and propositions and the historical social conditions they seek to explain. Given the past predominance of these objectivist and idealist ideas, to argue that social knowledge must be tied to a form of social practice has been to risk the accusation that one is jeopardizing truth by subordinating it to an instrumental purpose. Criticism of these ideas is therefore necessary to the development of this study, both as an explanation of how the social images in present curricula have been produced and justified, and as further elucidation of the position from which the later analysis is derived.

One traditional view has been based on an objective empiricist epistemology: schools were to pass on the facts which science produced. While the model was the natural sciences, the term 'science' was seen to apply to any discipline which sought such objectively verified facts, and historians, geographers, sociologists all felt justified in claiming membership. By the early years of this century, objective empiricism and positivism were widely accepted as providing the criteria for rational knowledge, and 'scientism', the belief that social progress would result from the application of factual knowledge, was well established.

However, developments in the theory of knowledge have shown these views to be inadequate. Philosophers of science have rejected the empiricist assumption of the primacy of facts, and theorists of social science are developing a consensus that the study of society cannot use the natural sciences as a model of procedure. Indeed, these conclusions have been so frequently drawn and are so widely accepted that it is not necessary here to set down the complete chain of reasoning. But its main thread will be given, and its implications for the social education debate discussed.

Briefly, the argument in the philosophy of science runs like this.[41] What we know about perception shows that people can look at the same thing and 'see' different things, for 'seeing' is a constructive and selective process. Further, when perceptions are articulated, people must rely on the categories of language, which predetermine the ways in which they can describe experience – thus the now common distinction between observing phenomena and stating facts. Since all observation statements must draw on the definitions and assumptions which legitimate their use, they are not pure observations arising from the experience or the phenomena. Thus theories can not be developed by induction from pure observations, for observation statements can be made only from the base of some theoretical language.

It is worth considering an example taken from the context of the present study, in which a recommended school text describes the scientific method of economics.

> Positive statements are those which deal only with facts. 'Britain is an island', 'British Leyland employ × thousand workers', 'Smith obtained a grade A in Economics', are all positive statements. If a disagreement arises over a positive statement it can be settled by looking to the facts and seeing whether or not they support the statement.
>
> Positive statements must be either true or false, where the word 'true' is taken to mean 'consistent with the facts'.... Scientific enquiry, as the term is generally understood, is confined to positive questions. It deals with those questions which can be verified or falsified by actual observations of the real world (i.e. by checking the facts). One major objective of science is to develop theories. These are general statements or unifying principles which describe and explain the relationships between things we observe in the world around us. Theories are developed in an attempt to answer the question 'Why?'. Tides rise and fall at regular intervals of time, a city is afflicted by smog at certain times of the year, the price of strawberries falls sharply during the summer months. When some definite regular pattern is observed in the relationships between two or more things, and someone asks why this should be so, the search for a theory has begun.[42]

An important issue here is the status of facts. The examples cited in the second sentence hinge on terms which specify relations between phenomena e.g. island, employ, grade. We might ask how 'workers' is defined, and whether 'obtained' is preferable to 'was granted' as a description of Smith's achievement. However economics would be trivial indeed were it restricted to facts of this kind, and other examples can be cited which are more complex. Take for instance the statements: 'In 1978, £x million worth of goods and services were produced in the United Kingdom'; '56 per cent of the population is in productive employment'; 'Country A has a higher standard of living than country B'. Such descriptive statements are ubiquitous in economics, but they cannot be taken as given facts.

The first two statements depend on conventional classifications of what is to be included in goods and services, and what is to count as productive employment. There are many potential controversies here, but the most significant is the case of the housekeeping spouse, who certainly produces goods and services, but because she or he is not paid is not regarded as producing anything of value. The third 'fact' is controversial for its reliance on a descriptive statistical index. The common problem is whether an arithmetic mean (commonly gross national product per head of population) is an adequate basis for such a judgment, or whether provision should be made for other aspects of the distribution. The decision will be made according to the goal of the enquiry and some criteria of importance, but it cannot be verified or falsified by observations of the real world. Would the economist quoted refuse to deal with such matters? Of course not, but he has said that scientific enquiry is 'confined to positive questions which can be verified or falsified by actual observations of the real world'.

The second paragraph in the quoted passage suggests that theories are developed after observations have identified regular patterns which need explaining. But regularity and pattern can be identified only within some framework which establishes the relationships. A fall in the price of strawberries is significant only against a background of some real or hypothetical expected uniformity, and 'price' is significant only in the context of a theory of value and exchange. The example cited is not an atheoretical 'pure' observation statement. No statement is a pure observation; in the present study of the ways human nature and society are depicted in schools the theory-impregnated nature of description is of fundamental importance.

Many philosophers of science have made a virtue of this necessity, by placing theories at the heart of scientific knowledge, and accepting the falsificationist view of scientific progress. Popper's notion of scientific method as a process of conjectures and refutations, and later versions like Lakatos' sophisticated falsificationism, see scientific progress as the critical development and assessment of theories, which can never be proved, but rather can receive confirmatory support by explaining what we already know and producing new facts; or they can be falsified on their own terms. When it can be shown that a new or rival theory explains more than an older one, or produces new facts, or solves problems which the older one could not, the new theory replaces the old, and is itself subject to critical test.[43] The significance of this is that if 'science' is to be the model for social knowledge, then the social disciplines must be based on falsifiable theories and not on the primacy of facts; they must be able to create new knowledge; they must always be subject to criticism and competing theories; and they must always be held tentatively, as any theory may be falsified.

The notion of theory used here needs some clarification, largely of what it does not imply. For this discussion, a theory can be taken to mean a framework of ideas which articulates problems by identifying and defining relevant elements, and by hypothesizing the nature of the relations among them, with a view to solving the problems. The tests of the theory are its ability to solve the problems to which it is addressed as well as others which it might subsequently articulate and solve. Neither theories nor tests are necessarily predictive, in the sense of saying what must happen at a future time. The definition includes the use of a theory to reinterpret past writings, throwing new light on problems, framing the problems in a different way.[44] Similarly, explaining human behaviour will involve interpreting acts in terms of a theory of action: of what elements of the situation were considered relevant to the decision, of what options were considered feasible, of what seemed reasonable grounds for action, of the relation between situation, reasons, motives and action, and so on. Again the interpretations can be tested on the evidence. To accept a theory based view of knowledge does not tie the discussion to prediction or determinism.

However, no theory can fully comprehend the facts it seeks to explain. A theory will need to make assumptions and draw on other theories to explain the facts to which it addresses itself. Thus when scientists use an optical microscope to make observations to test a theory, they accept the theory on which the microscope has been developed.[45] When geographers study locational decisions they must make assumptions which rest on particular theories from psychology or economics (though the geographer may regard them as common sense, ignoring the fact that psychologists or economists would see the assumptions as problematic). All social disciplines make assumptions which would be seen as controversial by disputants in another discipline.

While social knowledge can be scientific to the extent that it is based on criticism of theories, it does however deny the possibility of objective empiricism in ways which natural science does not. First, social theories do not simply describe or explain social events; they are a part of the events themselves, constituting the rules and expectations by which the participants act. This relation between social knowledge and social events makes social concepts 'essentially contestable':

> The behaviour that is captured by the concept of a political party or a family or an army or a social class is itself behaviour informed by the concept in question. For a necessary condition of such behaviour is that the majority of those who engage in it shall have certain beliefs about what makes this particular party a case of a party, this army an army, and so on.[46]

The constitutive role of knowledge in social action is the clearest point of difference between the social and natural sciences. Examples of this are self-fulfilling or self-negating possibilities in the effects of any social theory. Thus economic forecasts can influence people to act in ways which confirm or destroy the validity of the prediction; and psychoanalysis is based on the belief that knowledge can lead to changes in how people see themselves and how they act. Nor is the effect limited to accurate knowledge, for people can act on beliefs which are erroneous, giving support to W. Thomas' famous statement that 'If men define situations as real, they are real in their consequences'.[47] People construe their environment or define their situations in ways which are theory dependent. Giddens shows how this distinguishes social from natural science:

> The concepts and theories produced in the natural sciences quite regularly filter into lay discourse and become appropriated as elements of everyday frames of reference. But this is of no relevance, of course, to the world of nature itself; whereas the appropriation of technical concepts and theories invented by social scientists can turn them into constituting elements of that very 'subject-matter' they were coined to characterize, and by that token *alter* the context of their application.[48]

Such effects can operate at widely ranging scales, as when individual managers or neurotics act to confirm or negate economic or psychoanalytic theories, or when whole societies absorb the premises of Marx or Freud into their everyday interpretations. In providing categories for interpreting the world, social theories contribute to the individual's judgments about what constitute reasonable grounds for action. Legal responsibility, the idea of reasonable conduct, and the predictability on which social interaction depends require 'more or less diffusely integrated patterns of belief which actors refer to in order to derive principled explanations of each other's conduct;'[49] these beliefs consist of what Giddens calls:

> generically 'mutual knowledge', interpretative schemes where-by actors constitute and understand social life as meaning-ful; this can be distinguished from 'common-sense', which can be regarded as comprising a more or less articulated body of theoretical knowledge that can be drawn upon to explain why things are as they are, or happen as they do, in the natural and social worlds. Commonsense beliefs typically underpin the mutual knowledge which is brought to any encounter by participants.[50]

An important part of these developments in social theory has been the increased attention to the role of language in social relations. Language is a structured medium: as the dominant means of com-municating ideas it is also the resource in which ideas are construc-ted. Forms and styles of language constrain the ideas which can be developed. There is again here the theory-based nature of observa-tion statements: while concepts do not determine beliefs, not all beliefs can be expressed in a given set of concepts.[51] Also, there is the common tendency for language forms developed in one social context to be transferred to others. Pocock[52] quotes Burke's obser-vation that Englishmen in his time tended to conduct debate largely in the language of common law and real property; a modern parallel is the widespread tendency for the language of economics to supply concepts like exchange, transaction and market mechanisms to explanatory models in social psychology and political science (see page 56). In studying any society, past or present, its language is fundamental, not only because it reflects aspects of social relations, but because it helps to constitute them: 'the paradigms which order "reality" are part of the reality they order ... language is part of the social structure and not epiphenomenal to it'.[53]

This discussion would be incomplete if it did not address the question of objectivity, for a frequent issue in curriculum discussion is whether social knowledge can be objective in the sense of being unbiased. Bias usually means intentional or unintentional error originating from a person's interests or situation, and is contrasted with truth. The theory-based idea of knowledge which is held here asserts that all knowledge is tentative. Therefore, if objectivity or lack of bias means certainty and lack of error, we can never attain the first, and can never know if we have finally attained the second. But there are senses in which objectivity can be claimed, and these lie in the criteria by which knowledge must be criticized.

One criterion is that the theory on which knowledge is based be objective. In Popper's words an objective theory is one which is 'arguable, which can be exposed to rational criticism, preferably a theory which can be tested: one which does not merely appeal to our subjective intuitions'.[54] A second criterion consists of the tests we are able to bring to bear in rationally criticizing theories and the knowledge they produce. This is a difficult point to argue, since the origins of procedures which are not themselves theory dependent are not clear. It can only be asserted here that there is an irreducible capacity in human thought and language which enables us to criticize all but the most fundamental theories.

These will include pragmatic and intersubjectively agreed criteria, but ultimately assume concepts and rules of the kind that Elliott cites as examples of mental powers,[55] or which Pring calls intellectual virtues.[56] While the articulation of these will be tied to forms of life, such concepts are basic to human experience, what the arch-relativist Winch has called 'limiting notions' fundamental to human life.[57] The combination of arguable theories and the processes of rational criticism are the means to, though no guarantee of objective, unbiased theory. While there is no such thing as absolute attainable truth, 'Truth plays the role of a regulative idea'.[58]

The theory of knowledge on which the present study is based takes as its starting point the problems which the human species encounters in practising its forms of life. These problems are recognized and articulated, their elements related and responded to through theories, making experience intelligible and providing the framework for action. The theories operate at the most fundamental level through logical processes and categories which characterize people as human, but their elaboration and particular form will show features of their historical contexts and the prevailing technological and social conditions.

Ideologies are the theories which articulate particular forms of social practice, and provide the framework within which social relations and institutions are related to beliefs and ways of under- standing the social world. The extent to which particular ideologies promote the interest of the species and individuals within it can only be revealed and tested by criticizing the theories through which the ideologies operate. All knowledge is ideological in this sense, but some may be so closely related to the universal concerns of the species that they are not generally controversial. An example might be the valuing of physical health and its understanding through medical research, though even here the universal interest will often not prevail.

More controversial and more variable will be the theories which explain conflicting social practices, where the interests of some are subordinated to those of others, where unequal power sustains injustice. In these cases, the dominant theories which sustain injustice must be revealed through criticism, for the existence of any human suffering is a threat to us all. In the conflict between these practices, certain theories, goals and beliefs will be crucial, others less relevant. Thus not all social knowledge is equally controversial; the task is to identify the central ideological issues and criticize the theories which claim to interpret and resolve them.

The implications of the perspective on the nature of knowledge argued here arise chiefly from three main aspects of the foregoing discussion. First is the idea that knowledge will always exist within a framework of theory, which provides a background of assumptions and principles by which the problem is isolated and defined, and which helps to select and state facts. The theory will be most evident in the nature of the questions asked, the explanatory models selected, and the terms and methods used. These will be manifest in common-sense beliefs about what things in the social worlds are related, how they influence each other, what will happen if certain actions are taken – in other words, the theories of everyday life; and, developing from these, the social disciplines, which in specializing, abstracting and seeking generalizations, have relied on similar properties of theoretical systems to provide a framework for relating events and phenomena.

The second major implication of the argument is the focus it recommends on the ideational content developed within theories. If procedures of concepts and methods are subordinate to problems and theories, these procedural elements will be inadequate substitutes for the prior and more general frameworks which integrate them. And it is the more general frameworks, the theories, which must be criticized, not merely particular facts they may generate. The ways theories colligate phenomena, the elements they consider relevant, the relationships they admit as possible, the criteria of acceptability they assume – these are the structures of ideas which theories formulate and the theoretical properties which define content.

From these perspectives, images can be viewed as representations of theories, and images of people and society will function in the theoretical way just described. How we conceive human nature and society, the theories we form about them, separately and in association, will determine what questions shall be asked, what evidence is relevant, what relationships are possible, what methods appropriate. Any theory of everyday life, any academic discipline dealing with social questions, must include, either as a central, explicit and defended principle or as a background assumption taken for granted, a model of human nature. This model will contain assumptions about how people should be conceived, what are their most potent or interesting characteristics, what motivates them or causes them to act, from whence derive their abilities, what is universal and what variable in them. Their relations with society will also be involved. How does the theory on which any social knowledge is based view the relations between the individual and society? Which of the two is the source of humanity? To what extent can one be thought to exist or be understood without the other? How does the relation operate?

Some of these questions will be central to some disciplines, providing the distinctive models or methods which characterize their special concerns. Others of them will be assumed to be irrelevant, or their answers taken to be stable in some particular form; either way they will not be subjected to conscious examination. These theories or images must be accepted as part of any social discipline's approach to its task; they are the slice of life to which that discipline addresses itself. As such they present a view of life from a selective perspective, and will normally ignore competing perspectives.

But if the perspective of the discipline is presented uncritically, or in isolation, if competing perspectives are not allowed, then what is only one possible view may appear and be accepted as the only one possible. Or assumptions which the discipline holds, if not examined, may be taken for granted as necessarily true. If views of human nature and society contribute to what people believe to be so, what they believe to be necessary or changeable, how they interpret their social relations, these beliefs become central aspects of their everyday lives, and critical analysis of them a major obligation of social education.

Ideological Content and The Nature of Social Images

Educational discussion of the elements of social thought has been fraught with a plethora of ill-distinguished terms. Beliefs, ideas, concepts, values, attitudes, opinions and other terms have been conscripted into service. This study's emphasis on social images requires some discussion of what is intended by the term, since it defines the area of concern, provides a unit of analysis and implies important features of the analytical method to be applied to the curriculum content.

Traditionally, curriculum content has been analyzed into smaller units. So-called cognitive objectives have generally been classified as facts, concepts, generalizations and theories, though most discussions have not gone beyond the level of concepts and very few have addressed theories. Cognitive objectives have usually been complemented by affective objectives dealing with attitudes and values. Curriculum planners have found this distinction useful as a means of drawing attention to the broad scope of course objectives, but in social education it has had the unfortunate effect of disguising the interrelatedness of the elements. For instance, facts are selected and concepts constructed in theories, and to study the first two without the third is dangerous, disguising the origin of facts and concepts in particular, often controversial, theoretical perspectives. Similarly, social science in general and particular theories within it are impregnated with ideological assumptions, and imply a set of values.

Also, psychological constructs frequently fail to explain the content of ideas, a claim which can clearly be aimed at the notion of attitude. To define attitudes as mediating constructs or predispositions is to obscure their relationship with belief, and to grant them an *a priori* independence which might be questioned, both on logical grounds and on the empirical evidence that measured attitudes are notoriously unreliable as predictors of behaviour, and can be changed by information. Similarly, to separate values as a category raises problems. Psychologists have usually studied either attitudes or values, dealing only briefly with the distinctions and connections between them, and the role of belief and cognition has seldom been made clear. The decision to treat the idea of 'justice' as either a concept or a value is a perplexing one, which is sometimes avoided but not illuminated by the label 'value concept'. Another example of the problems of analytic classifications is the following view that a person's ideology is a relatively stable set of beliefs.

> Psychologically an ideology is a system of beliefs about social issues, with strong effects in structuring thoughts, feelings and behaviour. Information processing and decision making are facilitated when established categories are available to reduce the complexity of any environment, although the use of defined categories may prematurely limit the search for new information. The functional constraints can become established as stable personality patterns.[59]

This view emphasizes the beliefs and established categories which are in some unexplained manner applied to experience. The implication is that the process is a relatively straightforward one of classification, and ignores the interactions of beliefs, goals and contexts which produce the variety of people's thoughts about society. The scheme is too static to capture the complexity of ideological thought. Its derivative in textual analysis, quantitative content analysis, is similarly inadequate.

For these reasons, the concept of image is an attractive alternative if it is seen as a more dynamic complex of ideas and processes generated by the wish to explain or interpret social events. The term is not new: it has often been used by authors who, seeking to discuss ideas about society, have felt constrained by more well established alternatives such as concept, theory or model. A tradition of use has developed in sociological studies of people's conceptions of social structure,[60] but the working class images studies have concentrated more narrowly on how people interpret class structure. When going beyond this to use the term more broadly, they have not clarified their use of the term, and have used it in different ways.[61]

The importance of theories in social knowledge has already been discussed, and an image can be seen as a representation of a theory or set of theories with their associated concepts, believed facts, conclusions and applications. A theory was defined as a framework of ideas which articulates problems by identifying and defining relevant elements, and by hypothesizing the nature of the relations among them, with a view to solving the problems. It is the structure, process and products of this framework which constitute the image.

The term has close connections with its literary use as a means of representing phenomena through metaphor, symbol, model, analogy, and similar devices. Social structure, social relations or aspects of human nature such as motive, character or personality are not observable objects, and will often be thought of metaphorically. The metaphorical use of language, the choice of concepts, the emphasis on certain relationships can be seen as indices of theories to be scrutinized for their ideological functions.

Another element of images which derives from their theoretical base is their selective nature. Theories guide perception in an intentional manner, for any social situation can be perceived in numerous ways. The selection and definition of relevant elements will proceed according to the significance of the situation for the problem as understood by the interpreter. Thus in text descriptions and explanation, ideas will be presented according to what are perceived as the problems addressed, and the problems and theories can be inferred from these ideas. Similarly, guiding theories and acknowledged problems will be revealed by what statements do not include, what the selective process has omitted as irrelevant. In seeking the problems and theories which have generated discourse, what texts do not say is as important as what they do say. As Lukes observes, echoing Cassirer: '... every way of seeing is also a way of not seeing'.[62]

Further, the problem oriented origins of theories mean that, at some level, all theories are programmatic, and imply goals and forms of social practice. At one level, the relationship between knowledge and human interests as outlined by Habermas[63] indicates this characteristic. As a specific instance, the use of market theory to explain pluralistic political systems accepts in its explanation the claims of the system it seeks to explain (see page 28). People wield theories in perception in a goal oriented way, and images construct definitions of situations organized around and providing direction for action.

The class image studies referred to earlier have shown that people 'hold a multiplicity of class images or meaning systems from which they will draw upon the most appropriate to explain a particular situation ...'.[64] As Davis concludes:

An image of society is for the most part a projection of the process of social construction rather than a depiction of social structure. As a projection of the processes in which the individual is caught up, it can no longer be seen as a representation with a precise content but as a creative act, as an exercise of the imagination.[65]

Images are not descriptions or concepts or models created from the application of stable categories, but dynamic responses to problems in particular situations, subject to test and alteration in experience. Their function is to create order, to explain, predict and justify, but the process is one of interaction and adaptation rather than simple application. The analogy is the conduct of a conversation rather than the application of labels.

This brings the discussion to its most recent point of development, for the language analogy has been widely taken up, and provides some interesting methodological possibilities. There is a growing consensus that ideological thought, the creation and use of social images, is a generative process in which interpretations are produced by the operation of a semantic system of symbolic meanings and a syntax of rules. Davis' sociological analysis of the class images research leads him to this conclusion: 'The concrete statements or elements of discourse are the clues in a search for rules and regularities which represent an underlying structure'.[66] In the tradition of political philosophy, we find a similar analogy: '... ideological thinking should be considered as the elaboration of a language rendering experience intelligible in the light of, or by reference to, some picture or conception of men as socially related beings.[67]

This realization is in line with the current popularity in social theory of structuralism and especially structural linguistics after Saussure.[68] Its application to how people construe and explain human nature and social events can be illustrated by two approaches which will act as starting points for the method employed in this study.

The first is Larrain's explanation of Greimas' structural semantics. Ideological discourse is seen as having a manifest content of denotative meanings, and a latent content representing an underlying structure of connotations, what Greimas calls a mythical level. 'According to this conception, if one can reach the logical model, if one can identify the structures which give coherence to the message, if it is possible to discover the principle which presides over the organization of discourse and which unifies its elements, the analysis of ideology has largely been completed'.[69] The procedure first establishes the principles of organization and combination of small units and tries to derive the rules by which these basic units combine. The details of the procedure are obscure, and Larrain is critical of the arbitrariness of such analyses, and their tendency to objectify textual meaning beyond the analyst's interpretation. However the ideas are suggestive and give some access to a method compatible with the linguistic analogy.

A quite different tradition has provided yet another linguistic interpretation of the explanation of social events. From the world of conceptual analysis and symbolic logic, a philosophical treatment of common-sense psychology achieves a very similar result. In analyzing how people explain social events, attribute motives and character, Morton argues that common-sense psychology is neither a body of empirical principles like a scientific theory, nor a set of fixed concepts, but that 'it consists in a constancy underlying innumerable improvisations and variations in the principles we apply and the concepts we use. . . . It is like . . . speaking a dialect of a language'.[70] Morton posits a surface pattern of explicit judgments, apparently independent of one another, and beneath it a stratification of implicit concepts, at some points organized by a body of principles. This scheme is subject to 'a set of conditions on the ways in which the implicit concepts are related to one another and in which explicit concepts may be related to them. . . . The main effect of the schematism is to constrain the possible combinations of beliefs involving the explicit concepts'.[71] The similarities between these two analyses are clear; their potential for explaining how images of human nature and society are created and operate in social explanation is encouraging.

Accordingly, and drawing together these threads from the theory of knowledge and the study of ideology, images are here used to represent the way theories construct and articulate goal related problems by generating and relating elements such as facts, concepts and generalizations. These relations are constructed according to rules of combination, association and inference. The whole will be manifest in and operate through language with its devices of connotation and metaphor. To identify images in social discourse, analysis must seek the problems, elements, rules and language which comprise them.

The structure of an image can be represented then by these four components. First, the image will contain elements whose combination creates the explanation or resolution of the problem. These elements may be relatively simple and discrete terms or concepts, or more complex entities like models, metaphors or other theories. Identifying them will normally be a relatively straight-forward matter, beginning with the colligations of the discourse itself and then analyzing or combining them to produce more homogeneous and distinctive elements. This is of course not simply an inductive procedure, but will be guided by hypotheses about the relations between the discourse and typical problems of the field of discourse, and must be informed by knowledge of the history of the field and the social context to which it relates. Clearly, this knowledge of the social context will itself be specifiable in terms of an image. The theory from which any analysis is conducted should be made clear.

Second, the problem to which the discourse is addressed will be identifiable by inferring the question to which the discourse could provide an answer. There will seldom be only one such problem, though some will be more influential than others in selecting and organizing the text explanation. The problem will be formulated and therefore expressed through the terms and concepts of the discourse itself. It should be seen as the synthesizing element of the image which determines the relevance of the other elements.

The third component is the set of rules by which the elements are combined and sequenced for any particular explanation, for the image is a dynamic framework which can generate a multitude of particular judgments, conclusions, comparisons and explanations when called on in any specific situation. These rules are likely to be the most difficult component to identify, requiring in most cases extensive testing of hypothesized rules of combinations and judgment.

Finally, the problem elements and rules will be embedded in a complex semantic system of jargon, metaphor and connotation, which will provide associations, tone and other elaborations of the structure. This component will pervade all the others, and is one reason why the analysis does not proceed in discrete steps as this outline might suggest. Rather the components form a complex whole, synthesized to varying degrees, but which is progressively outlined as the four components are identified in the analysis.

This study focuses on the concepts of human nature and society as the issues on which relevant images are identified. It has been argued earlier that what people believe to be the nature of individuals and society is an important influence on their hopes and expectations, and provides rules by which social relations are conducted. It was also shown that any social theory will contain implicit or explicit positions on these issues. Parekh argues the centrality of these concepts in political doctrines:

> The identity of a political doctrine is to be found neither in its philosophical nor in its programmatic part but in its conception of man and society. It is this 'middle part' that provides the most fruitful point of entry into its complex structure.[72]

By analyzing what texts say or imply about human nature and society, images can be identified which serve the ideological purpose of explaining why people do what they do and why society is as it is. In the present study, the analysis will be guided by the egalitarian, participative and expressive theories of human nature and society which characterize the stated goals of social education. These curricular theories and their implications as argued in earlier chapters provide the backdrop against which text images will be highlighted. Before beginning this analysis, some general observations can be made about alternative images of human nature and society, for certain basic images have characterized social thought, and will recur in the subsequent discussion.

Images of the Nature of the Individual and Society

Of the various images of the individual formulated by philosophers and historians of ideas, perhaps the most useful broad distinction is between what have been called the plastic and the autonomous 'models of man'. Hollis[73] analyzes the assumptions in the models of human nature which underlie competing theories of society. In economics, psychology, sociology and history, Hollis traces the opposing models of 'plastic man', a relatively passive being, from which ideas flow naturalistic and deterministic explanations, and 'autonomous man', where existentialism, the theory of self, and the everyday ethics of commonsense search for reasons rather than causes in explaining action (or, as in the plastic model, behaviour). Associated with the first model are a faith in planning or social engineering as programmes of social change, an extreme illustration being B.F. Skinner's utopian schemes.[74] The autonomous model has produced doctrines ranging from classical liberalism[75] to existentialist ethical individualism.[76] Most social theories, their methods of enquiry, and their programmatic implications will be locatable on a continuum formed by these models of individual human nature.

A second dichotomy lies in Lukes' distinction between the concept of the abstract individual and the concept of the person:

> ... the abstract conception presents the individual as consisting merely in a certain set of invariant psychological characteristics and tendencies – as having certain sorts of wants and purposes, as acting on certain sorts of motives, as having certain interests. Conceiving of an individual as a *person*, by contrast, presents him as the source of (yet to be discovered) intentions and purposes, decisions and choices, as capable of engaging in and valuing certain (yet to be discovered) activities and involvements, and as capable of (yet to be discovered) forms of self-development.[77]

An example of the abstract conception is the 'state of nature' argument which postulates a set of *a priori* human characteristics and concludes that particular social arrangements necessarily follow. The problem with this strategy is that its proponents can select the relevant characteristics only from within a social context and a related ideology. For instance MacPherson[78] has shown how Hobbes, in his famous example of this approach, looked at his own society and tried to imagine it without law and order; in so doing, Hobbes was forced to begin with a postulated model of a particular society, and not a model of human nature in an *a priori* state of nature.

The concept of a person is a more expressive image from which derive terms like self-actualization,[79] conscientization,[80] and other developmental or even teleological ideas. Again to identify development, with its association with maturity and progress, requires an *a priori* conception of possible end states to which preceding stages can be seen to contribute and according to which they are conceived. The conception of the end state will be an interpretation imposed by a theory.

Related to this is an important distinction between conservative theories, based on 'a philosophy of imperfection',[81] and theories which to some degree assume human perfectibility. Conservatism preaches the imperfectibility of human nature as a caution against optimistic calls for radical change, and thus advocates a limited style of politics. An example of an opposing view is the Marxian image of the fully humanized communist person, which emphasizes the creative, productive capacities of the species. These capacities can be realized only through a cooperative process involving the entire species. In the Marxian image, the ideal person:

> ... is, in short, a cheerful, well-integrated, expansive, social being who sums up in his life the greatness and wealth of his species. As long as any individual in any society fails to live this kind of life, the species suffers a loss, and its historic task of humanising nature remains unfulfilled.[82]

The interdependence of people in developing their capacities follows from the generic consciousness of the individual as a species-being.[83] This is an important difference from the liberal image which, in its classical form, sees the individual as prior to society, and social and political relationships as artificial constructs designed to counter the imperfections 'experienced by men competing for wealth and position whilst valuing privacy and leisure'.[84]

More specific images of the individual have been developed in particular fields of thought,[85] but most of them are applications or combinations of these basic alternatives, and will be discussed as they arise in later analysis. However, while images of human nature are one means of approaching the individual-society relationship, other traditions of thought have focused on images of society and its structure and operation.

Commentators have often noted the tendency to discuss society in metaphorical terms. Brown describes the idea of the root meta-phor, 'a fundamental image of the world from which models and illustrative metaphors may be derived', and identifies five principal examples in sociological thought: society as an organism or as a machine, and social conduct viewed as language, drama, or a game.[86] Of these, the mechanistic and organic images have the longest and most fertile history, and have received most attention.[87]

Before the eighteenth century, the terms 'organic' and 'mechanical' were synonymous descriptions of the properties of instruments or engines; but there then developed the distinction between biological and mechanical characteristics, and in Burke and Coleridge societies and institutions are described as 'organic' in contrast to the artificiality of 'mechanical' objects.[88] In the nineteenth-century utopians, especially Saint-Simon and Fourier, organic connoted organized, based on

rational human characteristics and a logical hierarchy....
Rational, cooperative organization would produce a quasi-
organic society within which individuals have predetermined
functional roles and tasks, proof against anomie.[89]

Since that time, however, the organic image has signalled the idea of
naturalness, spontaneity, wholeness, unity, evolutionary growth in
society, often with associations of social harmony through a supra-
individual ethos or energy.

The interdependence and integration of an 'organic society'
were invoked as a source of stability by Burke,[90] and in Saint-
Simon's idea of 'social physiology' we see the idea, found also in
Coleridge, that the whole is greater than the sum of its parts:

> ... it soars above the level of individuals who are, from its
> viewpoint, no more than the organs of the body politic
> whose organic functions it must study, as specialized physi-
> ology studies that of human individuals.[91]

This supra-individual level of social existence has been the
organic image's most consistent feature, usually expressed in the idea
of community. Most frequent in socialist thought, the idea of
community can be traced through the writings of Wilde, Morris,[92]
Hobson and Ramsay MacDonald.[93] Morris illustrates it well:

> Men are free when they belong to a living, organic, believing
> community; active in fulfilling some unfilled, perhaps un-
> realized purpose.[94]

But there is a history of use in more conservative thought also,
where the ethos of the organic society derives not from an evolving
humanistic spirit but from the common experience of tradition.
Leavis and Thompson invoke this notion in lamenting the loss of the
naturalness of Old England's organic community, as the 'rural
community' has been replaced by the 'organized modern state':

> The outward and obvious sign that the loss of the organic
> community was the loss of a human naturalness or normality
> may be seen in the building of the industrial era.[95]

The organic image thrives in the continued search in present social
thought for a common purpose in society on which to base a
programme of reform. Unger combines the idea of a common
human nature and its development through common experiences to

advocate a society of organic groups whose continuous evolution will resolve the conflicts in the division of labour:

> The hypothetical image of a universal community whose practices reveal the species nature of man provides an interpretation of a natural harmony.[96]

Polanyi and Prosch exhort us to seek a 'traditional devotion to the spiritual objectives, such as truth, justice, and beauty' which can be implemented only in a society whose affairs 'would be managed through the development of various *spontaneous* orders – ordered wholes that develop freely by means of mutual adjustments'.[97] In both these prescriptions, the organic image, once the conception of rational social planning and organization, is now most often a vehicle of faith, the image by which people can transcend the problems created by individualism and immune to its remedies.

It is in Leavis and Thompson's statement that we most clearly see 'organic' contrasted with 'organized', and artificial industry opposed to a normal community. The mechanical image in general has been criticized for its contrived and unnatural features, and is now often associated pejoratively with social engineering and control. Williams[98] traces its links with materialism, and its opposition to spiritualism and the organic image; and Barfield[99] cites its origin in the eighteenth century reverence for reason and order and its flowering in nineteenth-century science. A good example is provided by the evolutionary philosopher Haechel, who wrote in 1899:

> The great abstract law of mechanical causality now rules the entire universe, as it does the mind of man. It is the steady immutable polestar, whose clear light falls on our path through the dark labyrinth of the countless separate phenomena.[100]

Few social thinkers would willingly use the mechanical analogy today, tainted as it is with materialistic and behaviourist assumptions. The humanism of the organic image is more popular. But despite the Romantic antipathy to mechanism and its contrast with organicism, there are common elements in the two metaphors.

Wolin sees them both as manifestations of the shift in thought which, after Hobbes, brought the dominance of the idea of society as a self-activating unity. Strong in Locke and Adam Smith, and developed by the utopians, the idea is current in both the organicists' idea of community and the rationalists' 'spare metaphors of mechanics'.[101] This development has rendered irrelevant considerations of the political order, for society has been seen not as ordered by power or authority but by automatic self-adjustment, and the utilitarian laws of economics. If society is an organism or a mechanism, its structure and its operation will not be explained by considerations of how people interpret authority or justice, or by how they wield power and influence. It will be explained by natural laws which relate the parts to each other and to the whole in biological or physical terms. Wolin castigates both organic and mechanical images for their contribution to the decline of political theory.

The similarities between the organic and the mechanical can be further demonstrated by the modern development of yet another image – the image of the system developed in systems theory and cybernetics, for it is of the essence of cybernetics that the laws of control, operating through the flow of information, do not depend on the dichotomy between organic and inorganic systems. In fact, cybernetics has been defined as 'the science of control and communication in the animal and the machine'.[102] And it is not surprising that when this most recent combination of organic and mechanical images is applied to social theory, it should be criticized in terms reminiscent of Wolin:

> ... in the imagery of social cybernetics there is an atrophy of the very vocabularies of citizenship, moral responsibility, and political community. Instead, the machinery of governance, initially conceived as serving human values, tends to generate its own self-maintaining ends.... The polity – the arena for the institutional enactment of moral choices – dissolves upward into the state, or downward into the individual whose intentionality is now wholly privatized and whose actions, uprooted from an institutional context, are bereft of social consequence and hence of moral meaning.[103]

It has already been shown that the systems approach to the study of politics has been criticized for its implied support for the existing system and its effective exclusion of alternative political arrangements. Indeed Birnbaum[104] has argued that organicist analogies, systems theory and cybernetics are explanatory models which serve to idealize harmonious functioning, with the result that consensus through apathy and lack of conviction are seen as virtues.

Another image with a longer and more continuous history and

now found in economics, politics and social psychology, is that of the market as the model for society as a whole, and exchange as the analogy of its operation. As we have seen, Wolin[105] ties this to the devolopment of the notion of 'society' as a self-maintaining system, with its organic and mechanical metaphors, its disguising of the political process and the supplanting of political theory. In discussing the classical economists of the eighteenth century, he claims that their aim was to seek order in human relationships through regularized economic behaviour by which the relationships were integrated into a rhythmic pattern, thus avoiding the need for compulsion. The economist's model of society was anti-political in that it posed economic transactions from which coercion was absent as the alternative to the idea of a politically directed system, and all behaviour could be seen as explicable in economic terms.

> The next step was natural and almost inevitable. If economics was the knowledge of society, nothing save humility could prevent the economist from assuming that society's relationships and multifarious activities, in short, society's life, could be summarized through various economic categories.[106]

It seems that humility was not adequate to the task: a submission by the Economics Association to a governmental enquiry describes economics as 'the core subject of the social sciences'.[107] But though Wolin suggests that the battle was won and lost in the eighteenth century, it is still very much alive, for power and exchange continue to be advocated as alternative central concepts in the study of politics. The significance of this dispute, and the potential importance of the choice of images in general, can be illustrated by analyzing the differences between the concepts, and what is involved in choosing one rather than the other.

Blondel discusses the role of exchange, 'trade-off' or 'bargaining' in political thought, comparing its advantages in certain contexts with those of 'power' in others. He concludes:

> Trade-offs occur where there is near-equality between the various actors; when there is gross inequality there *is* influence domination, and various other forms of power.[108]

So the choice of explanatory concept rests on a judgment of the extent of equality or inequality, and as there are no satisfactory ways of determining the boundary between 'near-equality' and 'gross inequality', political theorists must presumably assess the degree of equality for themselves, a most controversial assessment. The exchange model then has built into it an assumption of equality.

All social explanations assume a theory of human nature and society. Whether clearly and systematically constructed as in systems theory, or vague and implicit as in Leavis' ideas of an organic society, the history of social thought can be traced in terms of its metaphors, models and analogies. More interesting is the way such images have been derived from and made possible by changes in society itself. With capitalism came the market analogy; industrialism stengthened the mechanical image; and social cybernetics has grown with large organizations. There has always been a programmatic and tendentious element in the use of images: the utopians' images were persuasive devices;[109] imperialists and slave owners found in Social Darwinism a justification;[110] the organic metaphor suggests a better world to Burke, Saint-Simon, Morris, Unger, and a worse one to Wolin.[111]

Images have given sense and order to complexity, but their usefulness may obscure their dangers. Beardsley's[112] list of problems in the use of metaphor applies more widely to some aspects of the images discussed here. First, the complexity of an image leaves it open to misunderstanding. It may not be clear which of its elements are being referred to, so that the organic image may be intended to highlight complexity, common purpose among members, interdependence of function, natural law-like operation, or all of these. Second, the meaning of the image trails off to a margin of subtle and vague associations, so that its total effect will be difficult to predict in advance and even assess on reflection. For instance, does the mechanical image suggest dehumanization, the necessity for machine-like control, the idea of one fixed place for every part? Beardsley points out that metaphors are highly sensitive to context. While the concept of exchange or trade-off might be useful in certain cases in the politics of international diplomacy, how do its implications change when applied to relations between classes? Other problems arise from changes in society which may in turn change the meaning of the image, as when the biological image took on a new significance with the development of eugenics.

It has been shown how a choice of image can limit alternative lines of thought, and how the assumptions built into a model can immunize it against certain conclusions, as, for example, when the market analogy in politics reduces the significance of the idea of power, or when systems theory implies stability and harmony as the goal of social relations. Images can suggest a future in another way, for what may be intended as metaphorical devices may be reified into immutable facts. The suggestion that society is an organism or a machine does not sit easily with the notion that change is possible. If society is a self-adjusting system in dynamic equilibrium what encouragement is there for the individual to try to influence it? If the direction of social development is determined by biological evolution there is little point in political activity to promote ideals.

Conclusion

Inequality of human welfare and opportunity is incompatible with the egalitarian and participatory ethos of social education; yet inequality is maintained in the currently prevailing political system and attendant ideology. If social education is to achieve its aims, it must be based on a clear understanding of the relationship between its ideals and the reality of the existing political order.

Pluralist elitist democracy is neither egalitarian nor participatory. It holds that social knowledge need not be universally accessible, and that the rational application of people's ideals to political practice is dangerous. Liberalism and empiricism share the view that theory is unreliable, that concrete experience is the best basis of understanding and judgment, that substantive values are inimical or irrelevant to science and a successful political system.

But social knowledge is inevitably theoretical, and is constructed in solving problems thought worth addressing. It is bound by the language, metaphors and frames of reference of its historical context, and helps to constitute the social relations it seeks to describe and explain. It cannot therefore be seen as objective or value free in the sense these terms most often intend. All social knowledge is ideological in that it is reflexively related to sets of social relations and forms of social practice. Social education imbued with ideals of human welfare must attend to any disjunctions between these ideals and the ideology of the prevailing order.

This will involve criticizing extant theories, how they articulate problems, and what they deem relevant to solving them, for what will count as problems and acceptable solutions will be influenced by the theories' position with respect to some ideology and political culture. One way of representing the theory which underlies any text is to construct an image of it, that is to infer the problem the text addresses, to identify the terms in which the problem and its discussion are couched, and to show how these elements are related to produce acceptable interpretations and explanations. The history of social thought provides many examples of images of individual human nature and society which have been the basis of attempts to describe and explain, but which also imply political doctrines, accepted values or programmatic goals.

This study began with the hypothesis that curricular problems in social education could be understood in terms of the social control debate. It has further explored important relationships amongst the political culture, social knowledge and educational aims, and has suggested terms and procedures for criticizing the ideological content of existing curricula. The following chapters explore ideological images of human nature and society presented in a selection of texts written for British secondary schools. For each of the subjects addressed, implications are drawn for the issues of social inequality, human welfare and social education outlined above.

Notes and References

1 EGGLESTON, J. (1977) *The Sociology of the School Curriculum*, London, Routledge and Kegan Paul, p. 41.
2 See note 2, p. 4.
3 This assumes (a) that there is no reason to believe that redistribution of wealth will involve smaller total production; (b) that even if it did the non-material benefits for human dignity would compensate for some material loss, though there might be some limit to this, beyond which increased equality would become unjust in the Rawlsian sense. See ATKINSON, A. (1974) *Unequal Shares: Wealth in Britain*, Harmondsworth, Penguin, Chap. 5; RAWLS, J. (1967) 'Justice as fairness' in LASLETT, P. and RUNCIMAN, W. (Eds.) *Philosophy, Politics and Society*, Second Series, Oxford, Blackwell.
4 BELL, D. (1960) *The End of Ideology: On the Exhaustion of Political Ideas in the Fifties*, Glencoe, Free Press, p. 402. The relevant British statement was Laslett's 1956 claim that 'political philosophy is dead'. See the discussion by LASLETT, P. and RUNCIMAN, W. (1962) 'Introduction' in LASLETT, P. and RUNCIMAN, W. (Eds.) *Philosophy, Politics and Society*, Second Series, Oxford, Blackwell.
5 This assertion is most readily supported by reference to 'positional goods' in which 'there is no such thing as levelling up'. HIRSH, F. (1977) *Social Limits to Growth*, London, Routledge and Kegan Paul, p. 176.
6 It could be argued that the legitimating processes have become part of the hidden curriculum, the 'prevailing social arrangements in which

schooling takes place and the implication that children infer modes of thinking, social norms, and principles in these arrangements'. DREEBEN, R. (1976) 'The' unwritten curriculum and its relation to values', *Journal of Curriculum Studies*, 8, 2, p. 112. For instance, Miliband confines his discussion to the hidden curriculum and pressures on teachers to avoid controversy, but does not scrutinize curriculum content itself. If this carries the implication that the overt curriculum is free of ideological function it is incorrect for the reasons argued. MILIBAND, R. (1973) *The State in Capitalist Society*, London, Quartet Books, pp. 214–19.

7 MACPHERSON, C. (1977) *The Life and Times of Liberal Democracy*, Oxford, Oxford University Press, p. 77.

8 LIVELY, J. (1978) 'Pluralism and consensus' in BIRNBAUM, P., LIVELY, J. and PARRY, G. (Eds.) *Democracy, Consensus and Social Contract*, London, Sage, p. 188. Benewick reviews the particular form of British pluralism, highlighting the role of the Civil Service and the idea of representativeness as distinctive characteristics, but in all respects Britain reveals the features listed. BENEWICK, R. (1973) 'Politics without ideology: the perimeters of pluralism' in BENEWICK, R., BERKU, R. and PAREKH, B. *Knowledge and Belief in Politics: The Problem of Ideology*, London, George Allen and Unwin.

9 The experts comprise politicians themselves (that is, people who make a career of government), the civil service, the full-time advocates and administrators of the major pressure groups, and the range of advisers and consultants clustered around these components of the political elite. PARRY, G. (1969) *Political Elites*, London, Allen and Unwin; JOHNSON, T. (1972) *Professions and Power*, London, Macmillan.

10 MACPHERSON, C. (1977) *op. cit.* p. 78.

11 LUCAS, J. (1976) *Democracy and Participation*, Harmondsworth, Penguin.

12 DAHL, R. (1956) *A Preface to Democratic Theory*, Chicago, University of Chicago Press, p. 151.

13 PLAMENATZ, J. (1973) *Democracy and Illusion: An Examination of Certain Aspects of Modern Democratic Theory*, London, Longman.

14 OAKESHOTT, M. (1962) *Rationalism in Politics and Other Essays*, London, Methuen.

15 MACPHERSON, C. (1977) *op. cit.* p. 81.

16 BIRNBAUM, P. (1978) 'Consensus and depoliticization in contemporary political theory' in BIRNBAUM, P., LIVELY, J., and PARRY, G. (Eds.) *op. cit.* p. 182.

17 PARRY, G. (1978) 'Citizenship and Knowledge' in BIRNBAUM, P., LIVELY, J., and PARRY, G. (Eds.) *op. cit.* p. 51.

18 PLAMENATZ, J. (1973) *op. cit.* p. 186.

19 *Ibid.*

20 *Ibid.* p. 185.

21 CRICK, B. and LISTER, I. (1978) 'Political literacy', in CRICK, B. and PORTER, A. (Eds.) *Political Education and Political Literacy*, London, Longman, p. 41.

22 VINCENT, J. (1978) 'In the country of the blind', *The Times Literary Supplement*, 21 July, p. 815.

23 PLAMENATZ, J. (1973) *op. cit.* pp. 176–9.

24 *Ibid.* p. 190.

25 HAYEK, F. (1973) *Law, Legislation and Liberty. Volume 1: Rules and Order*, London, Routledge and Kegan Paul.

26 OAKESHOTT, M. (1962) *op. cit.*

27 See for instance the basic political concepts of the political education programme of the Hansard Society, which includes the study of general images of the world through concepts of justice, order, freedom and others. The Hansard Society's programme could not be described as wholly rationalist, since there are elements of the evolutionary empirical tradition in their approach to politics which might well derive from Oakeshott. Nonetheless, the advocated application of abstract ideals to political practice is anathema to the Oakeshottian tradition. CRICK, B. (1978) 'Basic concepts for political education' in CRICK, B. and PORTER, A. (Eds.) *op. cit.*

28 BARKER, R. (1978) *Political Ideas in Modern Britain*, London, Methuen.

29 HOWELL, D. (1976) *British Social Democracy: A Study in Development and Decay*, London, Croom Helm.

30 OAKESHOTT, M. (1962) *op. cit.* p. 127.

31 Quoted in BARKER, R. (1978) *op. cit.* p. 193.

32 ANNAN, N. (1959) *The Curious Strength of Positivism in English Political Thought*, Oxford, Oxford University Press.

33 MacPHERSON, C. (1977) *op. cit.* pp. 84ff.

34 TAPPER, T. and SALTER, B. (1978) *Education and the Political Order: Changing Patterns of Class Control*, London, Macmillan, pp. 27ff.

35 BRZERZINSKI, Z. (1968) 'America in the technetronic age', in *Encounter*, January, p. 18.

36 WOLIN, S. (1961) *Politics and Vision: Continuity and Innovation in Western Political Thought*, London, Allen and Unwin.

37 HAYEK, F. (1973) *op. cit.*

38 WOLIN, S. (1961) *op. cit.* p. 344.

39 A useful discussion of American evidence is Voege's study of the rise of Keynesian theories in economics textbooks. A lag of twenty years for implementation of educational ideas had been suggested by other American research, and was supported by Voege. VOEGE, H. (1975) 'The diffusion of Keynesian macroeconomics through American high school textbooks, 1936–70' in REID, W. and WALKER, D. (Eds.) *Case Studies in Curriculum Change*, London, Routledge and Kegan Paul.

40 GRACE, G. (1978) *Teachers, Ideology and Control: A Study in Urban Education*, London, Routledge and Kegan Paul, p. 239.

41 BARNES, B. (1974) *Scientific Knowledge and Sociological Theory*, London, Routledge and Kegan Paul; CHALMERS, A. (1978) *What is This Thing Called Science? An Assessment of the Nature and Status of Science and Its Methods*, Milton Keynes, Open University Press; HARRIS, K. (1979) *Education and Knowledge: the Structured Misrepresentation of Reality*, London, Routledge and Kegan Paul.

42 STANLAKE, G. (1976) *Introductory Economics*, London, Longman, pp. 4, 5.
43 CHALMERS, A. (1978) *op. cit.*
44 For instance, C.B. MACPHERSON postulates relations among elements of Hobbes' ideas and his milieu, and elaborates and develops (tests) the theory in the context of Hobbes' writings. The theory is in principle falsifiable since the interpretations based on it must be reasonable, supportable on the evidence, and open to criticism. MACPHERSON, C. (1962) *The Political Theory of Possessive Individualism*, London, Oxford University Press.
45 KEAT, R. and URRY, J. (1975) *Social Theory as Science*, London, Routledge and Kegan Paul, p. 47.
46 MACLNTYRE, A. (1973–74) 'The essential contestability of some social concepts', in *Ethics*, 84, p. 3.
47 Quoted by Janowitz in the introduction to THOMAS, W. (1966) *On Social Organization and Social Personality* (Ed. M. JANOWITZ), Chicago, Chicago University Press, p. xi.
48 GIDDENS, A. (1976) *New Rules of Sociological Method: A Positive Critique of Interpretative Sociologies*, London, Hutchinson, p. 179.
49 *Ibid.* p. 115.
50 *Ibid.* p. 114.
51 KEAT, R. and URRY, J. (1975) *op. cit.* p. 218.
52 POCOCK, J. (1971) *Politics, Language and Time. Essays on Political Thought and History*, London, Methuen, p. 21.
53 *Ibid.* p. 38.
54 POPPER, K. (1976) *Unended Quest: An Intellectual Autobiography*, Glasgow, Fontana, p. 138.
55 ELLIOTT, R. (1975) 'Education and human being. 1' in BROWN, S. (Ed.) *Philosophers Discuss Education*, London, Macmillan, p. 48.
56 PRING, R. (1972) 'Knowledge out of control', *Education for Teaching*, 89, p. 21.
57 WINCH, P. (1970) 'Understanding a primitive society' in WILSON, B. (Ed.) *Rationality*, Oxford, Blackwell, p. 107.
58 POPPER, K. (1972) *Objective Knowledge: An Evolutionary Approach*, London, Oxford University Press, p. 30.
59 BROWN, L., (1973) *Ideology*, Harmondsworth, Penguin, p. 179.
60 BULMER, M. (1975) 'Some problems of research into class imagery' in BULMER, M. (Ed.) *Working Class Images of Society*, London, Routledge and Kegan Paul.
61 WILLENER, A. (1975) 'Images, action, "us" and "them"' in BULMER, M. (Ed.) *op. cit.* pp. 183–4; ALLCORN, D. and MARSH, C. (1975) 'Occupational communities – communities of what?' in BULMER, M. (Ed.) *op. cit.* p. 214.
62 LUKES, S. (1973) *Individualism*, Oxford, Basil Blackwell, p. 149.
63 HABERMAS, J. (1971) *Knowledge and Human Interests*, London, Heinemann.
64 BELL, C. and NEWBY, H. (1975) 'The sources of variation in agricultural workers' images of society' in BULMER, M. (Ed.) *op. cit.* p. 96.

65 DAVIS, H. (1979) *Beyond Class Images*, London, Croom Helm, p. 29.
66 *Ibid.*, p. 48.
67 ROBINSON, T. (1980) 'Ideology and theoretical inquiry', in MANNING, D. (Ed.) *The Form of Ideology*, London, Allen and Unwin, p. 68.
68 GIDDENS, A. (1979) *Central Problems in Social Theory: Action Structure and Contradiction in Social Analysis*, London, Macmillan.
69 LARRAIN, J. (1979) *The Concept of Ideology*, London, Hutchinson, p. 133.
70 MORTON, A. (1980) *Frames of Mind, Constraints on the Common-sense Conception of the Mental*, Oxford, Clarendon, p. 1.
71 *Ibid.* p. 16.
72 PAREKH, B. (1975) 'Introduction' in PAREKH, B. (Ed.) *The Concept of Socialism*, London, Croom Helm, p. 3.
73 HOLLIS, M. (1977) *Models of Man: Philosophical Thoughts on Social Action*, Cambridge, Cambridge University press.
74 SKINNER, B. (1973) *Beyond Freedom and Dignity*, Harmondsworth, Penguin.
75 MANNING, D. (1976) *Liberalism*, London, Dent, p. 17.
76 LUKES, S. (1973) *op. cit.* p. 15.
77 *Ibid.*, p. 146.
78 MACPHERSON, C. (1962) *op. cit.*
79 MASLOW, A. (1971) *The Farther Reaches of Human Nature*, Harmondsworth, Penguin.
80 FREIRE, P. (1972) *Cultural Action for Freedom*, Harmondsworth, Penguin.
81 O'SULLIVAN, N. (1976) *Conservatism*, London, Dent, p. 12.
82 PAREKH, B. (1975) *op. cit.* p. 59.
83 *Ibid.* p. 47.
84 MANNING, D. (1976) *op. cit.* p. 14.
85 LUKES, S. (1973) *op. cit.*
86 BROWN, R. (1977) *A Poetic for Sociology: Toward a Logic of Discovery for the Human Sciences*, Cambridge, Cambridge University Press, p. 78.
87 PEPPER, S. (1948) *World Hypotheses: A Study in Evidence*, Berkeley, University of California Press; STARK, W. (1962) *The Fundamental Forms of Social Thought*, London, Routledge and Kegan Paul.
88 WILLIAMS, R. (1963) *Culture and Society 1780–1950*, Harmondsworth, Penguin, p. 256; WILLIAMS, R. (1976) *Keywords: A Vocabulary of Culture and Society*, Glasgow, Fontana, p. 190.
89 GOODWIN, B. (1978) *Social Science and Utopia: Nineteenth Century Models of Social Harmony*, Sussex, Harvester, p. 36.
90 WILLIAMS, R. (1963) *op. cit.* pp. 30, 31.
91 Claude Henri Saint-Simon quoted in GOODWIN, B. (1978) *op. cit.* p. 182.
92 WILLIAMS, R. (1963) *op. cit.*
93 BARKER, R. (1978) *op. cit.*
94 William Morris quoted in WILLIAMS, R. (1963) *op. cit.* p. 210.
95 LEAVIS, F. and THOMPSON, D. (1933) *Culture and Environment: The Training of Critical Awareness*, London, Chatto and Windus, p. 93.

96 UNGER, R. (1975) *Knowledge and Politics*, New York, Collier-Macmillan, p. 260.
97 POLANYI, M. and PROSCH, H. (1975) *Meaning*, Chicago, University of Chicago Press, p. 203.
98 WILLIAMS, R. (1976) *op. cit.* p. 168.
99 BARFIELD, O. (1954) *History in English Words*, London, Faber and Faber, p. 187.
100 Quoted in *Ibid.* p. 188.
101 WOLIN, S. (1961) *op. cit.* p. 140.
102 BEER, S. (1977) 'Cybernetics' in BULLOCK, A. and STALLYBRASS, O. (Eds.) *The Fontana Dictionary of Modern Thought*, London, Fontana, p. 150.
103 BROWN, R. (1977) *op. cit.* p. 230.
104 BIRNBAUM, P. (1978) 'Consensus and depoliticization in contemporary political theory' in BIRNBAUM, P., LIVELY, J. and PARRY, G. *op. cit.*
105 WOLIN, S. (1961) *op. cit.*
106 *Ibid.* p. 300.
107 BURNS, R. and ANTHONY, V. (1971–72) 'The Economics Association and the training of teachers', in *Economics*, 9, 3, pp. 171–4.
108 BLONDEL, J. (1978) *Thinking Politically*, Harmondsworth, Penguin, p. 115.
109 GOODWIN, B. (1978) *op. cit.* p. 136.
110 HIMMELFARB, G. (1968) *Victorian Minds*, London, Weidenfeld and Nicholson.
111 Evidence of the importance of such matters can be found in the revisions to language conducted in Nazi Germany in 1936. In reviewing the changes, Mueller shows how mechanical and organic terms were overused; words normally used to describe inanimate objects were applied to society, while organizations and objects were described with adjectives normally reserved for people or other living beings:

> Thus the ideal German was like steel (stahlern) and lived in an organic community of people (organische Volksgemeinschaft) which was charged with power (aufgeladen) as a result of predestination (Vorsehung).

MUELLER, C. (1973) *The Politics of Communication: A Study in the Political Sociology of Language, Socialization and Legitimation*, New York, Oxford University Press, p. 29.
112 BEARDSLEY, M. (1967) 'Metaphor' in EDWARDS, P. (Ed.) *The Encyclopaedia of Philosophy. Volume 5.* New York, Crowell Collier and Macmillan.

3   Environment, Space and Technology: Images in Geography

Geography in English schools has been a staple of the curriculum in the social subjects. In 1860, inspectors' reports indicated that history was taught in about one school in three, while geography was found in 85 per cent of them.[1] Overtaken by history in the 1920s and 1930s, geography has in recent years again become the most popular social subject, at the first School Certificate level at least.[2]

'Popular' would hardly be the word for the Victorian geography curriculum, for contemporary comments paint a picture of unrelieved boredom. The principal nineteenth-century rationales for geography were that it provided useful information, either as background knowledge for classical studies in the public schools, or equipment needed by any citizen of a commercial and imperial nation.[3] A contemporary advocate, Sir George Robertson, called geography 'The science of the merchant, the statesman and the strategist'.[4] These pressures sustained the notorious 'capes and bays' geography of the time,[5] and it is hard to disagree with Hurt that the constraints on geography teaching resulting from the Revised Code were no great loss.[6] However, in whatever form, geography was established as a school subject, and strengthened by its inclusion in the 1858 Code for the training of pupil teachers.[7]

While present discussions of geography teaching continue to assert the need for information about the world, often as a background to international understanding or current events, what was to become the most influential paradigm of geography, environmentalism, developed in the last quarter of the nineteenth century. In emphasizing the centrality to geography of the society-environment relation, its advocates gave the subject a new direction for growth. Initiated by the Royal Geographical Association and promoted by individuals such as J. Scott Keltie, Sir Halford Mackinder and A.J.

Herbertson, the revival led to the formation in 1893 of the Geographical Association, and with Herbertson the Secretary, to the publication in 1901 of *The Geography Teacher*. The important point to note is the zeal of Mackinder and Herbertson and their followers, and their great interest in schools. Mackinder and Herbertson taught in summer and extension courses, and both wrote textbooks published in extraordinary numbers,[8] and showing surprising longevity. One of Herbertson's works, *Man and His Work*, originally published in 1899, was still in print in the late nineteen-sixties.[9] Graves has said of Herbertson: 'It is probable that his influence on what was taught in British schools was enormous and has since been unsurpassed'.[10]

Mackinder and Herbertson established two major features of subsequent geographical study – the unity of the society-environment relationship, and the region as a framework for study. But the unity they sought was developed in a context which emphasized the physical at the expense of the social. While Mackinder fought to redress the imbalance of the time towards physical geography, and saw political geography as the 'Crowning Chapter' of geography,[11] he nonetheless held that 'no rational (human) geography can exist which is not built upon and subsequent to physical geography'.[12] Herbertson was the more influential of the two in schools. Mackinder had noted that Herbertson was 'weak' on the historical side,[13] and the need for a precise and more scientific basis for the regional division led to Herbertson's most influential contribution to English geography – the idea of the natural region.[14] There is some disagreement over the extent to which this framework led Herbertson to distort explanations of human activity. Gilbert refers to 'the crudity of some of his deterministic statements',[15] while Graves holds that 'there was never any crude environmental determinism in Herbertson's view of geography – yet there existed a subtle suggestion in his textbooks, that man's life and work were shaped by the physical environment in which he lives'.[16] This implication can be located in the strength of Darwinist assumptions of the time. Freeman notes this influence, and in doing so quotes W.M. Davis writing in 1902:

> The need, therefore, was to study the inorganic environment and then 'all these responses by which the inhabitants from the lowest to the highest, have adjusted themselves to their environment'. From this definition as from other sources, the phrase 'response to environment' has become commonplace among students: it is clearly of Darwinian origin.[17]

It was this paradigm of geography which rescued the subject from its arid nineteenth-century state, providing a framework for explanation it had previously lacked. But the framework produced tensions in the ways geography could contribute to general educational aims, for a subject based on an environmentalist paradigm was an unlikely source of insights into the relationships among people. Yet many advocates of geography in the curriculum claimed that it did provide such insights.

It has already been noted that Mackinder saw geography as a contribution to social understanding: in 1887 he described the subject of geography as 'the interaction of man in society and so much of his environment as varies locally'.[18] The interwar period saw constant references to the social values of the study of geography. In a book first published in 1926, Fairgrieve continues the tradition of commercial utility:

It pays to have some knowledge of the conditions under which people live, who are purchasers or possible purchasers of British goods; the more geography is known the better trade is likely to be served....

the real value of geography lies in the fact that it helps man to live; it helps man to place himself (the word 'place' is used advisedly) in the world, to learn his true position, and what are his duties....

Better than most subjects, because it has a warmth of sympathy tempered by dispassionate accuracy, it is fitted for the promotion of goodwill throughout the world.[19]

Fairgrieve's view that geography was a humane study, whose greatest value lay in helping to understand social problems, was widely shared in the nineteen twenties and thirties. Barker's 1927 statement[20] reiterated the benefits to commerce and international goodwill, while the three editions of Barnard's book between 1933 and 1949 advocated geography teaching whose 'ultimate aim should be a training in citizenship':

The man to whom our countryside can unfold innumerable interests, who can understand the traditions and aspirations of our busy towns, will gain the sanest and most lasting inspiration to live and work for his native-land.[21]

Garnett's book, again spanning two decades from its first edition in 1934 to its second in 1949, continued the theme:

> It should be a humanist subject, considering the life and work, interests and thoughts, ideas and ideals, of mankind the world over, enabling those who study it to see their own lives more nearly in perspective, and calling for a broader outlook and visions, a deeper understanding and sympathy.[22]

The Spens Report gave this widespread view official sanction:

> Geography also can give a conception of the world and of its diverse environments and peoples, which should enable boys and girls to see social and political problems in a truer perspective, and give them sympathetic understanding of other peoples.[23]

While this view of what was worthwhile about geography was continued in the Norwood Report[24] and post-war curriculum writings, it was tempered in the nineteen-sixties by a scepticism which has caused writers to look elsewhere for justification of the teaching of geography. Gopsill warned that 'Teachers of geography might well be cautious of approaching their subject with a missionary zest which encourages them to believe that it is a part of their job to set the world to rights'.[25] The true benefits of geography are intrinsic in the nature of the subject:

> ... the study of geography is a profitable one for children, not because it prepares them for this or that, but because it can provide them with interesting material which has immediate significance and also offers opportunities for exercise in the discipline characteristic of the subject.[26]

This intrinsic argument of justification is not new. The distinction between intrinsic and instrumental rationales appears in Barker's observation in 1927 that 'To the truly educational value of geography there may thus be added its usefulness as a contribution towards the understanding of the peoples of the world',[27] and current writers tend also to allow both types of justification, while generally themselves preferring the intrinsic argument.[28]

Of more interest here is the fact that geography is still seen by many as a contribution to social understanding. A survey of European nations showed that the secondary schools of most countries, including England, regarded geography 'as a means of acquainting pupils with the political, social, and economic problems of the world as a whole'.[29] A recent Schools Council curriculum project in geography has included in its aims that the pupil will respond to ordinary life situations with a 'readiness to search out meanings, that is, the feelings and purposes that prompt the communications and actions of other people and the spatial patterns that result from their decisions, even when these implicit meanings are unfamiliar or disagreeable', 'the ability to develop his own feelings and values which, for example, resolve conflicts between personal convenience and the good of the community', and 'understanding of what it is to work with others towards the partial solution of complex long-term problems'.[30]

These are laudable aims, but it must be remembered that geography is a diverse subject with many fields of interest, such as urban geography and climatology, having little connection with each other. The social aims of geographical education will not be realized by all selections from the discipline, and may not be realized by any of the current dominant paradigms. The history of the discipline is traceable through competing paradigms, and educational arguments complicate the possibilities of geography course content. Whatever the merits in general terms of the various arguments, the interest here is how the curricula they have produced present particular ideas about the nature of people, society, and the relations between the two. An investigation of relevant curricular sources reveals some interesting patterns.

Social Images and the Concept of Geography

While there have always been geographers whose main interests lay in explaining human activity from an environmental or spatial perspective, until recently there have been relatively few who have sought to do this within the specialized form of the discipline known as human or social geography. However, increased interest in human geography has made it a 'growth area' in the subject. Changing social conditions have in most people's views increased the importance of the study of settlement, urban studies and migration; improved technology and greater emphasis on planning have made the case of the environmental determinist even harder to sustain; the demand in academic circles for relevance to social problems such as population pressure and human inequality have strengthened claims that human geography should be the core of the subject.

But there are those who see such a specialization as divisive and damaging to the distinctive benefits of the study of geography. Herbertson's call of seventy-five years ago was for a synthesis of the physical and the human to bring 'diverse and apparently unrelated elements into a naturally constituted complex',[31] and he is echoed today in one examination syllabus whose 'subject content aims to preserve geography as a unitary study, avoiding sub-divisions, such as "human", "physical", and "economic"'.[32] It should not surprise that there is very little in the syllabus that follows which would be recognized as human geography by modern exponents of the subject. Unity is sought at the expense of scope.

However this is indeed the overwhelmingly dominant pattern in the syllabuses reviewed here, where the environmental tradition clearly prevails, and human activities, while a criterion of relevance, are not the major substance of study. Examination syllabuses have generally assumed that the nature and content of geography are clear and universally understood, a surprising state of affairs in light of the diversity of views of the discipline. There seems to be an acceptance of Herbertson's 'naturally constituted complex' of phenomena, usually referred to as 'general geography'. In those syllabuses using this term, there is, as table 1 shows, a consistent emphasis on the physical environment, mining, agriculture and manufacturing, and where human geography is the focus at all, it is seen as the study of population distribution and related problems. This assumed consensus of the generality of geography is indicated by such unexplained statements as the syllabus direction 'It is assumed that the total geography of each area will be studied'.[34] To the extent that the notion of 'general' geography indicates the nature and scope of the discipline, human geography has a negligible place in the scheme.

But it could be thought that syllabus planners see the true geographical approach to people and society in the study of regional geography where human activity can be seen in more detail and in closer connection with real environments. If this is so, the perspective of people and society provided is little different. The over-riding emphasis is on the physical environment as the background to human activity, and the basis on which this activity should be understood. There is no better indication of this than the syllabus content which presents to pupils the geographical perspective on their own society and environment. Almost all geography syllabuses at the 16+ examination level contain a major regional study of the British Isles. Table 2 summarises the content descriptions of these

...tterns of General Geography in 16 plus examination board syllabuses in geography, 1979–80[3.3]

Syllabus and preamble	Map work	Terrestrial movements	Geology and/or Geomorphology	Meteorology and/or climate	Vegetation	Primary industry (extractive and agricultural)	Secondary industry (including power generation)	Population and settlement	Transport	Other topics
Oxford Local Examinations GCE O Level *General* Candidates are expected to have a knowledge of the elements of general geography set out below.	✓	✓	✓	✓	✓	✓	✓	✓	✓	
Joint Matriculation Board GCE O Level 1980 *General Geography* This paper will test general principles illustrated by specific examples			✓	✓		✓	✓	✓		
University of Cambridge Local Examinations GCE O Level 1978/79 *General Geography*	✓		✓	✓	✓					
University of London GCE O Level Syllabus A 1979–80 'The syllabus aims to provide a topic and systematic approach to the fundamental concepts of geography.'		✓	✓	✓	✓	✓	✓	✓	✓	The inter-relationship between man and his environment: resource management and conservation; river control, irrigation, reclamation; soil conservation; air and water pollution; urban problems.
Southern Universities Joint Board GCE O Level 1979 *Principles of Geography*		✓	✓	✓	✓	See note	See note	✓	See note	Note: Economic activities combined in the following statement 'The nature, distribution and problems of man's economic activities in relation to his environment.'
The South-East Regional Examinations Board CSE 1979–80 *General World Geography*				✓	✓					The names and location of the continents and oceans, important countries, principal rivers, mountain ranges and cities. ...major products. Latitude and longitude

sections. The common emphasis again falls on physical features, extractive industry and agriculture, manufacturing, and the provision of services such as fuel, power and transport. The study of human geography *per se* provides little more than a brief culmination.

The image presented can be summarized as follows: the most important human activities are those by which people use the resources of the environment to fulfill their needs. An understanding of this process lies in seeing what possibilities, limits and influences occur in the natural environment and how people have responded to them. This response is best studied at the general level of the 'industry', for industry provides the essential link between the natural environment and other aspects of human activity such as population distribution and density, and settlement, the most important elements of human geography from this perspective.

This is the view most consistently presented in the syllabuses and textbooks reviewed. It largely explains the popular sequence of study from physical background to primary to secondary industry and thence to population distribution. It has clear historical origins in physical and commercial geography, and it is, presumably, widely believed to be the most successful way of integrating the concerns for knowledge of the physical world, familiarity with places on the earth's surface, and an understanding of why people do what they do in those places.

But it also emphasizes a particular model of human beings and excludes aspects of human experience which would contribute to a more comprehensive image of what people are like and why they are like that. The model is predominantly that of the 'plastic' individual[35] and its two strongest elements are environmental and economic determinism.

Environmental Determinism

Textbook writers are increasingly wary of the difficulties of explaining phenomena and events from an environmental perspective, for only a thin line separates it from the discredited principles of crude environmental determinism. A typical example of this crudity, and one of interesting vintage, is the following:

> Food is the raw material of labour, and where geographical conditions make it possible to produce food cheaply and abundantly, as in the Ganges valley, the population will be

dense and labour will be cheap and abundant. In contrast to this in Switzerland, where, because little food can be produced locally and much has to be imported at great expense, labour is comparatively sparse and dear.

Moreover, labour is not uniformly good. Climatic, and other factors too, will create differences, but generally speaking, man in the cool temperate regions is vigorous, energetic, and progressive while in the hot lands man is indolent and slow.[36]

More recent writers have grappled with the problem by qualifying their statements and phrasing them in more tentative tones:

These regions, which are neither too hot nor too cold and which enjoy variable weather conditions, have been acclaimed as being *climatically the best for human activity, stimulating physical and mental effort.* Seldom, too, do the climatic conditions prevent man from working out of doors. If the correlations between maps showing regions of stimulating climate and areas of highly developed civilization are acceptable, this implies that good health and energy promoted by such a climate must be counted among the conditions necessary for human progress and, therefore, that the *high degrees of progress and civilization* in most of the cool temperate regions is not surprising.[37]

There is in this passage no analysis of the exceptions to the relationship or discussion of the alternative cultural and historical explanations, quite apart from the assumptions of progress and civilization. Geographers are interested in the environment, and this is the explanatory base.

The central position of society-environment relations, while producing inadequate explanations like those above, also has a selective effect on content, for it is not difficult to see how regions and topics will be chosen which best illustrate the effect of environment. An instance is found again in a perennial text whose first edition was published in 1936, but whose most recent impression (the twenty-sixth) was printed in 1974:

Each country or region described has been chosen because it exemplifies a certain combination of geographical elements which, more or less, control present population density and dictate certain modes of life.[38]

Table 2: Contents of studies of the British Isles in 16 plus examination board syllabuses in geography, 1979–80[40]

Syllabus	Relief and drainage	Climate and/or weather	Fishing and/or forestry	Mining and/or energy	Agri-culture	Manufac-turing	Population and its distribution	Settle-ment patterns	Recrea-tion and/or tourism	Transport and/or commu-nication	Other topics
Associated Lancashire SEB CSE 1979				✓	✓	✓			✓		Urban renewal and New Towns
East Anglian EB CSE 1979	✓	✓		✓	✓	✓				✓	Local geography
Welsh Joint Education Committee GCE O Level 1979	✓	✓		✓	✓	✓	✓				London as a conurbation. A major port, a market town, a regional centre, a holiday resort
Welsh Joint Education Committee CSE 1973	✓	✓		✓	✓	✓			✓	✓	Unequal development of different regions and its consequences. Britain's overseas trade
Oxford and Cambridge SEB 1979	✓	✓		✓	✓	✓	✓	✓		✓	Resource and amenity conservation. Problems of large urban centres
North West REB CSE 1979	✓	✓			✓	✓				✓	
Metropolitan REB CSE 1980	✓	✓			✓	✓					Ideas of urban structure and its problems
The Associated Examining Board GCE O Level 1979		✓	✓	✓	✓	✓		✓		✓	
Southern Regional Examinations Board CSE 1979		✓		✓	✓		✓	✓	✓	✓	

	Water supplies	Location	Trade	Vegetation	Water supply	Resources and amenity conservation
South Western Examinations Board CSE 1979						
East Midland REB CSE 1980						
The South-East Regional Examinations Board CSE 1979–80						
University of London GCE O Level Syllabus B 1979						
University of Cambridge Local Examination Syndicate GCE O Level 1978–79						
Joint Matriculation Board GCE O Level 1980						
Oxford Local Examination GCE O Level 1979						

This selective principle leads to an emphasis on those human activities which are most directly affected by environmental conditions. Dury has pointed out that agriculture, forestry and fishing combined employ only 1 in 70 of the paid workers of the United Kingdom. Mining and quarrying take an additional 1 in 50, but all primary production accounts for only about 1 in 30. Using contribution to gross national product as an alternative criterion, over 50 per cent is contributed by finance, public services and defence, transport, communication and related activities; 35 per cent by manufacturing; 8.5 per cent by mining, quarrying and construction; and even less by agriculture, forestry and fishing.[39] What, then, can explain the overwhelming proportion of space and time devoted in syllabuses to the study of primary industry and manufacturing (see tables 1 and 2)? What underlying assumptions can account for the apportionment of contents of an O level text entitled, note, *Human and Economic Geography*, shown in table 3?

The human geography in this list is difficult to find, neglected by the prior commitment to environment and resources as central to geographical study. To the extent that people are more than this they are not of interest to the environmentalist. Unfortunately, there is a frequent tendency for environmentalism to be equated with geography itself. Simons has pointed out the incongruousness from the spatial viewpoint of the use of the term 'geographical factor',[42] but the difficulty he sees in its implicit equation of geographical with physical is still common in the syllabuses and texts. The geographical

Table 3: Contents of human and economic geography[41]

1	Types of communities	13	Minerals: general information
2	Foods from grasses	14	Iron and steel
3	Food from animals	15	Five base metals
4	Food from the sea	16	Other minerals
5	Drinks and sugar	17	Coal
6	Fruits, tobacco and spices	18	Petroleum
7	Vegetable oils	19	Hydro-electric power
8	Timber	20	Atomic power
9	Rubber	21	Trade
10	Wool and cotton	22	Transport
11	Silk and other fibres	23	Latitude, Longitude, time and maps
12	Farming types, methods and problems	24	Population and settlement

factors that help East Anglian farmers are soils, flat land and climate[43]. Physical factors are referred to as 'geographical' while historical and political ones are 'non-geographical'[44]: 'religion is not bound by any political frontier or geographical barrier'.[45]

> Man is shown as an inhabitant not of a particular state but of a natural region, and his varied activities and problems are viewed against the geographical environment of each region.[46]

While environmentalism can paint people as respondents to environmental controls, or explorers of environmental prospects and limits, the sequence of study and the selection and emphasis of content most often suggest the former. The danger is aggravated by the likelihood that even if environmental explanations are presented in a qualified and careful manner, the explanatory sequence of the underlying model will be the predominant result in learning and the careful qualification lost. The evidence lies in examiners' complaints of naive environmentalist answers:

> The general weakness was that many were unaware that cities are the hub of functional regions and that position and importance cannot be explained by site factors alone.[47]

> The majority of answers contained rote-learned optimum conditions which were indiscriminately and often erroneously applied to a wide variety of named areas.... Frequently explanations went no further than climatic factors.[48]

> Too many of the answers were written in vague generalizations – 'Bad climate, poor soils, no jobs' proved to be the problem for nearly all areas, while 'Better climate, better soils, more jobs' were the panacea for all ills.[49]

Other reports have mentioned the popularity of physical rather than human geography among teachers and pupils.[50] Environmental determinism is a major line of geographical thought, to some a necessary one,[51] but until it is able to explain human activity in ways which adequately reflect its complexity and the significance of human values and culture, it is likely to remain the source of misleading determinist accounts of human nature and society.

Related to the environmentalist approach is the view that it is the productive activities of society which are most important, and that productive activities are those where the use of natural resources is most direct. Whether this physiocratic tendency is a consciously chosen model of human activity, or a result of the environmental determinist emphasis is of little consequence; the result is that 'economic man' is the main concern, hewing a living from nature, subject always to the factors which influence what people can do and where they can do it. In this case the universal male gender is appropriate, for the nature of the emphasis finds little of interest in the work of women. It has already been noted that the focus on primary and manufacturing industry reflects neither the proportions of people involved nor the gross national product accounted for in the industries. Rather it seems that these industries are chosen because they are thought to best reflect the society-environment relation, and the operation of the ubiquitous factors of location. The practice persists of explaining industrial location in terms of nearness to raw materials, labour and market, ineluctable forces which 'explain' the location of industry and settlement with reliable regularity. It is true that increasing numbers of writers are acknowledging the complex relationships between the opportunities provided by a location, individual or group enterprise and historical circumstances,[52] but the majority stand condemned by Pounds' observation:

> In the final analysis location results from a human decision to locate some activity in a given place.... It is not difficult to show that the distribution of much economic activity, once explained so conclusively and so naively, is in fact a great deal less than rational.[53]

Although in the British Isles government planning policy has become a major influence on location decisions, political and policy considerations are almost totally absent from the text discussions. Again this fits the developing pattern of an image of people as moved more by environmental or economic forces than by intention, whose role is to respond to circumstances as they present themselves rather than to create them.

Progress and Technology

While the forces of nature and economic law may be powerful, they are also beneficent, and if society can only learn to accommodate their demands, they offer a clear path to progress. This progressivist view of social change is another consistent theme revealed in the text material in a variety of ways.

The first is the common and, given the premises just discussed, quite natural tendency for geographers to see history as a process of society's increasing success in coming to terms with the environment. The agricultural and industrial revolutions are the most significant of past events, and while some writers acknowledge that they brought difficult problems, the general view is that these are no longer with us, and that modern society can be pleased with its achievements of technological advance and material prosperity. This impression is most commonly established by descriptions of change which focus on achievements while ignoring the possibility of detrimental side effects, or the reality that few social changes benefit all to the same extent.

Typical of this is the optimistic tone of the following account of how people's demands lead to automatic improvements:

> Many of the chapters have mentioned the influence which the changing demands of individuals and groups of people have had on our towns and countryside. People are no longer satisfied with the poor living and working conditions which our cities have inherited from a less prosperous past. Demands for better houses, schools, shops, and roads have resulted in large renewal schemes near the centre of many cities, vast suburban estates at the edges of most cities and in the development of New and Expanded Towns.[54]

A similar note of optimism can be seen in the following conclusion of a regional study:

> The Government is encouraging the development of industries in the South West. Trading estates are being built on the fringes of even the smaller towns. The variety of jobs available is increasing, and the higher earnings are reflected in better housing and improved amenities. Around the larger towns and cities the villages are taking on a new function as dormitory areas. As new industry is introduced the economy is becoming more varied, balanced and stabled. Despite all this progress the South West has retained its character and remains one of the most distinct regions in the British Isles.[55]

These passages illustrate the effect of tone and selectivity in presenting text book images. The structure of the passages, with their optimistic hyperbole, and their underlying temporal sequence of progress, culminates in an approbation of the present. Their failure to qualify the picture of prosperity with the realities of inequality and the political difficulties of regional development give a less than full account of how such development is achieved, and at what cost. There are other less acceptable instances of the following kind, where the pictures painted are so benign as to be distorted.

In the first example, the progress is in housing for Welsh coal miners, where apparently the only obstacle to complete material bliss is the difficulty of the relief of the area:

> Anita's home ... is nearly seventy years old ... built without a bathroom, because in those days miners were not expected to want such luxuries. Now times have changed, Anita's father and his friends (those, that is, who are still working in the pits) earn good wages, and most of the houses have been thoroughly modernised. But in this steep-sided valley there is little room to lay out housing estates on modern lines, and it is proving a slow job to provide good houses for everyone.[56]

Another example is Hull's picture of life in London:

> There is an account of the many sides of London: the historic capital city, the centre of industry and trade, a target in war and the scene, in peace, of great projects in building and transport. There are sections on London's river and port. The events leading to London's massive growth and transformation are shown as having occurred in a physical basin, now including most of the New Towns of the 'London Region'. There is reference to the social aspects of the capital which is a famous centre for recreation and entertainment, but which is now a new home for many races.[57]

This glowing picture is reflected in the content of the book (see table 4, page 85), but it is interesting to look more closely at the 'social aspects' of London referred to in the final chapter. This comprises a brief description of the multi-racial population, the Green Belt, recreation, and the dormitory towns; no mention of problems of housing, employment, or redevelopment, and the only reference to poverty is as an explanation of why immigrants leave their homelands and travel to London.

Yet another vivid example highlights this widespread tendency to neglect unpleasant realities and depict change as a natural working out of the progress of society. In this case, the process is the enclosure movement, described by one historian as 'a plain enough case of class robbery, played according to fair rules of property and laid down by a parliament of property-owners and lawyers'.[58]

> Gradually larger farms were formed by joining up some of the open field strips into bigger fields. Fences and hedges were put up to enclose land. All kinds of new methods were brought in – growing crops in rotation, breeding better animals, draining marshy land and using more and more machines in farming. These machines meant that fewer people were needed on the land and so large numbers began to leave the small farming village and move into the growing towns where there were other jobs and more began working at full-time jobs outside farming. In turn, these larger mechanised farms could now produce the extra food needed for the growing town populations.[59]

Again the meaning of the passage lies as much in its style, its structure and what it omits as in its literal sentences. The passive tense depersonalizes the process, and suggests a functionalist necessity in which 'fewer people were needed', and the rural consolidation is nicely balanced by urban growth. The technological and economistic emphases exclude more political and humanistic considerations. Contrast the totally beneficial version of the enclosures above with this more balanced but rarer presentation:

> In their social aspects, the emergence of a labouring class, the division of rural society into farmers and labourers, the pauperising of many countryfolk can only be condemned. These accompaniments of enclosure were not wholly compensated by the rise of a class of independent farmers, some of them secure in ownership or in long leases. Technically, however the agricultural revolutioin was wholly beneficial. It enabled the country to be fed during the Napoleonic Wars, and to support the rapidly growing towns of the early years of industrialization.[60]

There are some interesting sidelights to this concern for technological achievement and the social progress it inspires. In the first place geographers writing school texts have for a long time thought it important that pupils know the processes involved in production, especially in manufacturing. A part of this predilection for technical detail derives from the implications for industrial location and movement which result from particular processes, their raw material demands and by-products. But the technical detail goes far beyond these requirements, and the history of steel processing, the production of hydro-electric power, the washing, carding, combing, spinning and weaving of textiles and many other processes, with the full complement of terms, seem to reveal the fascination with technology which pervades the material. One author explains that 'Reference to processing has been made wherever possible, which should prove of value to both technically- and academically-minded students'.[61] Another text[62] sees the geography of British industry in a way better described as the economics of technology; in its 390 pages there are only eight maps, no reference to political or social matters, but pages of detailed description of industrial processes from shipbuilding to rubber production. This approach to industry is often what passes for a study of 'people at work', and is a revealing indication of the place of human beings in the geography curriculum.[63]

Related to this is the interesting treatment in the texts of strikes, one of the more frequent social issues dealt with in the economically oriented geographies. It seems that here again technological progress takes precedence over social concerns, for strikes are with few exceptions regarded as unfortunate obstacles to production, rather than social problems in their own right; geography texts are less than neutral on the issue of the strike as a political or economic weapon. A clear example is presented in one text which discusses strikes in the context of the motor industry, citing as its only example a strike in protest at the dismissal of two workers caught smoking in a non-smoking area. The book's epilogue concludes:

> On the one hand are the international giants, such as Shell Petroleum; on the other are small family businesses, quietly pursuing their skills in small country towns. And there is still a place for the rugged individualist, who like Mr Jones of Vyse Street runs a one-man business. He has no staff problems, and he never goes on strike.[64]

Most commonly, strikes are mentioned as a 'problem' of the industry, explained in terms of boredom[65] or not analyzed at all.[66] It is indicative of the general perspective in the books reviewed that the most sympathetic reference to strikes was the following, and yet even here the concern is clearly for the damaging lost production, rather than the 'different' wages and conditions.

> Labour relations have always been difficult in the motor industry: the boring nature of many assembly-line jobs, and the ease with which disruption in a small part of one factory can affect others, have prompted many damaging strikes. In 1969, BLMC lost production of vehicles worth £70 million through strikes. Mergers have drawn attention to different wages and conditions among the many factories, while the sheer numbers, 170,000 BLMC workers in Britain, add to the difficulties.[67]

The clear implication is that the geographer's concern with strikes is a 'problem' for industry, rather than what they mean for the people involved, and the observation of the examiner's report that 'all too frequently labour disputes were deemed to be the sole reasons for economic decline'[68] is not a surprising outcome.

If technological achievement provided the possibility of social progress, and if careful attention to the environmental and economic determinants of production will produce such achievement, then progress is attainable and even assured so long as people plan skilfully and rationally. The economistic image of human nature emphasizes its materialistic rationality, and the geographical manifestation of this image is people deploying resources in space.

The texts exude a strong faith in planning, the expectation of continued and universal progress. The possibility that planning is not fully rational, that it is subject to political pressures, that planning decisions are usually made from numerous options each of which will benefit some more than others, all involving costs as well as benefits – these difficulties are not part of text book geographers' approach to planning, and the texts present a naive picture of how planning decisions are made, and what they mean. Exercises frequently simulate planning with no element of economic or political constraint or controversy, and the process of planning becomes a technical exercise amenable to solution on rational location principles: 'Sometimes the planning decisions made by the experts are wrong, because they did not take into account all the facts'.[69] What assumptions about the purposes of planning would prompt the following suggestion?

Planners should always bear in mind the needs of the people because there will be a demand for more houses, better working conditions and efficient transport.[70]

Hugh Stretton[71] has discussed the social theories implicit in approaches to urban planning, identifying four main images or models of cities which underlie them: consensual theories of cities as communities; theories viewing cities as battlegrounds for conflict between classes or other groups; cities as market places dominated by the rules of economic competition, consumption and efficiency; and cities as machinery, emphasizing planning by rational expertise. According to this classification, the images of cities and the corresponding approach to planning most common in the materials are a combination of the first and the last. Cities are seen as communities of people sharing inevitable and common problems, which are to be solved by rational planning. In common with the modern orthodoxy in planning and the 'new geography' (discussed on page 88), the effect is to demand of the geography of planning rigorous, quantitative, abstract and technical methods and problems.

Though premature at this point, it is interesting to note Stretton's contrary recommendations for a diversity of approaches to prevent methods dominating the selection of problems; concreteness to preserve the complexity and wholeness of life against the inevitably selective and narrow perspective of abstract analytical theory; and recognition of the need for social purposes to dictate the selection of methods in planning. Much of what Stretton argues for in his approach to planning would profitably be applied to its study in schools, as further discussion will reveal.

The social content of the geography curriculum described so far is determinist in explanation, narrowly materialistic in assessment of social priorities, and neglects a wide range of social issues having obvious spatial significance. It is optimistic in its description of change, and ignores the complexities of many of the issues it touches on. To illustrate further the cumulative effect of these features of the material, take the seven texts which deal with the geography of London, whose contents are outlined in table 4.

The predominant pattern illustrates the tendencies previously described. The emphasis is on economic functions and industry; these are manifest in the visible landscape of buildings, factories, roads and docks; the selection of industries studied is quite disproportionate to their significance as employers; and human geography

Table 4: Contents of seven texts on the geography of London

Allison: *Greater London*
1 The Thames in London
2 Central London
3 The port of London
4 Power for London
5 Manufacturing industry
6 London's water supply
7 The route centre of Britain
8 Inner and outer boroughs
9 The Green Belt and beyond
10 The future of London

Dancer and Hardy: *Greater London*
1 Central London: the City
2 Central London: the West End
3 The port of London
4 Settlement and industry in the Lower Thames Valley
5 The growth of London's inner suburbs
6 The Lea Valley zone
7 The Great West Road
8 London's Water Supply: the outer suburbs and the Green Belt
9 The New Town of Crawley
10 The Greater London Council

Gowing: *London*
1 What a place!
2 London's growth!
3 What makes London tick?
4 Homes for people
5 The new Londoners
6 Traffic in towns
7 Noise
8 Water
9 Room to breathe

Hull: *London*
1 The physical scene
2 The making of London
3 London the capital
4 A central point
5 Buildings
6 River and port
7 A business centre
8 Industry
9 Transport
10 People at work and play

Morris: *Britain and Beyond Book 4*
1 The size of London
2 The regions of London
3 The London basin
4 The functions of London
5 The port of London

Padget: *London*
1 The great metropolis
2 The position of London
3 London's history
4 The port of London
5 The City
6 Communications and markets
7 London: capital and tourist centre
8 The problems of London
9 London's future

Rayns: *The London Region*
1 The Thames Basin – Introduction
2 Structure of the London Basin
3 London's water supply
4 Relief, soils and vegetation of the London Basin
5 Climate of the London Basin
6 Farming in the London Basin
7 Towns and industries of the London Basin
8 Roman London
9 An historical outline
10 From the LCC to the GLC – 1888–1965.
11 From 1965 onwards: the GLC and some possible future developments
12 The functions of London
13 London as a centre of communications
14 London as a centre of industry   .
15 The port of London

is poorly represented. Social problems are largely ignored, the one exception being the text by Gowing[72] which, in its approach to London through the study of social problems, is in stark contrast with the others. Padget[73] lists the problems of traffic and over-crowding as the only matters for concern while Hull's[74] picture of people at work and play is a rosy review of recreational land use. The other texts complete the pattern, one posing the question 'Why are there no problem areas in the Outer Boroughs?',[75] another allocating twice as much space to a description of the West End as to the suburbs.[76] The important point is that not only do these treatments neglect large areas of human experience and social problems which are clearly important in themselves, but the neglected issues are matters to which a geographical perspective has much to contribute, as Gowing's book admirably illustrates.

The Approach to Controversy

Quite apart from the selective bias deriving from the environmental and commercial traditions of geography, and the relative youth of a specifically human geography, the neglect of social and political issues is most likely due also to the difficulties of dealing with controversial issues. These are genuine problems, and while the easiest solution might be to ignore such sensitive issues, it is neither academically nor morally acceptable to do so. If the geographical perspective on political and economic questions is productive and helpful in under-standing them, the integrity of the subject demands that its potential usefulness be demonstrated; more importantly, if there are clear gains to be had from the discipline in pupils' understanding of their political and economic relations with others, it is difficult to see how a systematic avoidance of such perspectives by curriculum or text writers or teachers can be justified. But avoidance there is in two main forms.

First is the practice already touched on whereby certain ques-tions are not raised. Inter-urban and rural-urban migrations are dealt with, but intra-urban movement ignored. Few writers ask why some people, groups, classes, occupations move more than others, whether movement is by choice or otherwise, what social con-sequences arise for the people involved. Political policy is taken as a given influence on location of industry, but almost never do texts raise questions about the political process or decisions themselves, again despite the existence of a thriving branch of geography devoted to such matters.[77] Traffic is consistently seen as a problem, but never why some groups have higher rates of car ownership than others, nor why it is that these groups are concentrated in some parts of the city and not others. Differential employment opportunities across regions are mentioned, but not how such regional differences are or might be responded to by governments. Regional variations in political allegiance are never discussed.

But the study of geography, while perhaps neglectful of many important though controversial questions, inevitably touches on others. Here again however, the treatment is evasive, and it is instructive to analyze how such issues are dealt with. A common strategy in the texts is for the issue, once confronted, to be turned back to the reader, in the form of a question calling for an expression of opinion. The conflict is not analyzed, but acknowledged and implicitly classified as 'a matter of opinion' about which the text can say no more. Typical examples are the brief reference to the potential conflict between development and conservation, followed by the question 'Which side would you take? Why?';[78] and the following list of problems:

You may have heard people discussing such points as these:

1 If the railways lose money, should they charge higher fares, or should the government make up the loss, or should some rail services be cut to save money?
2 Should people be forbidden to carry heavy goods by road, or to use very big lorries?
3 Is it worth while to spend a lot of money on modernising the canals?
4 Should private motoring be forbidden in very crowded areas, such as Central London?
5 What do you think about any of these questions?[79]

Both authors raise important questions, but in neither case do they present evidence for positions which might be taken, or show how geographers or planners might approach the issues, or discuss the range of criteria relevant to such judgments. The suggestion is that such decisions are matters of opinion outside the province of geography. If they are to be developed at all it must be by the teacher, who is, presumably, in a better position to conduct the treatment of controversy. But text writers cannot avoid the accusation that by omitting the kind of material needed for any informed pursuit of the questions they raise, they are offering a clear judgment that these matters are peripheral to their subject.

This avoidance of controversy, and its tacit relegation to the realm of the unknowable is of course consistent with the positivist and empirical traditions within which geography has developed. Long aspiring to the status of science, geographers have adopted the required premises of what counts as valid academic knowledge, with all that this implies about the dangers of addressing policy issues, of making moral judgments, or of attempting humanistic forms of understanding or explanation.

It is for this reason that the images of human nature and society remain a valid cause for concern in the 'new' geography; for its considerable success in establishing itself as a scientific pursuit, while eradicating much of the crude determinism and the selective bias in content of the environmental tradition, offers no guarantee that social understanding will be greatly advanced. For a review of the texts deriving from the quantitative spatial analysis of the 'new' geography reveals difficulties for those concerned with social education as here conceived.

The 'New' Geography and Spatial Analysis

Part of the strong attraction of the 'new' geography, with its emphasis on quantification, correlations of distributions, testing of models and formulae, derives from the opportunities offered for skill development, itself a popular educational concern of recent times. Calculating rank size rules, rent-bid curves, spheres of influence, least-cost locations, indices of centrality or primacy, constructing maps of distributions or journeys to work, or applying the hypothetical models of von Thunen, Burgess or Christaller provide a wealth of useful practice in wielding statistics, graphs, tables and maps. But the danger is obvious, and not unknown to some of the authors:

> Finally, a word of warning: techniques are only a means to an end, and not an end to themselves. It is vitally important that in all quantitative studies the techniques remain of lesser importance than the actual problem under consideration.[80]

Such dangers are of course difficult to avoid. Frequently the fault lies in the treatment of an important issue as an opportunity to focus on a technical skill, as when 'The Quality of Housing' becomes the cue for teaching survey methodology[81] or an entire chapter on 'Contrasts in Living Standards' is devoted to the problem of deriving indices to measure standard of living.[82] At other times hypothetical models seem to become ends in themselves rather than partial aids to understanding. This impression results largely from the common practice of presenting and explaining the model first, rather than focusing on the problem which the model attempted to solve.[83] While the difficulties of ideal models are usually pointed out, and their differences from reality noted, the emphasis is on the logic of the model, so that departures from it become aberrations best ignored.

> These models are easily criticised because they are not perfect. However, instead of criticising the obvious weaknesses, it is more profitable to consider the accuracies and usefulness of these ideas.[84]

The impact of scientific models as explanatory paradigms is to emphasize further how human activity is determined, not now by environment, but by the tyranny of space. Efficient spatial distribution becomes the criterion of optimal social conditions, and other criteria become secondary considerations which may or may not be accommodated. Note the interesting effects of this tendency in the following passage, where modern transport has rendered many earlier settlements unnecessary from the efficiency criterion, though in some cases, for obscure 'social reasons', alternative provisions may be possible:

> In all three areas which we have considered in this chapter we have noted that too many settlements came into existence. The landscapes of western countries are relics of the pre-motor age, but they are now changing.

> Fewer settlements are needed, especially fewer smaller centres. Where low order services cannot be sustained they can be supplied by travelling vans. This enables the hamlet to be preserved for social rather than economic reasons.[85]

The dilemma of these writers is a good example of how ideas can be constrained by the premises of an explanatory model. While they acknowledge and may even show concern for 'social' issues, and though they realize these may conflict with economic efficiency, their starting point is a spatial economic model of settlement hierarchies, which is not designed to accommodate 'social reasons'. These reasons are not pursued.

A Dehumanizing Language

While many assumptions about human nature and society can be found in environmental or economic or spatial models of explanation, and while images can be shown to be shaped by selection of content or avoidance of controversial social issues, there are less tangible or at least less direct ways in which the texts imply conclusions about human nature. For there seems also to be a pervasive tone, a normal way of referring to events which is so taken for granted that it is not immediately obvious. It lies in the words and phrases, the stock language of geographers, the normal conventions of their trade. It could be called the commonsense of geographical discourse, but it is not, on reflection, unproblematic or inconsequential.

Derived from deterministic forms of explanation, the language denies intention in human activity, phrasing events instead in passive terms, where people behave in response to casual forces, rather than act as constructive agents. Events are explained as outcomes of mysterious processes of which people are, if not unaware, clearly not in control. 'Change is an inevitable and essential part of life, and any big change makes problems for the men and women who have to adapt their lives to it'.[86] 'Working in the steel or chemical industries is a natural thing to do if you live on Teesside',[87] while another region 'acted like a magnet, attracting people from all over Britain'.[88]

The earlier description of the enclosure movement (page 81) described it with an air of inevitability, as if it were the only natural sequence of events, but natural inevitability is still with us:

> We are living in an age when great changes are affecting all aspects of human activity. The forces which have been steadily gathering during the first half of the present century have burst forth since the Second World War, and are in process of altering the whole of the human way of life.[89]

Given the statistical evidence of lack of change in important aspects of human welfare, this is a highly selective exaggeration. Its metaphorical denial of human intention is paralleled elsewhere by a way of referring to people as powerless and almost unimportant in the process of economic development:

> The ingredients of production, namely raw materials, labour and power, are of primary concern in the location of industry. For extractive and reproductive industries, locations are chosen where natural conditions are favourable. Workers, machinery, and power are taken to those places where natural resources are available; and the permanence of the location is determined by the continuance of such conditions as a favourable climate and the abundance and quality of raw materials.[90]

Effects of agricultural mechanization are alleviated as 'industry-based towns can absorb the surplus labour force'.[91] Developing nations become an illustration of variety in settlement patterns[92] while 'The level of unemployment is a good indicator of the economic health of a country'.[93] In Cardiff, 'The different parts of the city provide homes for different kinds of people so it is possible to divide the city into "social areas"'.[94] Ironically, this dehumanization of people is in contrast to the universal practice of personifying inanimate objects. Towns have problems, industries move and grow, and regions prosper.

Geographic Images of Human Nature and Society

The features of geographic discourse highlighted in this analysis can be traced to their origins in earlier social trends – physiocratic emphases to nineteenth century commerce, environmental determinism to Darwinism, spatial models to positivistic science, faith in planning to ideas of progress. All these ideas are connected with the view that existing social arrangements can bring prosperity to all through diligence and expertise, subject to acceptance of the constraints of physical and economic laws.

If the features of the image are related to each other the aggregate can be represented diagrammatically as shown in figure 1. The basic explanatory principles derive from the combination of universal human needs and frailty with the uncompromising laws of nature, space and economic activity. Success is determined by the extent to which human effort can wisely exploit these lawful condi-

Figure 1: The geographic image of human nature and society.

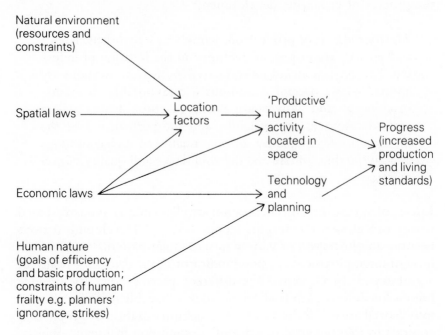

tions through technology and planning, avoiding the 'problems' of human frailty.

The dominant image is of 'plastic' individuals forming part of a total and ultimately determining system, for human activity is seen as a part of the total system with similarly given characteristics. Stoddart[95] has traced this fundamental organic image to Darwin and Comte, and to Herbertson's use of the term 'macro-organism' to describe the complex of human and physical geography. Its persistence is due to the popularity of systems analysis whose attraction is that 'it appears to offer a way of resolving the dualism between human and physical geography'.[96]

But the organic image is the constraining one castigated by Wolin, rather than the transcending one which inspired Morris or Unger (see pages 53, 54), for it shows no distinctively human features. In fact, when social models are directly used, as in the case of urban geography, they are static and mundane, revealing nothing of the ideals and conflicts of human culture. In Stretton's terms, the image is of a consensual community pursuing its basic needs through mechanistic rational planning. In glossing over inequality, controversy, even visions of desirable futures, the human geography presented is a poor attempt to realize its subject.

There is no consensus about the aims of geography either as a research discipline or as a subject for study in schools, but there is general agreement that understanding the results of human activity, aspects of social organization and social change are essential parts of it. If the arguments presented in Chapter 2 are accepted, the differences between explaining physical processes and human action makes impossible a unified society-environment study based on a single explanatory paradigm. Explanatory models which serve for one cannot serve for the other. The dominance of the traditions of environmental and economic determinism are a handicap to further profitable application of geographical knowledge to human affairs. As one geographer has pointed out:

> ... until subject matter theories with different epistemological characteristics have been formulated, the focus of our spatial planning must continue to be on supermarkets, roads and airports, and not on the needs and desires of those individual human beings that the facilities allegedly are constructed to serve.[97]

This tradition and its inherent contradictions have been noted before, as when an historian of the discipline wrote almost twenty years ago:

> Many geographers have never been deeply concerned with ultimate objectives of social character, and some would sincerely regard efforts to provide directives for human action as presumptuous and arrogant. But sooner or later writers ask whether geography really is a human study at all, possibly because some writers on human geography appear to have studied almost everything except the people.[98]

That environmentalism may be superseded in schools, as it appears largely to have been in universities, by the locational analysis school is no guarantee of a more appropriate form of explanation. For, as has been suggested in the texts reviewed, the old paradigms may merely be replaced by a new form of determinism, this time based on space. Here again the results of human activity are explained without recourse to conscious human agents or social contexts. The locational analysis school can be said to have reified 'the spatial' as the basis of the subject matter of the discipline. At the same time it diverted attention away from the underlying structural explanations of society and economy, as part of a general process of 'mystification' whereby surface manifestations are confused for root causes.[99]

Thus statements in the text material which attribute spatial differences to 'different kinds of people', or government planning, or factors of location such as the availability and stability of a labour market, have arbitrarily stopped the causal chain at a point which omits social, economic and political considerations. To claim that explanation in geography can go no further is only to say that it is inadequate to its task, and ignores the fact that many geographers are going further:

> Geographical differentiation is a detail – albeit an important detail – and a result of the operation of social systems. It is not a fundamental property of such systems. The space-economy for example is simply the spatial pattern of organization created by the industrial economy; it is not an independent variable. This point has been clearly demonstrated by recent reconsiderations of, for example, the nature of uneven regional development and economic under-development which show that both processes, whilst creating spatial patterns are, more fundamentally, outcomes of the operation of the economy rather than the result of autonomous geographical factors. To concentrate on the latter is not only superficial, it is also incorrect.[100]

The images of human nature and society built into the explanatory paradigms which dominate school curricula and texts are inadequate. They restrict the extent to which human action can be understood, substituting explanations based on a plastic model of the individual and a narrow and amorphous model of social relations and structure. In focusing on concrete outcomes of social activity, and explaining them through natural causal models, geographers have disguised the social origins of these outcomes and the political assumptions and implications of their theories. Olsson, in his analysis of urban geographical theories and their usefulness, concludes that:

> the explanatory power and potential planning applicability of

geographic theory does not depend on the employed and usually specified spatial axioms but rather on the unspecified axioms about individual and group behaviour.[101]

Until these underlying images of individual and society are recognized, and their study given the explicit attention it deserves, the significance of geographical knowledge for social practice will not be realized, nor the constraints it currently imposes overcome.

Notes and References

1 HURT, J. (1972) *Education in Evolution: Church, State, Society, and Popular Education 1800–1870*, London, Paladin, p. 206.
2 In 1926, 89.8 per cent of candidates studied history, with 69.2 per cent taking geography; in 1937 the figures were 82 per cent and 69 per cent respectively. However, in recent years CSE and GCE examination entries in geography have exceeded those in other subjects. GREAT BRITAIN BOARD OF EDUCATION (1938) *Report of the Consultative Committee on Secondary Education with Special Reference to Grammar Schools and Technical High Schools*, London, HMSO, p. 99.
3 BARNARD, H. (1949) *Principles and Practice in Geography Teaching*, London, University Tutorial Press, p. 3.
4 Quoted in GREGORY, D. (1978) *Ideology, Science and Human Geography*, London, Hutchinson, p. 18. The connections with imperialism are documented in HUDSON, B. (1977) 'The new geography and the new imperialism: 1870–1918', in *Antipode*, 9, 2, pp. 12–19.
5 GILBERT, E. (1972) *British Pioneers in Geography*, Newton Abbot, David and Charles, p. 128.
6 HURT, J. (1972) *op. cit.* p. 206.
7 GRAVES, N. (1975) *Geography in Education*, London, Heinemann Educational, p. 47.
8 GILBERT, E. (1972) *op. cit.* p. 194.
9 GRAVES, N. (1975) *op. cit.* p. 31.
10 *Ibid.* p. 28.
11 GILBERT, E. (1972) *op. cit.*
12 This 1887 statement by Mackinder is quoted in GREGORY, D. (1978) *op. cit.* p. 16.
13 GILBERT, E. (1972) *op. cit.* p. 188.
14 GRAVES, N. (1975) *op. cit.* p. 31.
15 GILBERT, E. (1972) *op. cit.* p. 199.
16 GRAVES, N. (1975) *op. cit.* p. 31.
17 FREEMAN, T. (1961) *A Hundred Years of Geography*, London, Duckworth, p. 74.
18 GILBERT, E. (1972) *op. cit.* p. 172.
19 FAIRGRIEVE, J. (1946) *Geography in School*, London, University of London Press, pp. 7, 8, 10.

20 BARKER, W. (1927) *Geography in Education and Citizenship*, London, University of London Press.
21 BARNARD, H. (1929) *op. cit.* p. 219.
22 GARNETT, O. (1949) *Fundamentals in School Geography*, London, Harrap, p. 19.
23 GREAT BRITAIN BOARD OF EDUCATION (1938) *op. cit.* p. 174.
24 GREAT BRITAIN BOARD OF EDUCATION (1943) *Curriculum and Examinations in Secondary Schools*, Report of the Committee of the Secondary Schools Examination Council appointed by the President of the Board of Education in 1941, London, HMSO.
25 GOPSILL, G. (1966) *The Teaching of Geography*, London, Macmillan, p. 11.
26 *Ibid.* p. 2.
27 BARKER, W. (1927) *op. cit.* p. 168.
28 GRAVES, N. (1975) *op. cit.*; UNDERWOOD, B. 'Aims in geographical education', in *Cambridge Journal of Education*, 6, 3, pp. 151–6.
29 MARCHANT, E. (1971) *The Teaching of Geography at School Level*, Council for Cultural Cooperation of the Council of Europe, London, Harrap, p. 17.
30 TOLLEY, H. and REYNOLDS, J. (1977) *Geography 14–18: A Handbook for School Based Curriculum Development*, Basingstoke, Macmillan, p. 21.
31 Quoted in BRAMWELL, R. (1961) *Elementary School Work 1900–1925*, London, Institute of Education, University of London, p. 31.
32 JOINT MATRICULATION BOARD (1978) *General Certificate of Education Regulations and Syllabuses 1980*, Manchester, p. 65.
33 Sources for this table are as follows: OXFORD LOCAL EXAMINATIONS (1979) *General Certificate of Education 1979. Regulations and Syllabuses*, Oxford; JOINT MATRICULATION BOARD (1978) *op. cit*; UNIVERSITY OF CAMBRIDGE LOCAL EXAMINATIONS SYNDICATE (1976) *Syllabuses. General Certificate of Education, 1978*, Cambridge; UNIVERSITY OF LONDON (1977) *General Certificate of Education Examination, Regulations and Syllabuses. June 1979 and January 1980*, London; SOUTHERN UNIVERSITIES' JOINT BOARD FOR SCHOOL EXAMINATIONS (1978) *General Certificate of Education 1979. Regulations and Syllabuses*, Bristol; THE SOUTH EAST REGIONAL EXAMINATIONS BOARD FOR THE CERTIFICATE OF SECONDARY EDUCATION *Certificate of Secondary Education Examinations 1979–80. Regulations and Syllabuses*, Royal Tunbridge Wells.
34 THE ASSOCIATED EXAMINING BOARD FOR THE GENERAL CERTIFICATE OF EDUCATION (1979) *Syllabuses 1979. Section III*, Aldershot, p. 107.
35 HOLLIS, M. (1977) *Models of Man: Philosophical Thoughts on Social Action*, Cambridge, Cambridge University Press.
36 FOX, F. and FAIRS, G. (1967) *A Rational Economic Geography*, London, Cassell, p. 4. This text does not fall within the criteria of selection of this study, which is limited to texts printed since 1969. However, while the original edition of this text was published in 1937, it has seen numerous revisions and printings, including ten editions from 1959 to 1967, and two printings of the eleventh revision published in 1967, from which the statement is quoted.

37 ROBINSON, H. (1976) *Economic Geography*, Plymouth, MacDonald and Evans, p. 187.
38 ARCHER, A. and THOMAS, H. (1958) *Geography. First Series. Book 4: The Grouping of Peoples – From Desert to City*, London, Ginn, p. 3.
39 DURY, G. (1973) *The British Isles*, London, Heinemann Educational, p. 2.
40 Sources for this table are as follows: ASSOCIATED LANCASHIRE SCHOOLS EXAMINING BOARD (1979) *Regulations and Syllabuses. Certificate of Secondary Education. 1979 Examination*, Manchester; EAST ANGLIAN EXAMINATIONS BOARD FOR THE CERTIFICATE OF SECONDARY EDUCATION (1979) *Regulations and Syllabuses – 1979*, Colchester; WELSH JOINT EDUCATION COMMITTEE (1979) *General Certificate of Education. Certificate of Secondary Education. Regulations and Syllabuses*, Cardiff; OXFORD AND CAMBRIDGE SCHOOLS EXAMINATION BOARD (1979) *Regulations for Certificate Examinations for the year 1979*, Cambridge; NORTH WEST REGIONAL EXAMINATIONS BOARD CERTIFICATE OF SECONDARY EDUCATION *Syllabuses for the 1979 Examinations. Section 1*, Manchester; METROPOLITAN REGIONAL EXAMINATIONS BOARD *Regulations and Syllabuses 1980*, London; ASSOCIATED EXAMINING BOARD (1979) *op. cit.*; SOUTHERN REGIONAL EXAMINATIONS BOARD (1978) *Syllabuses for the Examinations for the Certificate of Secondary Education 1979*, Southampton; SOUTH WESTERN EXAMINATIONS BOARD FOR THE CERTIFICATE OF SECONDARY EDUCATION (1977) *Regulations and Schemes of Examination 1979*, Bristol; EAST MIDLANDS REGIONAL EXAMINATIONS BOARD (1979) *Regulations and Syllabuses for the Certificate of Secondary Education 1980*; SOUTH EAST REGIONAL EXAMINATIONS BOARD (1979–80) *op. cit.*; University of London (1977) *op. cit.*; UNIVERSITY OF CAMBRIDGE LOCAL EXAMINATIONS SYNDICATE (1976) *op. cit.*; JOINT MATRICULATION BOARD (1978) *op. cit.*; OXFORD LOCAL EXAMINATIONS (1979) *op. cit.*
41 CAIN, H. (1975) *Human and Economic Geography*, London, Longman.
42 SIMONS, M. (1966) 'What is a geographical factor?' in *Geography*, 51, pp. 210–217.
43 MORRIS, R. (1974) *Britain and Beyond. Book 4: Britain, Europe, and World Problems*, Glasgow, Blackie.
44 ROBINSON, H. (1976) *Human Geography*, Plymouth, MacDonald and Evans, p. 18.
45 *Ibid.* p. 41.
46 DOBSON, F. and VIRGO, H. (1974) *The Elements of Geography in Colour*, London, The English Universities Press, preface.
47 UNIVERSITY OF LONDON (1975) *General Certificate of Education Examination. Subject Reports.*
48 JOINT MATRICULATION BOARD (1974) *General Certificate of Education Examiners' Reports.*
49 JOINT MATRICULATION BOARD (1975) *General Certificate of Education Examiners' Reports.*
50 UNIVERSITY OF LONDON (1975) *op. cit.*; ASSOCIATED LANCASHIRE SCHOOLS EXAMINING BOARD (1973) *Reports of the Chief Examiners and the Chief Moderators.*

51 MARTIN, A. (1951) 'The necessity for determinism: a metaphysical problem confronting geographers', in *Transactions of the Institute of British Geographers*, 17, pp. 1–13.
52 MINSHULL, R. (1968) *Human Geography from the Air*, Basingstoke, Macmillan; TOLSON, A. and JOHNSTONE, M. (1976) *A Geography of Britain*, London, Oxford University Press; WATTS, D. and JONES, S. (1974) *Industrial Location in Britain and Ireland*, London, Ginn.
53 POUNDS, N. (1976) *Success in Geography: Human and Regional*, London, John Murray, p. viii.
54 HOPKINSON, I. *et al.* (1972) *Living Geography. Book 4*, Edinburgh, Holmes McDougall, p. 164.
55 SECKINGTON, R. (1972) *South West England*, London, Ginn, p. 63.
56 YOUNG, E. (1975) *People in Britain*, London, Edward Arnold, p. 88.
57 HULL, O. (1970) *London*, London, Macmillan, p. 3.
58 THOMPSON, E. (1968) *The Making of the English Working Class*, Harmondsworth, Penguin, p. 237.
59 AYERS, A. *et al.* (1977) *Homescapes*, Edinburgh, Oliver and Boyd, p. 33.
60 DURY, G. (1973) *op. cit.* p. 52.
61 SIMMONS, W. (1976) *The British Isles*, Plymouth, MacDonald and Evans, p. v.
62 REES, H. (1970) *The Industries of Britain: A Geography of Manufacture and Power, Together with Farming, Forestry and Fishing*, London, Harrap.
63 ASKEY, G. BENYON, P. and JAMES, A. (1974) *Cardiff and the Valleys*, Edinburgh, Holmes McDougall; GADSBY, J. and D. (1970) *Looking at Britain*, London, A. and C. Black.
64 FEES, H. (1970) *op. cit.* p. 379.
65 SAUVAIN, P. (1974) *Man the Manufacturer*, Amersham, Hulton, p. 43.
66 MARSDEN, W. (1974) *Towns and Cities*, Edinburgh, Oliver and Boyd.
67 WATTS, D. and JONES, S. (1974) *op. cit.* p. 41.
68 JOINT MATRICULATION BOARD (1969) *General Certificate of Education Examiners' Report*, p. 19.
69 REDDIN, T. (1971) *Town Studies*, London, Macdonald, p. 24.
70 ASKEY, G. *et al.* (1974) *op. cit.* p. 34.
71 STRETTON, H. (1978) *Urban Planning in Rich and Poor Countries*, Oxford, Oxford University Press.
72 GOWING, D. (1975) *London*, London, Longman.
73 PADGET, S. (1972) *London*, London, Macdonald.
74 HULL, O. (1970) *op. cit.*
75 ALLISON, R. (1978) *Greater London*, London, Hodder and Stoughton, p. 132.
76 MORRIS, R. (1974) *op. cit.*
77 COX, K. (1973) *Conflict, Power and Politics in the City: A Geographic View*, New York, McGraw Hill.
78 CRISP, T. (1975) *Industry*, London, Nelson, p. 12.
79 YOUNG, E. (1975) *op. cit.* p. 84.
80 WOODCOCK, R. and BAILEY, M. (1978) *Quantitative Geography*, Plymouth, MacDonald and Evans, p. vi.
81 REDDIN, T. (1971) *op. cit.*

82 DUNLOP, S. and MacDONALD, D. (1978) *Social Geography*, London, Heinemann Educational.

83 ADAM, A and DUNLOP, S. (1976) *Village, Town and City*, London, Heinemann Educational; BRIGGS, K. (1974) *Introducing Towns and Cities*, London, Hodder and Stoughton.

84 WOODCOCK, R. and BAILEY, M. (1978) *op. cit.* p. 4.

85 ADAM, A. and DUNLOP, S. (1976) *op. cit.* p. 75.

86 YOUNG, E. (1968) *Britain and Ireland: Their Changing Patterns of Life and Work*, London, Edward Arnold, p. 62.

87 YOUNG, E. (1975) *op. cit.* p. 105.

88 JOHNSON, M. (1974) *Towns*, London, Evans, p. 11.

89 PARKER, G. (1972) *The Geography of Economics*, London, Longman, p. 1.

90 STONE, W. *et al.* (1972) *Geographic Fundamentals*, London, Heinemann Educational, p. 220.

91 NESS, T. (1971) *Scotland's People. Where They Live and Work*, London, Heinemann Educational, p. 7.

92 ADAM, A. and DUNLOP, S. (1976) *op. cit.*

93 NESS, T. (1971) *op. cit.* p. 26.

94 BOLWELL, L. (1974) *Wales*, London, Ginn, p. 81.

95 STODDART, D. (1966) 'Darwin's impact on geography', in *Annals of the Association of American Geographers*, 56, pp. 683–98.

96 GREGORY, D. (1978) *op. cit.* p. 45.

97 OLSSON, G. (1972) 'Some notes on geography and social engineering', in *Antipode*, 4, 1, pp. 1–22.

98 FREEMAN, T. (1961) *op. cit.* p. 182.

99 SMITH, D. and OGDEN, P. (1977) 'Reformation and revolution in human geography', in LEE, R. (Ed.) *Change and Tradition: Geography's New Frontiers*, Department of Geography, Queen Mary College, University of London, p. 54.

100 LEE, R. (1977) 'Anti-space: geography as a study of social process writ large', in LEE, R. (Ed.) *op. cit.* p. 72.

101 OLSSON, G. (1972) *op. cit.* p. 13.

4   *In the Palm of the Invisible Hand: Ideology in Economics*

The relative neglect of economics in schools is surprising, for there is a potentially strong instrumental argument for its inclusion in the curriculum, a long if interrupted history of the teaching of the subject, and frequent claims of its importance in social education. Its nineteenth-century manifestation, the lessons of political economy in the natural laws of society, was seen, in the report of the Newcastle Commission of 1861 and the 1871 Elementary Code, as a necessary part of schooling[1] at least in the elementary schools. A hundred years later, the subject is taught only to a minority, but official reports continue to claim its importance[2] and its advocates, in this instance the Economics Association, have felt justified in calling it 'the core subject of the social sciences'.[3] The failure of economics to realize this central position claimed for it must be attributed in large measure to the controversy surrounding the subject itself, a controversy which contributed to its demise in the last century, prevented its revival for much of the twentieth, and is closely related to the central problem of this study.

The Decline of Political Economy

Political or social economy has been well documented by historians of nineteenth century education, who have repeatedly cited its intentions of social control.[4] But the propagandist ideas of the political economists were not new. Rather they gave a new basis to the moral and political edicts previously drawn from Christian moral teaching by writers like Hannah More and Sarah Trimmer.

The scientific study of political economy flourished in the early decades of the nineteenth century. Ricardo and McCulloch built on the earlier works of Smith and Malthus, and their ideas were widely disseminated by popularizers such as Mrs Marcet and Harriet Martinau.[5] In the 1830s Richard Whately added to the tradition, which soon found a place in both the National and British schools. 'Virtually every reader published by religious bodies of the late 1830s to 1880 had its quota of Whately, or imitations or adaptations of his articles'.[6] Later William Ellis gave pride of place to social economy in the Birkbeck Schools founded between 1848 and 1865, his influence extending to the London Board Schools in the 1880s.[7]

In 1824, McCulloch had proclaimed that 'the errors with which Political Economy was formerly infected have now nearly disappeared, and a very few observations will suffice to show that it really admits of as much certainty in its conclusions as any science founded on fact and experiment can possibly do'.[8] That such a strong base existed for certain social and political conclusions was appealing to many public reformers. Lord Brougham had enlisted the support of Harriet Martinau to bring the authority of science to bear on the government's attempts to popularize the Poor Laws. Sir James Kay-Shuttleworth, in pointing to the dangers of the 'volcanic elements' of misery, vice and prejudice in the labouring classes of 1839, called for 'a good secular education to enable them to understand the true causes which determine their physical condition and regulate the distribution of wealth among the several classes of society'.[9] This sentiment was echoed over twenty years later in the Report of the Newcastle Commission of 1861:

> Next to religion, the knowledge most important to a labour-ing man is that of the causes which regulate the amount of his wages, the hours of his work, the regularity of his employ-ment, and the prices of what he consumes. The want of such knowledge leads him constantly into error and violence des-tructive to himself and his family, oppressive to his fellow workmen, ruinous to his employers, and mischievous to society.[10]

The solution to the violent dissatisfaction with their lot of which the working class were capable was thought, or at least said, to be, not in the oppression of one class by another, or in persuasion or indoctrination, but in the revelation of the laws of nature, including the interdependence of men and women of all classes, and the fundamental necessity in society of property and inequality. If these were the features necessary for the survival of society, then the school's task was to develop the required attitudes and personal qualities on which these features depended. Interesting for its direct and concrete translation to the school level is the following extract from the prospectus of the first of the Birkbeck Schools in 1848, describing the subject of social economy:

1   Instruction is the means by which wealth or the comforts and necessaries of life are produced; this inquiry leading to the conviction in the minds of the pupils, that industry, skill, economy, and security of property must prevail in society, in order that this production may be abundant:

2   Instruction in the advantages of the division of labour, of the co-operation of labour and capital and in the arrangements which facilitate interchange; the study of these subjects furnishing the pupils with arguments which demonstrate beyond all doubt how honesty, sobriety, punctuality, and moral discipline must obtain amongst a people for these arrangements to be fully serviceable:

3   Instruction on the influence upon the general well-being, of the prevalence of parental forethought or of parental improvidence.[11]

The ideas of the popular science of political economy were an interesting accommodation of the theories of Malthus, Smith, Ricardo and the like to the realities of economic and political power at the time. Thus Ricardo's labour theory of value was accommodated by interpreting capital as the fruit of past labour, and the King was no different from the meanest mechanic in receiving his just reward for labour. Competition was the guarantee of progress, and the laws of the economy operated to reward those who, by skill, knowledge and hard work produced the wealth of the land. From this description of the immutable principles of society, necessity became a virtue, and the conclusions drawn from fact were easily translated into moral prescriptions. Inequality was necessary to progress, and therefore could not be limited, as witnessed by a character in one of Mrs Marcet's stories:

All that you have said reconciles me, in a great measure, to the inequality of the distribution of wealth, for it proves that, however great a man's possessions may be, it is decidedly advantageous to the country that he should still endeavour to augment them.... It is ... an addition to the general stock of wealth of the country, by which the poor benefit equally with the rich.[12]

Or the British and Foreign School Society lesson book of 1864:

> Nothing is more certain than that, taking the working classes
> in the entire mass, they get a fair share of the proceeds of the
> national industry.[13]

Thus attempts at reducing inequality were misguided, unjust, and harmful, a commonly stated result being that beggars would no longer have anyone from whom to beg! Hard work was not its own reward in any Christian ethical sense, but rather the necessary contribution of each to the society, whose laws would ensure a just return. Shirking, ignorance and strikes were thus to be condemned, and nothing should be allowed to prevent nature taking its course in respect of these transgressions. Self-help, perseverance, temperance and thrift were the prime human virtues, and Malthus was used to preach abstinence for those who could not support their offspring.

The cynicism of a century's hindsight, and the frequent ridicule now aimed at much naive political economy has inured the modern reader to offence and even surprise at such a calculated defence of injustice in the name of science. And there is evidence of opposition from parents to such class interested teachings.[14] But for most of the nineteenth century elementary social education for the middle and lower classes consisted wholly or in large part of political economy, designed and executed to defend inequality, inheritance of wealth and injustice. Such a system was obviously threatened by a widening franchise and a more professional education, and the decline of political economy can be seen in this light.

Despite the recommendations of the Newcastle Commission, the Revised Code ended the development of political economy, as it had geography; but unlike geography political economy did not recover. The reasons for this can only be surmised. To begin with, political economy did not have the broad base across various types of schools which history and geography shared. But there was a more general change in the climate of economic thought, along two separate lines.

First, adherents to political economy became disenchanted. As early as 1847, J.S. Mill in his influential *Principles of Political Economy* had eroded the certainty of natural law, distinguishing, as he describes in his *Autobiography*, between:

> ... the laws of the Production of Wealth, which are real laws
> of nature, dependent on the properties of objects, and the
> modes of its Distribution, which, subject to certain con-

ditions, depend on human will. The common run of political economists confuse these together, under the designation of economic laws, which they deem incapable of being defeated or modified by human effort; ascribing the same necessity to things dependent on the unchangeable conditions of our earthly existence, and to those which, being but the necessary consequences of particular social arrangements, are merely coextensive with these.[15]

If political economists were to see distribution and even property as manipulable, and open to reform, as Mill later did, then the subject, rather than being ideologically safe, was positively dangerous. As socialism and reformist movements grew in influence, discussion of such matters became even more controversial. Also the writings of humanists like Ruskin were moderating the scientific approach of political economy. William Ellis's later writings in the 1870s show signs of this change,[16] as does the work of the idealist reformers of the Oxford Social Science Club and the extension movement.[17] In rejecting strongly scientific approaches, and incorporating more history into social science, influences such as these can be seen as the origins of the civics courses introduced into elementary schools in the 1890s.[18]

The second line of development was the rise of the highly theoretical marginalist approach to economics. Ushered in with publications in the first half of the 1870s by Jevons, Menger and Walras, it established a revolutionary theory of economics, and with it an abstract and difficult methodology. It became the orthodox theory of economics, and in the work of Alfred Marshall, 'the dominant influence on economic theory from the 1890s to the depression of the 1930s, especially in English-speaking nations'.[19]

In modifying theory it was revolutionary, but its ideological base was far from new. Among its founding fathers, Jevons, Menger and Pareto were avowedly anti-democratic,[20] and Marshall feared that the consequences of reformist zeal, especially socialism, would interfere with the rights of private property and free enterprise (beyond a minimum of protective legislation). A utilitarian ethos of unlimited individual want, a market theory of value, an economic system whose central dynamic was substitution at the margin, and a natural tendency to long-run equilibrium in the factor market, were major tenets of the doctrine. It was the adherence to the importance of private capital, the free market and the profit motive that was to be the controversial foundation of economic theory in the twentieth century, for these ran counter to the collectivism and egalitarian motives of socialist thought and the rising Labour Party.[21]

While this conflict was no doubt a handicap to any major attempts to introduce the new economics in schools, a more important, though related obstacle was the methodology of the modern analytical economics. The assumptions required for partial equilibrium analysis, the reliance on differential calculus as a technique for studying marginal change, and the increasing use of indices for measuring economic variables had created a complex set of methods essentially related to the theory. Fearing that any study of economics which did not comprehend these features would be distorted and abused, economists were reluctant to advocate its inclusion in schools. In fact, a long list of notable persons, including William Beveridge in 1921, Hugh Gaitskell in 1939, Lionel Robbins in 1955 and Lord Kahn in 1976, have warned against the teaching of theoretical economics.[22] These views were shared by the contributors to the Spens Report who were 'not convinced that a serious introduction to ... economics is within the capacities of normal grammar school pupils under 16'.[23] Such views helped to restrict the study of economics to a negligible level between the wars, despite occasional references to its importance in education for citizenship.[24]

Given these uncertainties, the post-war increase in economics courses and enrolments is all the more impressive, with a four-fold increase in total GCE entries in the twenty years to the mid-seventies dwarfed by a twenty-fold increase in economics entries.[25] But such a rapid growth can not be taken to indicate the solution of the problems of difficulty and controversy which so long hindered the subject's growth, for the conflict amongst economists over the proper study of their subject and the concern amongst educators about bias are probably greater now than ever before. Since many of these controversies turn on the concept of human nature which economics assumes, and the model of society it presents, they are central to the present study, and will be discussed in the context of the images themselves.

Images in Economics: Economic Individualism

Few social sciences are as clearly based on an orthodox and explicit image of the individual as modern positive economics. In developing an explanatory model, economists have focused on certain postulated universal human characteristics, allowing economic theory to treat individuals as atomistic and therefore amenable to simple aggregation and generalization. The universal characteristic which renders all people anonymous is unlimited wants, and the feature which requires an atomistic approach is the complete subjectivity of preferences. The texts reviewed reveal the central elements of the image.

First the theory of unlimited wants is universally established by considering the individual, whose subjective preferences are given. 'Each individual subconsciously arranges his wants according to his preferences; the economist says that he has a scale of preferences'.[26] These preferences must be material ones, for 'the general economic motive', for businessmen, professionals and manual workers is '... the motive for self-betterment. The businessman looks for the best profit he can get, the wage earner, singly or through his union, looks for the best wage.... They all try to act in the way which will *pay* best'.[27] This desire for self-betterment knows no bounds, for 'the more we have, the more we want ... *Our wants are never satisfied*'.[28] The extremes to which this can lead are illustrated in the following statement from one apologist for economics:

> ... the economist sees man as a being with an insatiable appetite, not just for food, but also for shelter, warmth, clothing, and less essential products of many kinds. No limit to his demands has ever been recorded: once he has a bicycle he desires a small car, then a larger car, then two cars – and even three-car or four-car families are now not unknown.[29]

It is not for the economist to enquire into the origins or merits of these preferences, and there are no economic grounds for giving a meal to a starving Asian rather than an English millionaire;[30] utility derives from the individual alone, is therefore completely subjective, and cannot be compared. But this is no cause for concern, for '... we are dealing with "economic man", who is not motivated by Christian feelings or patriotism but who seeks merely to maximize his own income – sordid, isn't he? But society turns his greed to good account by using it to attract him to the position where he is most needed'.[31]

The device by which society does this is the offering of incentive which appeals to the universal profit motive. 'Without profit as an incentive, our land, labour and capital would lie idle and production would not take place. There would be no jobs for us or goods in the shops for us to buy'.[32] 'Efficiency is achieved simply by using the incentive of private profit'.[33] This necessitates inequality of income, for 'There would be little point in a man training if inducements to do so were lacking'.[34]

The theoretical convenience of the image of economic individualism is its reliability. It is the source of a constant and stable demand, a universally applicable motive which reacts predictably to the incentives of the market, and there are no exceptions. 'We have found from long experience that when prices are lower, people buy more; when prices are higher, people buy less. The Law of Demand is a general rule of human behaviour'.[35] 'Even the philanthropist would like more to give away'.[36] What fluctuations do occur are attributed to the fickle difficulties of taste[37] and best ignored as aberrations.

It should not surprise that the ideal type of economic individual is the one who combines these traits – one who is motivated by an unlimited competitive urge to profit, who is skilled in accommodating to the laws of the market, and whose unique character deserves free rein to create prosperity. Just as nineteenth-century socialists and radicals found in the labour theory of value the justification for higher wages, positive market economics lauds the abilities of the entrepreneur, but with such vagueness and contradiction that one seems justified in suspecting special pleading.

First, entrepreneurial ability is like no other human ability.

> To make a sure profit, a profit in the economic sense, there must be *ability*, of the special business kind which consists in a knack of judging whether this or that (risk) is not worth taking for the expected return. This is very different from the technical skill which makes a good workman, or the professional skill which makes a good lawyer or teacher, or the artistic gifts which make a good novelist, singer or actor.[38]

In applying this skill to the market, the entrepreneur's functions 'are so specialized and distinctive as to require separate consideration and treatment'.[39] 'They are rare qualities and in the main they cannot, probably, be taught in schools and universities, as they are aspects of character'.[40] It is a 'mysterious gift of personality and flair'.[41] 'It requires qualities of initiative, leadership, organization, and control. The relatively few people of first-class ability who possess such qualities are able to operate effectively in almost any industry'.[42]

While one text author allows that enterprise is 'a highly artificial concept',[43] there is otherwise widespread agreement about the reality and uniqueness of this prized quality, but there is little consensus on just what it comprises. Thus profit is explained as a reward for special organizational ability in bringing the factors of production together, for leadership of workers, for shrewd judgment, or as a return on personal investment or risk taking. But whatever the exact nature of the contribution, there is no doubting the central role ascribed to the entrepreneur by the conventional text, for the economic system depends on such people.

> The entrepreneur may be considered as representing an *intermediary between the forces of demand and supply*, as a co-ordinator between market forces, represented by effective demand and potential supply. In this role the entrepreneur must attempt to 'interpret' consumers' actual and likely wants, and he must act, therefore, as a *link* between those wants and available resources.[44]

In performing these functions, entrepreneurs are only fulfilling their 'duties' to the system, which include controlling output in both quality and quantity, and controlling the labour force.[45]

Economic individualism assumes that human qualities originate ultimately in the individual. Wants are not socially conditioned, nor utility systematically varied by circumstance. The economic individual's most valued attributes are mysterious gifts, the wants infinite, the motives uniform. And the texts repeatedly argue that there is no point in distinguishing producers and consumers, for every individual is both a producer and a consumer. The individual is an atom, and since people are autonomous and in essence owe nothing to society, social relations become contracts freely entered into by quite independent parties naturally following their own self-interest.

The nature and origin of the image of the rational economic individual have been well documented,[46] and its deficiencies are increasingly widely voiced. The assumptions of profit maximization has been found to conflict with the evidence of real motives;[47] and to deny the possibility of interpersonal comparisons of utility seems to contradict everyday experience.[48]

More fundamentally, individual behaviour cannot be understood in isolation, divorced from the social context. The major difficulty arises when economists try to break the chain of interaction between individual and society by taking the atomistic individual as the basic unit of analysis and the starting point for study, and assume that utility and preferences are completely subjective and given. But preferences and their expression are influenced by position in society and income, and there are systematic variations in these:

> A man who is landless will estimate the 'sacrifice' and 'disutility' involved in hiring himself to a master at much less than will a peasant farmer possessed of land and instruments of his own, since the destitute position of the former causes him to place a lower subjective valuation on his own labours in terms of the necessaries of life. The same will be true of workers backed by a trade union, as contrasted with un-organized workers with a traditionally low standard of life.[49]

Thus, the attempt to build society from individuals and their essential characteristics ignores the social input into these characteristics, and results in a circular behaviourism, such that people act on their preferences, but their preferences are revealed only in how they act,[50] or that entrepreneurial ability causes success in business, but is such a mysterious quality that it is revealed only by such success. In seeking an unambiguous unit of analysis, economists have introduced a bias which assumes a basic equality of individuals, so that individual consumer sovereignty is assumed, even to the extent of comparing it, if in a qualified way, with the democratic equality of the electoral process:

> ... society 'votes' to have some human resources directed into particular activities, resulting sometimes in certain lucky people getting paid 'more than necessary'....[51]

> Under a free price system, therefore, consumers decide to a great extent what shall be produced because they 'vote' for the production of particular articles by showing that they are prepared to buy these rather than others.[52]

The image ignores structural aspects of society which make such an atomistic approach untenable, as Hollis and Nell point out:

> Utility functions describe preferences, which are formed by family consumption patterns, which depend in part on work habits, which are largely dictated by the organization of production and so ultimately by the technology in use. Hence utility functions will shift with movements *along* the production function, that is with changes in the ratio of

labour to machinery and equipment. But this ratio is supposed to be determined on the basis of given preferences. If neo-classical models are to be adapted to allow for such interaction, it will mean dropping or modifying the doctrine of Consumer Sovereignty and most central positions of welfare economics. The formation of preferences is not a topic upon which conventional economists can afford to dwell.[53]

To extend the study of individual economic behaviour to the total economy, the uniformity of individual motivations and the infinitely varied nature of preferences and utility allows for a procedure of simple aggregation. There is a tempting simplicity in extending the postulated regularities of micro-economics to the macro-economic stage, as illustrated in Jevons' observation a century ago that 'The general forms of the law of Economics are the same in the case of individuals and nations, and, in reality, it is a law operating in the case of multitudes of individuals which gives rise to the aggregate represented in the transactions of a nation'.[54] The modern version is little different, as presented in the texts:

> The market demand for a commodity is the sum of individual demands and, as we would expect, it will show similar characteristics to the demand of the individual consumers who make up the market in which the commodity is sold.[55]

And the more hesitant:

> In principle, there should be no difficulty in going from the analysis of the reactions of a single consumer of a good to an analysis of the reactions of all consumers of that good; i.e. in going from the individual demand to market demand for a good. All that is needed is the ability to *add*.[56]

> ... the goods and services demanded by a nation will be a reflection of individuals' decisions taken under varying circumstances.[57]

But the varying circumstances cannot be systematically studied in a discipline where the individual and the single firm are the units of analysis, and thus the fact of class, the power of business concentration or government, and the process of socialization to the group are excluded or seen as peripheral qualifications to the central idea. Such a view presents an unrealistic image of society which cannot be

defended by arguing that aggregation cancels out individual variations, since the variations are not simply individual ones, nor are
they random.[58]

The Market Model

While it is the individual who initiates economic behaviour free of
fundamental social determinants, and for his or her own material
self-interest, there is not an unlimited choice in the channels along
which a person's behaviour can operate. For to interact efficiently
with the other individuals in the society, all of whom share the same
basic characteristics of subjective utility and unlimited wants, people
must act in accordance with the laws of the market which such
interaction requires. The laws of supply and demand and the
tendency to equilibrium are the unseen hands which bring individuals harmoniously together. The image of the market is the central
image of society in economic theory.

> The price of any economic good, under market conditions
> such as we find in the capitalist world, is determined by the
> forces of supply and demand.[59]

> The price mechanism has been shown to involve a system for
> allocating scarce resources among competing uses, in which
> the relative values placed by consumers on different com-
> modities and their relative costs of production play a part. As
> it is sometimes put, the price mechanism helps to answer
> the questions of what shall be produced.[60]

> ... a form of social institution has evolved which allows
> producers and consumers to get in touch with one another.
> This institution is simply a market, and the communication
> that buyers and sellers have with each other is a monetary
> one, through the medium of what is known as the price
> mechanism.[61]

> ... the wishes of consumers and producers are harmonised
> through the price mechanism *in spite of* or rather *because of*,
> the fact that each individual in the market is doing his best to
> look after his own interests.[62]

In constructing a deductive theoretical system from the postulated characteristics of the economic individual, economists have

devised the model of the market which, from the dynamic of substitution and choice at the margin, and given certain assumptions about the conditions of the economy, serves to explain the inter-action of the individual units. These 'forces' are the result of general 'laws' or 'tendencies' which help to organize the economy. They are not the conscious design of any human agency – in fact, humans can sometimes hinder the proper operation of this mechanism:

> Undoubtedly, the price system does work, but it does not work perfectly. One of many reasons is that people do not always help the competitive process which would reduce prices to their correct, economic level, the level which would arise from the working of the laws of supply and demand.[63]

In using the concepts of equilibrium and the price mechanism under assumptions of perfect competition, economists have at times been guilty of clear bias. By applying perfect market assumptions to the study of real problems, by denying the effects of institutional power and historical influences on market behaviour, by implying that the 'perfect' market is the best, and therefore the model to be emulated, by assuming without question ends of gross maximization of productivity to the exclusion of other ends, by basing notions of system efficiency on Pareto optimality conditions, by empha-sizing harmonious aspects of the market over conflict, the perspec-tive of economic theory has been that of the liberal capitalist state, and its teachings have supported that perspective.[64]

Some authors are aware of these dangers, noting the irrelevance of the idea of equilibrium to arguments of social justice[65] or warning of the pitfalls in 'traditional' approaches to price determination, competition and monopoly.[66] But economists from the left and the right have frequently claimed that the price mechanism explains only some aspects of supply and demand over only certain time scales,[67] and that it quite ignores other influences on these variables. Text writers offer no alternative explanations. Rather they either reject explicit theory for a descriptive approach; or salvage the discredited theory by increasing and emphasizing the assumptions, by dealing only with those aspects of real life which can be accommodated to the model, or, even more alarmingly, by continuing to teach the original theory using only hypothetical examples.

The dilemma is illustrated in the words of one economics teacher; economic theory has reached the stage where academic rigour is no longer equated with explaining the real world:

The biggest challenge facing the teacher of supply and demand as part of an 'A' level or equivalent syllabus is that of combining 'academic rigour' and a firm grasp of the theory with an understanding of how pricing decisions are arrived at in the 'real world'. Perhaps even more than in other parts of the syllabus it is necessary to make generalizations and assumptions which further study may reveal to have been unwarranted, in order to enable the student to understand the essential elements of the theory.[68]

In explaining to pupils how this is done, text book writers are caught in the perennial difficulties they are trying to avoid. In emphasizing the differences between theory and reality, the two become further separated, and the former becomes a normative yardstick for the latter:

The economist's model of perfect competition is highly theoretical, but it does provide a useful tool of economic analysis and helps us to make some sense of real world conditions. The real world is much too complicated to understand all at once; it is necessary to examine one feature at a time. The economist is able to use his model of a perfect market as a means of assessing the degree of competition in real world markets. He sets out the conditions necessary for a perfect market and then contrasts these with the situations found in the markets for goods and services. The degree of competition in these real markets is based upon the extent to which they approximate to the model of perfect competition.[69]

Metaphors of the Market System

Despite the criticisms of the positive economists' theory of the market, and its associated bias, it survives in a more qualified but still inadequate form. The language of the market continues as the model of society, and market metaphors present the appropriate images of the economy. The relationships of the economic system are likened to

the relationship of the blood system and the nervous system with the parts of the human body. If anything is amiss in the nervous or blood system of humans, all of the parts can be affected. And, if something goes wrong with one of the parts, it can affect the system as a whole, which in turn affects other parts.[70]

While there are other references to organic metaphors, where the economy is said to behave as if it were an animate creature,[71] more common is the notion that the economy is a machine, and there is nothing in principle which prevents us from treating it as such:

> It is not yet possible for governments to fine tune the economy as though it were an engine; partly because not enough is known about the operation of the economy, and partly because economic analysis has not been sufficiently developed.[72]

> We can think of money as being the lubricant which facilitates the smooth working of the economy. Without an adequate form of money the intricate mechanism based on intense specialisation would sieze up.[73]

> ... the economic system may be likened to one of tanks, at different levels above the ground and interconnected by pipes. If these tanks were filled with water capable of finding its own level quickly, equilibrium would soon be restored following an alteration in the position of one tank.[74]

> The Budget '... should be in fact a kind of control lever to the economic machine, increasing or reducing the voltage according to the engineer's reading of the appropriate gauges' though '... the gauges which must be read before the engineer knows what to do are still rather imperfect'.[75]

Common to both organic and mechanistic metaphors is the notion of a self motivating system whose structure is given. While human agents may be able to 'fine tune', 'lubricate' or regulate the machine, its fundamental structure and operation are as immutable as the laws of gravity or the circulation of the blood; and if the system seems to operate less than perfectly, it is because we do not yet know how to operate it, rather than because the system itself is faulty. This is a longstanding image in economic thought.[75] Its implication, that the economy in its present form is to be accepted because it cannot be changed, is, in effect, a means of socialization to the *status quo*.

The Social Aggregate

Again at the macro- or societal level, interesting patterns of usage appear when text writers refer to the society as a whole. In keeping with the aggregative tendency mentioned earlier, texts are almost unanimous in seeing society as an essentially homogeneous unit comprising many individual elements harmonized into a close knit system. The term which represents this is 'community': 'Economic activity has its origins in the wants of a community' and the 'fundamental economic problems' are those of the 'community'.[77] The reason why office buildings, schools and luxury flats are built when many people do not yet have houses is because 'the community as a whole is willing to pay these factors to come into producing things other than houses'.[78]

> The community must decide which goods it is going to produce and hence which goods it is *not* going to produce. Having decided the range of goods to be produced, the community must then decide how much of each good should be produced.[79]

The texts seldom enquire into just how this community consensus is established, though one author seems to think that the present political system has long been satisfactorily performing the task. 'In Britain, the tendency throughout this century has been for the choices to be made on behalf of the community by the Government which, through the political system, is responsible to the community'.[80]

The tendency to ignore or deplore sectional interests is seen in the use of aggregative measures of welfare, where the community is again the unit, and systematic variations within it are neglected. The division of labour, mechanization and increased output are valued for providing 'a *higher standard of living* for the community at large...'[81] 'The living standards of a community rise if the volume of goods and services available for use increases faster than the size of the population wishing to use them'.[82] Modern positive economics has a long tradition of using aggregative measures of welfare, usually gross national product per capita, and Pareto optimality criteria of efficiency, both of which gloss over systematic inequalities of distribution. Of the twenty-seven books reviewed, only one treated the issue of inequality of the distribution of wealth in any comprehensive way.

For the rest, the concept of community was a way of avoiding this controversial issue.

While the theory requires this aggregating approach, descriptive institutional approaches do acknowledge divisions in the whole other than individuals. The most common is that between state and private enterprise, and many texts can be placed in one of two camps. There are those whose comparisons obviously favour private enterprise, phrased in tendentious terms which contrast 'free enterprise ... organized and controlled by individuals' with 'state control'.[83] Or again: 'Thus it is the individual who has the final say under Capitalism. Hence it is directly opposed to Collectivism, where the State decides what the people want and often produces what it considers is good for the people'.[84]

The second camp contains the defenders of the state. Here state activity is not pejoratively described as 'control' or 'interference', but rather in terms of an admiring paternalism:

> Anything which the consumer needs but which cannot be individually bought; anything which, because of poverty or ignorance or recklessness, the consumer cannot be trusted to buy in sufficient quantities, or at a sufficiently high standard, for the general good ... must be either supplied by the state or made cheaper by state subsidies.[85]

The overall picture is one of the desirability of market forces as the solution to the economic problem, combined with the acceptance of state regulation to avoid possible defects. But this issue is of secondary importance here since it does little to change the image of the relations of the individual with society. People are the anonymous bearers of unlimited wants and unique, self-initiated preferences, and this anonymity is the basis of the image of society as a community of essentially equal individuals. Homogeneous in content, the community operates as an economic system where the basic rules are given, as natural as organisms and as rigid as machines. Whether the channel is the consumer in the market, or the voter in an election, the system is still said to operate in the individual's interests. The image implies that the individual can influence both big business and big government. The consumer in the market and the voter in the election are both kings. And in neither free market conditions nor paternalistic collectivism are there any fundamental divisions within the system, no properties of the system that negate the equality of individuals.

Individualism and Social Rewards

But how is this combination of striving self-seeking individuals and harmonious economic community achieved? How is it that individuals who are to be regarded as equals in some of their relations with the economy are to be accepted as unequal in others? How does the competitive system operate to ensure a fair allocation of positions on the economic ladder and a reasonably just distribution of rewards? In presenting images of the individual and society, economics must be able to show how the two are combined. The issues which explain how the.two images become one are the division of labour and the distribution of income.

Of all the concepts of elementary economics, specialization and the division of labour are, in one respect at least, among the easiest to teach. The simulation of a production exercise analogous to Adam Smith's much quoted example of pin making, allows for a concrete illustration of the principle rarely found in the teaching of other economic concepts. This is fortunate, for the division of labour, specialization and consequent exchange are fundamental to the study of the subject, and, indeed, to some authors become an article of faith: 'Proper organization of labour is essential if the maximum output is to be secured. Not only must we avoid putting square pegs in round holes, but the principle of the division of labour must be applied whenever it increases output'.[86]

The image developed is that of a naturally occurring allocation of tasks according to ability and merit in the interests of increased production and efficiency for the group's welfare. Since this allocative mechanism integrates the images of rational economic individuals and the total economic system, it is important to see how this is done. The texts emphasize, often exclusively, the idea that each person finds the position best suited to his or her abilities.

> To sum up, then: division of labour makes it possible for each worker to concentrate his particular natural ability on the job he can do best and to avoid those he can do least well.[87]
>
> ... each person *concentrates* on the task which he can do best....[88]
>
> People differ in natural ability and some occupations require a high level of intelligence, or particular natural aptitudes

which are only possessed by a certain proportion of the population. For tl.is reason occupations such as surgeons, physicists, mathematicians, designers and entertainers are restricted to a relatively small proportion of the population.[89]

The suggestion that everyone has one thing which he or she can do best, and that the actual allocation of economic roles in society is in any predominant way related to such a notion seems incredible. At the heart of this system of explanation, as previously noted in the operation of the entrepreneur, is the all-embracing notion of natural ability. For again, as economic explanation rests on an individualistic image of society, the origin of the allocative process must lie in the individual. Thus division of labour results from individual ability, and its results are not only beneficial but necessary. 'The clever people can devote all their time to the difficult jobs so that their valuable talents are not wasted in doing simpler jobs which others can do equally well'.[90]

What is most alarming about this view is the practice of citing only the most extreme examples as evidence. The mutually convenient specialization of the surgeon and the gardener typifies the arrangements for society as a whole. Because society is willing to pay dearly for scarce skills, the competition generated by this incentive guarantees that the selective process is efficient, and determined by inherent natural ability. This model of the allocative mechanism may be plausible in part in the occupations most clearly requiring specifiable skills, such as artists, craftsmen, and some professions, and, in keeping with the style of argument, these are the most frequent illustrations. The great obscure mass of tasks which most of us perform must be thought somehow to fit with the model. And at the low end of the scale, as judged by the economist's yardstick of scarcity and market value, the explanations become quite odd, as instanced by the following perplexing example of a man who has *no* natural ability to do *anything*:

> What of the man who has no natural ability to do anything? There are many people in this position and it might seem to you that there would be no place for them in a society of specialists. Happily, there are two reasons why there is a useful place for all of us and why we can all be specialists.
>
> Firstly, even if a man has no particular aptitude for a job when first he tries it, there is no doubt that the constant

practice involved in doing his job for the whole of every working day will eventually give him a facility for the work and a pleasant feeling of superiority in doing it better than other people.

Secondly, there are some jobs that can be done fairly well by nearly everyone, such as minding a simple machine, and many cleaning jobs.[91]

To preserve the power of the notion of natural ability in explaining allocation of tasks in the division of labour, Davies has had to concoct the idea of a person with no natural ability for anything at all. Another author chooses a different tack, in which the less valued tasks, far from revealing a lack of natural ability, actually demonstrate its existence:

Artists, musicians, great actors and craftsmen, for example, have some abilities that cannot be taught. What is less often understood are the limited numbers of people with abilities that training can develop for more common skills. Not everyone can be trained to inspect goods made in a factory, for inspection needs powers of concentration if faulty goods are not to slip by and reach customers. Not everyone has nimble enough fingers or the co-ordination of hand and brain to sew a fine seam. Nor does everyone have the courage needed to work in a mine or the patience to nurse the mentally sick.[92]

The fundamental deficiency in all this is, of course, that the concept of 'natural' ability is a very difficult one to define. The nature-nurture controversy of psychology is wholly absent from the economist's use of the idea, where it is taken for granted as an identifiable and specific element of human ability inherent in the individual.

It might be argued in reply that the origin of ability is irrelevant to the economist, since it is the task of economics to explain the result of such ability, irrespective of how it develops. This is an inadequate defence in two respects. First, the texts clearly state that the abilities are natural, that is, innate, inherent and predestined. If economists are to escape the obligation of defending this view, they cannot take such an unequivocal position on such a controversial issue. This might be thought especially important in schools where pupils are not likely to distinguish between what is actually so and what is taken to be so for the purpose of economic theory.

But the second difficulty is more fundamental. If the allocation of tasks in the economy is not based solely on ability; if the selection mechanism is affected by factors other than natural ability; if group membership and circumstances of upbringing will systematically influence one's fate in the division of labour; then no theory can be satisfactory which takes as its starting point an image of the atomistic individual who is the possessor of inherent natural abilities, and thereby excludes other necessary theoretical perspectives. The deficiency is hardly ameliorated by holding to the theory as the basic model of explanation while pointing out exceptions or modifying influences which change the general rule. What is needed is an overarching theory which accommodates the social influences and their interaction with individual experience, or recourse to rival theories which explain the phenomena which the orthodox one ignores.

Equally important is the assumption that such ability, if not the only influence on the allocative mechanism, is at least the predominant one, and the only one warranting systematic study. It is this exclusive concentration on one explanatory model that makes the texts inadequate, leaving so many questions unanswered. For instance, class constraints on social mobility are not dealt with, and economic questions like the dual labour market are simply not acknowledged. Only one of the books analyzed mentioned the effect of 'experience in holding positions . . . gained through the influence possessed by their friends or relatives, rather than . . . any particular qualifications . . .',[93] and it is interesting and possibly significant that this text, while recommended for school use, was the only one reviewed which was not specifically written for schools. After all, even if the concept of natural ability is accepted, it must still be demonstrated in the face of evidence to the contrary, that such ability is the major determinant of the allocation of roles, not merely in the case of artists and doctors, but in the economy in general.

Connected with the allocative mechanism of the division of labour is the distributive mechanisms of the determinant of income. One of the most difficult questions for economic theory, since one of the most hotly disputed in the society at large, wage determination and the distribution of income are, not surprisingly, the subject of much vagueness and some disagreement in the texts. The main difficulty lies in the attempts to apply market theory and its specific principle of the marginal productivity of labour in a situation where other influences are obviously very important, and even predominant. This is not the place to analyze the text writers' verdicts on such economic controversies as the determination of the quality of capital or the classification of the factors of production, for their own sakes, though these issues do affect the explanation of the distribution of income.[94] The interest here is how the explanation of this feature of the economy involves images of the individual and society.

In common with other elements of economics the process of wage determination allows of two main approaches: an analytical explanation based on the laws of market forces; and institutional approaches where human intentions, power and history are thought more potent sources of explanation. Orthodox economic theory prefers the former, using the latter to explain qualifications and exceptions to the general model. Such is the case with the marginal productivity theory of wages, where wages are explained by the value of the marginal product of labour as determined by the forces of demand and supply. The relationships between wages and market forces are variously explained as follows:

> In technical language, wages are limited by the *marginal productivity* of the labour concerned; the amount which is added to the total value of the product when an extra man is taken on, or lost when he is dismissed or leaves.[95]

> The key to understanding why some people receive higher wages than others is to recognize that a wage is a price.... Because wages are prices, the levels of wages for all of us are determined, just as prices are, by the forces of demand and supply.[96]

> The wage rate for any occupation is, in essence, no different from any other price. We should, therefore, be correct in thinking that it is determined by the forces of supply and demand for labour.[97]

> ... wages are the *price paid for labour*. They are determined by the laws of supply and demand – more will be available at a higher price, less will be required at this price.[98]

> Wages, then, are determined by the interaction of the marginal productivity of different types of labour (demand) and transfer earnings (supply). The working of these forces is influenced by the bargaining strengths of trade unions and by the immobility of labour.[99]

... the profit maximising firm will employ labour up to the point where the last unit of labour hired adds as much to the firm's revenue as it does to the firm's costs.[100]

About one-third of the texts reviewed took what might be termed a hard line on the application of demand and supply forces to wage determination. That is, they argued that wages are determined by the value of the marginal product as set by market forces. A more modest position is that influences on wage levels such as union power and non-monetary attractions, while not encompassed by a marginal productivity theory, can be interpreted by a more general and less precise theory of supply and demand. The remainder of the texts take a safer line, either explaining wages in institutional terms, or limiting the topic to a descriptive treatment. Only one text described the procedures followed in an actual wage case.

The temptation to apply the theory first, and to cover the remaining problems with exceptions or qualifications, or to fit the qualifications to the theory by broadening its terms, seems to have succeeded in this range of books. The confident presentation of marginal productivity seems misplaced in the light of its controversial nature among economists, and its tenuous links with reality, for, as Routh has concluded:

> The history of the National Board for Prices and Incomes in the United Kingdom, 1965 to 1971, is, in part, that of well-intentioned men (and two well-intentioned women) painfully discarding the tools of economic theory and coming to terms with a world in which pay levels are determined by the elemental forces of emulation.[101]

While there may be occupations or types of firms in which marginal productivity is a real and calculable influence, or where the unattractiveness of a job has allowed unions to justify high wage claims, it is just as easy to think of cases where marginal productivity can have no meaning at all, and unpleasant jobs which are amongst the lowest paid. Again the tendency is to demonstrate the principles with extreme examples – doctors, pilots and dustmen abound – with the implication that the principles apply universally. The image presented by the theoretical approaches to wage determination is once more that of a set of immutable laws whose application is extended far beyond what could possibly be warranted. Rather than being one perspective on some aspects of wage determination under certain assumed conditions, it is in many texts presented as the best explanation of the total process of wage determination in the real world.

The results of this confusion are unfortunate. For instance, clear distinction is seldom made between the application of marginal productivity to the micro-distribution of income in particular markets, where it is applicable in certain cases, and macro-distribution of income across factors in the total economy, where it is not. Pupils could be forgiven for thinking that the theory claimed to explain the total shares of wealth distributed to wages and capital. And here, as elsewhere, the problem arises of neglecting assumptions which qualify the application of the theory to the real world. Free entry to markets, mobility of labour and full employment are just some of the assumptions ignored, or mentioned and forgotten, or actually held to exist in the real world, as in the following case which assumes that the distribution of wealth is fixed, and that Pareto optimal efficiency has already been reached:

> Wise trade unionists will, therefore, interest themselves in productivity, knowing that only if production goes up can wages safely be raised.[102]

As an example of the inevitability of these market forces, irrespective of the intentions and powers of human agents, take the following illustration of the effects of legislative interference with the natural forces of the market on behalf of women. Since 'the long-term marginal productivity of men is higher than women' equal pay is doomed to failure.

> If equal pay is decided upon, and this means in effect, an over-generous minimum pay for women, then
>
> (i)   more men will be employed (marginal utility of remaining women will be higher – to level of new wage).
> (ii) more women will go to the already 'women dominated' trades so that wages will fall even lower there.
>
> If attempts are then made to fix a minimum wage in these trades, and it is too high, we will have more machinery, perhaps the end of some trades, and certainly unemployment.[103]

There are many questionable assumptions in this series of deductions. For instance, the statement does not mention the possible effect of equal pay on female investments in education, which would in fact increase the long term productivity of women.[104] But the most important for present purposes is that no legislation can control or compensate for the operation of the market. Human aspirations which seem to contradict the laws of the market are folly; the forces which are said originally to have arisen from contractual arrangements between individual persons become as immutable as physical laws.

The Theory of Knowledge in Economics Texts

In the light of the controversies surrounding many of the issues in academic debate, it could be expected that writers at the school level would be hesitant in proclaiming their certainty. But there is a strident element in many texts which suggests that conclusions are beyond doubt. Much of this can be attributed to the commitment to positivist theories of knowledge in the definition of economic method. Economics is '(a) based on the collection, arrangement and classification of facts; and (b) concerned with the possibility of deriving and formulating from those facts, by the use of appropriate methods, a series of hypothetical laws, in the form of general statements'.[105]

> If we are to make any sense at all of the complicated society, we must observe and, having done this, try to formulate laws governing human behaviour in relation to economic circumstances. In other words, *scientific method* must be employed.[106]

> Economics is a *science* which observes facts and on the strength of these facts tries to formulate laws of general validity.[107]

> When some definite regular pattern is observed in the relationships between two or more things, and someone asks why this should be so, the search for a theory has begun.[108]

> The study of economics imposes strict mental discipline based on accurate observation of facts and conclusions that may be deduced from these facts.[109]

Naive inductivism is rife in the presentation of economics at the school level, which seems ignorant of the criticisms which have elsewhere seen it discredited (see chapter 2). It is all the more surprising given the strong deductive nature of much of the theory. But this confidence in the present ability of economics to produce lawful generalizations is not always thought justified, some authors optimistically holding that it will, however, come about in due course.

> We must not, however, be discouraged by the fact that social
> scientists do not know how to predict these and other aspects
> of social behaviour with a higher degree of certainty. The
> subjects are young and developing fast.[110]

There is, then, a strong element in the texts which attributes to economic theory an authority which is neither valid, given the vagaries of experience, nor possible, given the nature of knowledge. A particularly unfortunate example of the predictability of economic behaviour cited by one author is the stability of the consumption function;[111] a recent study shows marked and quite unexpected fluctuations in this previously assumed stable relationship.[112] The long history of economic laws which turned out to be false has been reviewed by Samuelson, who concluded 'If these be Laws Mother Nature is a criminal by nature'.[113]

One tactic which contributes to the air of authority in the presentation of economic theory, and the suggestion that the present society as described in the theory is given, natural and inevitable, is the 'state of nature' argument. This technique, a common teaching strategy, postulates an individual or group of individuals in the state of nature, where ownership, division of labour, exchange and the other elements of the modern economy are unknown. The task is to suggest how these ahistorical and asocial beings might then organize their economic affairs. Robinson Crusoe and other shipwreck victims, lone survivors of nuclear disaster, and inhabitants of foreign planets all manage to choose the modern democratic capitalist state as the solution to their problems.[114] The result is that feudalism, enclosure, the industrial revolution, the history of institutions of property and labour are shown to be irrelevant to understanding the present economic system.

In presenting a positivist inductive image of a society whose main elements are natural, inevitable, inherent in human nature and society, economists risk the danger of reifying ideas, and of hypostatizing social inventions into immutable facts of existence. The problem is manifest in the language of economics where what might be intended as a figure of speech can, if interpreted literally, transform ideas and conventions into things.

An examination of an individual's demand curve shows by how much he will change his consumption of a good as the result of a change in its price.[115]

... a supply curve really indicates the state of mind of the supplier.[116]

... The price mechanism helps to answer the question of what shall be produced.[117]

The price system directs the economy towards the satisfaction of consumer demand.[118]

In transferring agency and power from people to mechanisms, and in imputing to people's minds economic inventions like supply and demand curves, economists abstract the reality of human actions, intentions and social interaction into reified variables and self-motivating systems. Thus elasticity becomes an element of goods, rather than human behaviour, and models of interaction become determinants of it. These are the classic signs of reification in social explanation, and there is evidence of their effect:

A strong impression was left that the (consumer demand) theory exists *in vacuo* unrelated to practical questions ... very few apparently realised that demand elasticity is a measure of behaviour rather than a determinant....[119]

It is clear that many candidates can describe a model and how it works without really understanding what a model is intended to be ... abstraction involves simplification, especially of human behaviour and motivation.[120]

The Economic Image, Explanation, and Education

Nineteenth-century political economy, in its attempts to explain the inevitability of the *status quo*, aimed at socialization to the existing economic system and the individual's fate decided by that system. However, current economic curricula are motivated by a more active design for the individual's welfare. The citizenship rationale is strong, arguing that economics provides people with knowledge by which they can promote their interests in society. In its strongest form, this reflects a participatory view of citizenship in which the individual can choose his or her fate:

The objectives of the syllabus are ... to enable candidates to appreciate, and participate actively in, the choices which are available as individuals and as a community, both nationally and globally.[121]

The principal purpose of studying economics is to enable people to exercise some measure of control over the economic aspects of their lives.[122] -

Economics is important as a study:
(a) Because it can help people to become well-informed citizens. It enables them to understand the economic institutions of the society in which they live, so that they may control them to their advantage.
(b) Because it is of immediate and practical value in business and commerce.[123].

While these may be laudable aims, their success is jeopardized by the nature of the courses used to achieve them. For there is a strong element in the texts reviewed which is likely to discourage active citizenship and a feeling of efficacy in economic affairs. The images of human nature and society presented seem more likely to engender submissiveness, hopelessness, frustration, even ignorance.

In essence, people are characterized as having unlimited material wants, but the ability to attain these is decided by natural ability, a mysterious and immutable quality which predetermines one's place in the division of labour, and therefore success in the competitive economy. Failure is due to individual deficiency in natural ability. Note however that the texts do not use the terms success and failure, presumably because the idea that natural ability determines the distribution of tasks makes the model of competition difficult to apply. The individual's problem in this view is to find the position which corresponds to one's abilities, rather than to compete with others for positions potentially available to all. Thus are deftly avoided issues of power, advantage and opportunity in the struggle for the unequal rewards of the economic system. Ability and the allocative mechanisms are not products of social invention, but are inevitable outcomes of natural processes. They derive not from a creative history but from the natural development of society from the state of nature, and are seldom questioned.

Figure 2 illustrates the basic components and structure of the image. Economic individualism is mediated through the given

Figure 2:   The economic image of human nature and society.

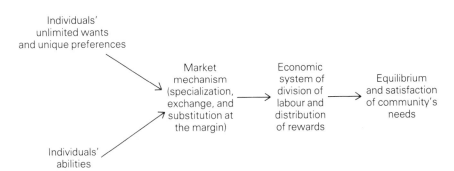

mechanism of the market to produce the economic system in which each individual finds a rightful place, and community needs can be satisfied. The image of the individual is a highly abstract one in Lukes' terms (see page 51), and the image of society, framed in both organic and mechanical metaphor, is the automatic system castigated by Wolin (see page 54).

The ontology of the market is not clear. It presumably is the rules and consequences of action which constitute substitution at the margin. These are derived in part from the image of the economic individual, which is explicit in the texts, but also, and this remains implicit, from a market theory of value. Power finds no place in this idea of a quite disinterested and natural system. The market is a reified mechanism, which we cannot change, but must try to understand in order to accommodate to its laws. Since such understanding is based on scientific theory derived from observable facts, it is not to be disputed. In explaining something as complex as the economy, there is little room for complicating factors, and, in the interests of simplicity, the intricacy of history, the variety of international comparisons, and competing theories are omitted.

The result is uncritical acceptance of the images dictated by the theory. It is seldom asked what historical factors have produced the ideas of property, entrepreneurship, labour or government on which the theory is based, or what alternatives there may be. International variations in features of the economy are not considered, and comparisons are not made. These omissions are important, for if the distribution of wealth is a natural process subject to market forces, how are marked international differences in the inequality of this distribution explained? What is the nature and extent of social mobility, and how is educational opportunity related to it, and to the postulated natural ability on which the theory so depends? The images identified here are vulnerable to the standard left wing critique.

Some qualifications are relevant at this point. It should be recalled that the criticisms have been illustrated mainly by reference to the theory of positive economics as presented in the texts, and that some of the exceptions to the theory are dealt with by authors in more descriptive institutional sections. Thus some texts reveal the curious practice of explaining wage determination in terms of marginal productivity in the theoretical section, while presenting it descriptively in terms of collective bargaining in sections on industrial relations, with few attempts to integrate the two.[124] But while the images are most clearly seen in theoretical approaches, many of the criticisms apply equally to institutional approaches for it must be remembered that the distinction is not as clear as might first appear, as shown by one text author:

> ... the bulk of the book is unadorned by a great deal of formal theory. Facts and institutions are, however, described and relationships put the way they are because of the existence of underlying and implicit theoretical justification.[125]

Further, texts sometimes point out that many of the issues dealt with are the subject of research in other social sciences, and that the texts present only the economic perspective. This could be seen as a defence against the kind of criticisms made here, in that the authors might be taken to imply that the images they present need to be criticized from other perspectives. Since none of the authors demonstrates by example how this might be done, it is a weak defence.

A more likely defence might be thought to lie in the role of assumptions in economic theory. Many of the difficulties of accommodating economic theory to the real world lie in its reliance on assumptions concerning human nature and the economic system, which allow it to study the operation of particular markets under relatively stable conditions. Criticisms of the texts because of the images they present may be rebutted by pointing out that the images are only assumptions, not intended to describe the real world. In fact, many authors would probably contend that some assumptions, such as profit maximization, are in the main descriptive of reality, assumptions being directed at their stability rather than their existence. After all, economic theory is not thought by its proponents to be an edifice of fictions. Other assumptions, such as the fully informed consumer or the non-existence of external economies, are accepted as fabrications for the sake of argument. Unfortunately, this distinction is seldom made, and assumptions, while usually stated at the outset, have a curious background role in the subsequent discussion. The result as evidenced in A level examiners' reports is not surprising:

> The idea behind this question was that the candidate should show his understanding of economic efficiency and critically evaluate the model of the operation of the free market economy advanced in most text books.... The assumption of a given distribution of income and wealth, the effect of external economies and the assumption of full employment all tended to be ignored.[126]

> Very few candidates explicitly contrasted, 'freedom of entry', the economist's prerequisite for price competition, with the more general view of competition as competitive behaviour. Similarly, there were few direct answers to the second part of the question which sought to contrast the model of resource allocation and income distribution in a competitive society with the existence of economies of scale and individualism in the real world. A few good candidates contrasted price and non-price competition but the majority of answers tended to be about the advantages of perfect competition and the evils of monopoly.[127]

There is reason to fear that the assumptions of economics, with their attendant false images, are not clearly distinguished as such. But even where the distinction is successful, the use of assumptions is open to serious doubt, for if the theory of economics does not describe and explain how things actually happen in the real world, it will be of little use to citizens managing their own affairs or trying to influence public policy. Such tasks require knowledge of how actions are related to their outcomes in an existential world, not merely that they are related in an abstract academic one. But the defence of unreal economic assumptions rests on this distinction, as put by Milton Friedman:

> ... the relevant question to ask about the 'assumptions' of a theory is not whether they are descriptively 'realistic', for they never are, but whether they are sufficiently good

approximations for the purpose in hand. And this question can be answered only by seeing whether the theory works, which means whether it yields sufficiently accurate predictions.

... The belief that a theory can be tested by the realism of its assumptions independently of the accuracy of its predictions is widespread and the source of much of the perennial criticism of economic theory as unrealistic. Such criticism is largely irrelevant, and in consequence most attempts to reform economic theory that it has stimulated have been unsuccessful.[128]

Since this view has been upheld in the school curriculum, as evidenced in a 1975 examiner's report,[129] and has important educational implications, it warrants some attention. Friedman's own example is of the expert billiards player, who does not need mathematical equations to succeed at his game, though they may be needed to explain why the ball goes into the pocket. A similar defence has been made for the marginal productivity theory of wages, where it becomes irrelevant how the firm decides on payment for the marginal product: the only important thing is that it does.[130] Whatever the scientific merits of this view of knowledge, its educational implications are clear: if the aim is to teach someone how to succeed in billiards, the list of mathematical equations will be of little help. As a major justification of economics teaching has been its practical value in the business of living, economic educators do not have the choice which Friedman might claim as a 'pure' academic. However well unreal assumptions may lead to successful prediction (which is doubtful if not demonstrably false, as evidenced in the variety of economic models presently used), they are not adequate to the task of economic education in schools. That the assumptions of modern economic theory are false, misleading and more harmful than helpful has been strongly argued:[131] these arguments have added force in the context of economics curricula for schools.

Conclusion

The economic images of human nature and society identified here are to a very large extent inimical to participatory and efficacious educational aims. The strength of these images in school texts is therefore surprising, especially when academic and professional economists seem to be reducing the emphasis on basic theory, and emphasizing economics as a method of analysis. School curricula may in time follow this shift, but the results will not necessarily answer the criticisms made here.

First, the methods are still connected with theories: cost-benefit analysis must assume a particular theory of value, and distributive issues requires a concept of efficiency. The move from utility to preference to choice theories has not changed the atomistic individualism which underlies them all. Definition of community interest is made no less controversial simply by acknowledging the costs of externalities. Second, an increased emphasis on techniques of analysis will simply divert attention away from substantive issues in ways already lamented (see pages 88–90).

Whatever the future of the images identified here, their recent position has been a dominant one, a clear example of a prevailing theoretical paradigm. Their perspective on central political and ideological controversies is clear. It is not, however, neutral, and is unlikely to help those whose interests lie in changing the system.

Notes and References

1 GOLDSTROM, J. (1977) 'The content of education and the socialization of the working-class child, 1830–1860', in McCANN, P. (Ed.) *Popular Education and Socialization in the Nineteenth Century*, London, Methuen, p. 102; GORDON, P. and LAWTON, D. (1978) *Curriculum Change in the Nineteenth and Twentieth Centuries*, London, Hodder and Stoughton, p. 14.

2 GREAT BRITAIN DEPARTMENT OF EDUCATION AND SCIENCE (1977) *Curriculum 11–16. Working Papers by H.M. Inspectorate: A Contribution to Current Debate*, London, HMSO.

3 BURNS, R. and ANTHONY, V. (1971–2) 'The Economics Association and the training of teachers', in *Economics*, 9, 3, p. 171.

4 GOLDSTROM, J. (1966–7) 'Richard Whateley and political economy in school books, 1833–80', in *Irish Historical Studies*, 15, pp. 131–146; GOLDSTROM, J. (1972) *The Social Content of Education 1808–1870: A Study of the Working Class School Reader in England and Ireland*, Shannon, Irish University Press; GOLDSTROM, J. (1977) *op. cit.*; JONES, D. (1977) 'Socialization and social science: Manchester Model Secular School 1854–1861' in McCANN, P. (Ed.) *op. cit.*; MARSH, J. (1977) 'Economics education in schools in the nineteenth century: social control', in

Economics, 13, pp. 116–18; STEWART, W. and MCCANN, P. (1967) *The Educational Innovators. Volume I. 1750–1880*, London, Macmillan.

5 ROUTH, G. (1975) *The Origin of Economic Ideas*, London, Macmillan.

6 GOLDSTROM, J. (1966–7) *op. cit.* p. 137. W.S. JEVONS acknowledged the influence of Whateley's *Easy Lessons on Money Matters for Young People*, especially in its theory of value based on utility rather than labour. HOWEY, R. (1973) 'The origins of marginalism' in BLACK, R., COATS, A. and GOODWIN, C. *The Marginal Revolution in Economics: Interpretation and Evaluation*, Durham, N.C., Duke University Press, p. 19.

7 STEWART, W. and MCCANN, P. (Eds.) (1967) *op. cit.* pp. 331, 340.

8 Quoted in MARSH, J. (1977) *op. cit.* p. 116.

9 Quoted in HURT, J. (1972) *Education in Evolution: Church, State, Society and Popular Education 1800–1870*, London, Paladin, p. 23.

10 Quoted in GOLDSTROM, J. (1972) *op. cit.* p. 159.

11 Quoted in STEWART, W. and MCCANN, P. (Eds.) (1967) *op. cit.* p. 332.

12 Quoted in ROUTH, G. (1975) *op. cit.* p. 184.

13 Quoted in GOLDSTROM, J. (1972) *op. cit.* p. 170.

14 STEWART, W. and MCCANN, P. (Eds.) (1967) *op. cit.* p. 330.

15 MILL, J. (1971) *Autobiography*, London, Oxford University Press, p. 148.

16 STEWART, W. and MCCANN, P. (Eds.) (1967) *op. cit.* p. 341.

17 GORDON, P. and WHITE, J. (1979) *Philosophers as Educational Reformers: The Influence of Idealism on British Educational Thought and Practice*, London, Routledge and Kegan Paul, p. 103.

18 STEWART, W. and MCCANN, P. (Eds.) (1967) *op. cit.* p. 340.

19 BÜRTT, E. (1972) *Social Perspectives in the History of Economic Theory*, New York, St. Martins, p. 201.

20 Ibid. pp. 178, 268; ROUTH, G. (1975) *op. cit.* p. 206.

21 The conflict between the collectivism of Marxism and the subjectivism of marginal theory is traced in MEEK, R. (1973) 'Marginalism and Marxism' in BLACK, R. COATS, A. and GOODWIN, C. *op. cit.*

22 SZRETER, R. (1965) 'Attitudes to economics for secondary schools, 1918–1945', in *Economics*, 6, pp. 85–88; KAHN, R. (1976) 'Political attitudes involved in teaching economics', in *Oxford Review of Education*, 2, 1, pp. 91–95.

23 GREAT BRITAIN BOARD OF EDUCATION (1938) *Report of the Consultative Committee on Secondary Education with Special Reference to Grammar Schools and Technical High Schools*, London, HMSO, p. 179.

24 SZRETER, R. (1965) *op. cit.*

25 RYBA, R. (1977) 'The recent evolution of economics education in EEC countries at the upper secondary level' in RYBA, R. and ROBINSON, B. (Eds.) *Aspects of Upper Secondary Economics Education in E.E.C. Countries*, London, Economics Association, p. 27.

26 NOBBS, J. (1975) *Social Economics*, Maidenhead, McGraw Hill, p. 6.

27 CROOME, A. and KING, G. (1971) *The Livelihood of Man*, London, Chatto and Windus, p. 19.

28 DAVIES, F. (1970) *Starting Economics*, Amersham, Hulton, pp. 6, 7.

29 HOUGH, J. (1976) 'Economics in the school curriculum', in *Trends in Education*, December, p. 38.
30 CHRISTIE D. and SCOTT, A. (1977) *Economics in Action*, London, Heinemann Educational, p. 9.
31 NICHOLSON, J. (1973) *Modern British Economics*, London, Allen and Unwin, p. 123.
32 DAVIES, F. (1970) *op. cit.* p. 58.
33 HARVEY, J. (1976) *Elementary Economics*, London, Macmillan, p. 18.
34 EDWARDS, G. (1970) *The Framework of Economics*, London, McGraw Hill, p. 309.
35 DAVIES, F. (1975) *op. cit.* p. 58.
36 SAPSFORD, D. and LADD, J. (1978) *Essential Economics*, St. Alban's, Hart-Davis, p. 11.
37 HARBURY, C. (1971) *An Introduction to Economic Behaviour*, London, Fontana, p. 16.
38 CROOME, A. and KING, G. (1971) *op. cit.* p. 171 (parenthesis added).
39 CURZON, L. (1975) *'O' Level Economics*, Plymouth, MacDonald and Evans, p. 39.
40 HADFIELD, J. (1969) *Basic Economics*, London, University of London Press, p. 58.
41 SHAFTO, I. (1971) *Introducing Economics*, London, Nelson, p. 54.
42 STANLAKE, G. (1976) *Introductory Economics*, London, Longman, p. 46.
43 HARBURY, C. (1971) *op. cit.* p. 25.
44 CURZON, L. (1975) *op. cit.* p. 41.
45 LANE, P. (1975) *Revision Notes for Ordinary Level Economics*, London, Allman, p. 68.
46 HOLLIS, M. and NELL, E. (1975) *Rational Economic Man: A Philosophical Critique of Neo-classical Economics*, London, Cambridge University Press; HUNT, E. (1980) 'A radical critique of welfare economics' in NELL. E. (Ed.) *Growth, Profits and Property: Essays in the Revival of Political Economy*, Cambridge, Cambridge University Press; LUKES, S. (1973) *Individualism*, Oxford, Basil Blackwell; MACPHERSON, C. (1973) *Democratic Theory: Essays in Retrieval*, Oxford, Clarendon Press: WEIS-KOPF, W. 'The image of man in economics', in *Social Research*, 40, pp. 547–563.
47 WILLIAMSON, O. (1977) 'Firms and markets' in WEINTRAUB, S. (Ed.) *Modern Economic Thought*, London, University of Pennsylvania Press, p. 188.
48 HOLLIS, M. and NELL, E. (1975) *op. cit.* p. 130; WARD, B. (1972) *What's Wrong with Economics?* London, Macmillan, p. 199.
49 DOBB, M. (1972) 'The trend of modern economics' in HUNT, E. and SCHWARTZ, J. (Eds.) *A Critique of Modern Economic Theory: Selected Readings*, Harmondsworth, Penguin, pp. 64, 5.
50 HIMMELWEIT, S. (1977) 'The individual as basic unit of analysis' in GREEN, F. and NORE, P. *Economics: An Anti-text*, London, Macmillan, p. 30.
51 NICHOLSON, J. (1973) *op. cit.* p. 124.
52 HADFIELD, J. (1969) *op. cit.* p. 19.

53 HOLLIS, M. and NELL, E. (1975) *op. cit.* pp. 119, 120.
54 Quoted in MEEK, R. (1972) 'The marginal revolution and its aftermath' in HUNT, E. and SCHWARTZ, J. (Eds.) *op. cit.* p. 90.
55 POWICKE, J. and MAY, P. (1977) *An Introduction to Economics*, London, Edward Arnold, p. 97.
56 CHRISTIE, D. and SCOTT, A. (1977) *op. cit.* p. 74.
57 *Ibid.* p. 107.
58 HOLLIS, M. and NELL, E. (1975) *op. cit.* p. 128.
59 STANLAKE, G. (1976) *op. cit.* p. 144.
60 HARBURY, C. (1976) *op. cit.* pp. 11, 12.
61 HARBURY, C. (1971) *op. cit.* p. 48.
62 *Ibid.* p. 50.
63 HADFIELD, J. (1969) *op. cit.* p. 20.
64 HELM, R. (1979) 'Values in economics', in *Economics*, 15, pp. 11–15; LEE, N. (1974) 'Concealed values in economics teaching' in WHITEHEAD, D. (Ed.) *Curriculum Development in Economics*, London, Heinemann Educational; SZRETER, R. (1972–3) 'The teacher of economics and the problem of political bias', in *Economics*, 9, pp. 353–7; WEBSTER, A. (1978) 'Ideology and "A" level economics textbooks', in *Economics*, 14, pp. 85–87; WRIGHT, N. (1979) 'Values' in WHITEHEAD, D. (Ed.) *op. cit.*
65 CHRISTIE, D. and SCOTT, A. (1977) *op. cit.* p. 87.
66 SHAFTO, T. (1971) *op. cit.* p. vii.
67 BRITTAN, S. (1975) *Participation without Politics: An Analysis of the Nature and the Role of Markets*, London, Institute of Economic Affairs, pp. 67–71; MOHUN, S. (1977) 'Consumer sovereignty' in GREEN, F. and NORE, P. (Eds.) *op. cit.*; ROUTH, G. (1975) *op. cit.* pp. 307–10.
68 MACLEHOSE, A. 'Supply, demand and pricing' in WHITEHEAD, D. (Ed.) *Handbook for Economics Teachers*, London, Heinemann Educational, p. 147.
69 STANLAKE, G. (1976) *op. cit.* p. 179.
70 CHRISTIE, D. and SCOTT, A. (1977) *op. cit.* p. 103.
71 POWICKE, J. and MAY, P. (1977) *op. cit.* p. 13; HARBURY, C. (1971) *op. cit.* p. vii.
72 CHRISTIE, D. and SCOTT, A. (1971) *op. cit.* p. 134.
73 POWICKE, J. and MAY, P. (1977) *op. cit.* p. 62.
74 EDWARDS, G. (1970) *The Framework of Economics*, London, McGraw-Hill, p. 132.
75 CROOME, A. and KING, G. (1977) *op. cit.* p. 307.
76 MEEK, R. (1965) *The Rise and Fall of the Concept of the Economic Machine*, Leicester, Leicester University Press.
77 CURZON, L. (1975) *op. cit.* pp. 5, 8.
78 LANE, P. (1975) *op. cit.* p. 15.
79 STANLAKE, G. (1976) *op. cit.* p. 3.
80 SHAFTO, T. (1971) *op. cit.* p. 154.
81 LANE, P. (1975) *op. cit.* p. 23.
82 SHAFTO, T. (1971) *op. cit.* p. 6.
83 BARON, D. (1973) *Economics: An Introductory Course*, London, Heinemann Educational, p. 134.

84 HARVEY, J. (1976) *op. cit.* p. 17.
85 CROOME, A. and KING, G. (1977) *op. cit.* p. 21.
86 HARVEY, J. (1976) *op. cit.* p. 313.
87 CROOME, A. and KING, G. (1977) *op. cit.* p. 37.
88 LANE, P. (1975) *op. cit.* p. 23.
89 STANLAKE, G. (1976) *op. cit.* p. 44.
90 DAVIES, F. (1970) *op. cit.* p. 40.
91 *Ibid.* p. 37.
92 SAPSFORD, D. and LADD, J. (1978) *op. cit.* p. 39.
93 HICKS, J. (1960) *The Social Framework: An Introduction to Economics*, Oxford, Clarendon, p. 68.
94 A review of the inadequacy of neo-classical theory on these points can be found in NELL, E. (1980) 'Introduction. Cracks in the neo-classical mirror: on the break-up of a vision' in NELL, E. (Ed.) *Growth, Profits and Property: Essays in the Revival of Political Economy*, Cambridge, Cambridge University Press.
95 CROOME, A. and KING, G. (1977) *op. cit.* p. 156.
96 DAVIES, F. (1970) *op. cit.* p. 93.
97 HARBURY, C. (1971) *op. cit.* p. 76.
98 LANE, P. (1975) *op. cit.* p. 81.
99 POWICKE, J. and MAY, P. (1977) *op. cit.* p. 150.
100 STANLAKE, G. (1976) *op. cit.* p. 227.
101 ROUTH, G. (1975) *op. cit.* p. 308.
102 HADFIELD, J. (1969) *op. cit.* p. 92.
103 LANE, P. (1975) *op. cit.* pp. 85–6.
104 These and other inadequacies in the neo-classical approach to women and employment are discussed in AMSDEN, A. (Ed.) (1980) *The Economics of Women and Work*, Harmondsworth, Penguin.
105 CURZON, L. (1975) *op. cit.* p. 5.
106 EDWARDS, G. (1970) *op. cit.* p. 19.
107 LANE, P. (1975) *op. cit.* p. 13.
108 STANLAKE, G. (1976) *op. cit.* p. 5.
109 TYRER, O. (1970) *Economics G.C.E. Further Model Answers*, London, Celtic Educational Services, p. 55.
110 HARBURY, C. (1971) *op. cit.* p. 176.
111 DAVIES, F. (1970) *op. cit.* p. 8.
112 WALTERS, A. (1978) *Economists and the British Economy*, London, Institute of Economic Affairs, p. 14.
113 Quoted in HUTCHINSON, T. (1977) *Knowledge and Ignorance in Economics*, Oxford, Blackwell, p. 148.
114 There is a nice irony here, since Defoe's character was calculating and unscrupulous capitalist, and even his island economy was based on slavery. Again the state of nature argument breaks down. For an economic analysis of Crusoe's exploits in Defoe's book, see HUMER, S. (1980) 'Robinson Crusoe and the secret of primitive accumulation' in NELL, E. (Ed.) *op. cit.*
115 CHRISTIE, D. and SCOTT, A. (1977) *op. cit.* p. 74.
116 NICHOLSON, J. (1973) *op. cit.* p. 150.
117 HARBURY, C. (1976) *op. cit.* p. 12.

118 MARDER, K. and ALDERSON, L. (1975) *Economic Society*, London, Oxford University Press, p. 106.

119 JOINT MATRICULATION BOARD (1972) *General Certificate of Education. Examiners' Reports*, Manchester, p. 54, parenthesis added.

120 JOINT MATRICULATION BOARD (1976) *General Certificate of Education. Examiners' Reports*, Manchester, p. 20.

121 The Associated Examining Board for the General Certificate of Education (1979) *Syllabuses 1979. Section III*, Aldershot, p. 88.

122 POWICKE, J. and MAY, P. (1977) *op. cit.* p. 152.

123 CURZON, L. (1975) *op. cit.* p. 8.

124 This practice has also been observed by LEAKE, A. (1979) 'The theory of distribution' in WHITEHEAD, D. (Ed.) *op. cit.*

125 HARBURY, C. (1976) *op. cit.* p. viii.

126 JOINT MATRICULATION BOARD (1974) *General Certificate of Education. Examiners' Reports*, Manchester, p. 54.

127 JOINT MATRICULATION BOARD (1976) *General Certificate of Education. Examiners' Reports*, Manchester, p. 62.

128 FRIEDMAN, M. (1953) *Essays in Positive Economics*, Chicago, University of Chicago Press, pp. 15, 41.

129 JOINT MATRICULATION BOARD (1975) *General Certificate of Education. Examiners' Reports*, Manchester, p. 54.

130 LIPSEY, R. (1979) *An Introduction to Positive Economics*, London, Weidenfeld and Nicholson, p. 402.

131 HOLLIS, M. and NELL, E. (1975) *op. cit.*, Chapter 8; HUTCHINSON, T. (1977) *op. cit.*, Chapters 3 and 4.

5   Images of the Past: The Ideology of School History

The great strength of school history is that it shows life not under a glass in a laboratory but in society, with all its clash of character, motive, in all its baseness and aspiration. No subject tears away the scales of prejudice and shortness of sight so readily and completely and no other subject has such a wealth of human interest. It has something for everybody and can be adapted to suit all stages and all pupils.[1]

Such fervour and superlative are not uncommon among advocates of history in schools. However, the striking feature of discussions of rationales in history is that so many people can ardently hold such divergent views on the nature and virtues of one subject. Having 'something for everybody' is one of history's strongest qualities, but ultimately one of its greatest problems. In 1941, the Norwood Report observed 'Perhaps no subject of the curriculum with the exception of English admits of more varied interpretation'.[2] While there are clear patterns in the range of views and their development, writers continue to uphold various aspects of the subject as those deserving emphasis. Teachers seem no less divided, if a small 197. survey gives an accurate picture in reporting 'no agreement on th. purposes of history teaching'.[3] Nonetheless, in analyzing debates on the purposes of history teaching, we can tease out important aspects of the ideological relationship between history content and underlying values.

Some commentators have sought to avoid altogether the pitfalls of specifying the valued outcomes of history in schools. In 1920, Hasluck rejected instrumental justifications such as training in citizenship, the study of human nature, or moral instruction, as 'false and shallow' justifications of history teaching which, though they are widely asserted, have no sound strength and consequently tend rather to weaken the really unimpeachable claims of history as a cardinal subject of modern Education.[4]

Hasluck's alternative is, evasively, that 'history interprets and illumines the whole of life', but in elaborating this he faces the problem, common to many intrinsic justifications, that his idea of the intrinsic worth of history is an abstraction from instrumental ones. Thus he cites broadening the mind, attacking prejudice, and understanding historical allusions in reading as ways in which history illumines life.

Half a century later Hasluck is echoed by similar rejections of utilitarian values which Jones believes introduce 'false criteria' into the study of history: 'the study of history has arisen out of curiosity to understand it'.[5] The only valid reason for the study of history, said Jones, is that pupils enjoy it; they should therefore be left to study problems in the way historians do. In the light of observations that a large proportion of pupils finds history boring,[6] this might be thought an unsatisfactory position, and it is certainly not a sufficient reason for offering history for study in schools. Surely Jones must mean that it is potentially interesting *and* valuable in some intellectual, psychological or moral way. Once this second element is allowed, instrumental considerations are clearly necessary, as, ultimately, they always are.

The Purposes of History

Instrumental considerations have long been recognized in official statements on the purpose of school history, where the teaching of history, rather than being seen as an entertainment for pupils or teachers, becomes the subject of public policy, whether at the school or system level. The discussion typically focuses on three aspects of history, as indicated in a public enquiry into history teaching in 1911. The history teacher, it was said,

> strives firstly to stimulate and train the mental powers of the child; then by means of those powers to bring the child to the comprehension of a certain body, and a particular kind, of truth; and finally by means of this truth to develop in him some grains of political wisdom and some notions of civic duty.[7]

The development of school history over the past century has seen these emphases (knowledge, skills and moral or civic purpose) compete for attention, but all have been represented in curricular debate throughout the period, and continue to provide a diversity of justifications. In the varying interpretations of the purposes of history we can see the roots of the contradictions and problems which now plague the subject.

School history in the nineteenth century and much of the twentieth consisted of the teaching and learning[8] of the facts of British political history. Booth attributes this emphasis to the nineteenth century public school concern 'that those who were destined to occupy influential positions at home and in the empire should be given a sound knowledge of the development of the British constitution', and argues that the state schools 'adopted a pale imitation of this syllabus . . . intended to give pupils a healthy respect for British institutions'.[9] The compatibility of this version of history with nineteenth-century views of knowledge and pedagogy, and its enshrinement in a repectable school of historical method under Acton guaranteed its early dominance. Its twentieth-century variant added more complex reasons, interpretations and trends, and social and economic history to the earlier isolated political facts, but it did little to change the basic epistemology of given information to be learned by rote, and has been sustained in the public examination system.[10] Its mark remains in the preface of a recent text, which suggests that questions provided be used:

> As catechisms, one of the oldest and best of teaching techniques. When a student can answer a set of questions from memory, he has gone most of the way towards learning the topic. He has, of course, not mastered it fully, until he can recall the essential information without any help.[11]

While examinations encourage rote learning, recent decades have also seen an emphasis on understanding. Causality, change, development, motive, trends have become at least implicit in much history teaching, and understanding how and why people acted, and how their actions were related to past institutions, and produced present ones, is a major preoccupation in discussion.[12] However in seeking more systematic explanations there has been a tendency to depersonalize events, as general social and economic developments are recognized as 'factors' producing 'trends' in history.

To elements of facts and understanding of social change has been added a third aspect of historical knowledge – the focus on imaginative experience, on understanding how and why people acted, not in a detached, analytical sense, but by appreciating what it was like to live at another time: empathy, sympathetic understanding, a sense of history are terms often used. Having philosophical roots in Dilthey and Collingwood, and gaining official impetus from the Ministry of Education pamphlet of 1952,[13] this aspect has sustained and in turn been popularized by progressive views on pedagogy and curriculum. Enquiry learning, the use of original sources and 'patch' studies have provided opportunities for this approach to history teaching.

Another basis of rationales for history teaching has been the so-called historical method and its associated skills. Again, this is not new, but the priority given to it has definitely changed. Early this century one of the first advocates of documentary analysis in schools claimed that, while 'it is as an introduction to the world of human nature that history is chiefly to be prized',[14] there had been too much emphasis on teacher exposition, to the neglect of the useful skills associated with the scientific method in history. As shown above, the London County Council Committee of 1911 assumed a progression from the development of mental powers to the comprehension of truth and thence of wisdom and civic duty. But in 1952 the Ministry of Education could still regard as 'extreme' the view that 'history is simply a scientific intellectual discipline, analogous to that derived from learning to multiply or to prove geometrical theorems, a matter of detecting and weighing evidence, analyzing motives, estimating results, irrespective of place or period'.[15]

While the view criticized by the Ministry would seldom be held in its entirety, the mathematical analogy is no longer a pejorative one:

> For history does for the arts what mathematics does for the sciences. If the subject is properly taught, it calls forth and develops, in teacher and pupil alike, the fullest exercise of their analytical powers.[16]

Once a means to an end, the development of skills and historical method have now become for a large and influential group '. . . the first purpose of teaching history, and the chief way of defending its place in the curriculum'.[17] In part, this view seems to have been arrived at by default: 'Arguments about the content of a syllabus can go on without end because of the infinite variety of history. . . . If we were to take greater concern for methodology, we might be on firmer ground'.[18] The result has been a proliferation of source books, document collections and a focus on primary sources as evidence and raw material for the exercise of historical method and skills. An example is the following textbook preface which enumerates the book's three purposes:

> The first is to present information to the increasing number of pupils who study this subject for their examinations. The second aim, which does not conflict with the first, is to give the pupils a taste of 'history' and 'the historian at work' by a plentiful use of original material in the Documents section. . . . The third aim has been to help pupils to acquire a number of skills – by asking them to write, research, compare, criticise, draw and paint.[19]

Of the three goals listed by the London County Council's Committee in 1911 – knowledge, mental powers, and civic duty – the last seems to have suffered most attrition in the ensuing years. With occasional exceptions prompted by considerations of war or international goodwill, history teaching has become increasingly wary of espousing overt moral or civic purposes. The dilemma of balancing a belief in objective knowledge with the social purposes of education has been a perennial problem, and the complexities of the issue have understandably led to some variety and even contradiction in educators' pronouncements. It is still the case however that commentators are reluctant to deny that history makes a contribution to moral or political aspects of citizenship. What has changed is the relative significance attached to this as an educational goal, and the nature of the presumed contribution.

Prior to 1950, the commitment to citizenship goals in statements on history teaching was almost universal. Some favoured direct instruction: others saw civic virtue arising automatically from the study of history, Typical of many approaches was that of the Norwood Report which, acknowledging that good citizenship requires first a good example in the 'general life of the school', held that 'instruction in the duties of the good citizen . . . springs most naturally and effectively from the study of ordinary school subjects, particularly history, provided that those subjects are treated, when appropriate, in such a way as to be of relevance and significance to the present day'.[20] The early advocates of history for citizenship spoke of responsibility, spirit of duty,[21] patriotism,[22] moral truth,[23] moulding of character,[24] and right attitudes,[25] all of which presupposed identifiable ethical and political stances to which pupils were to be led. But other discussions, especially official ones, tried to avoid the difficulties of this position by arguing that objective knowledge was the best quality history could supply the future citizen. An early example illustrates the difficulty of the issue:

> Nor was there ever an age when, in the multiplicity of issues and of interests, it was so necessary as now to be able to take one's stand in an impartial position, and, while allowing the fullest weight to opposing views, to hold the balance fairly in the interest of the whole. This is the temper which the study of History tends to foster, and our teachers do almost without exception strive to maintain it. Justice to all and veneration for the great are two indispensable conditions for its successful pursuit.[26]

The contradictions of trying to combine liberal means and traditional ends confound the intention. The modern reader will ask if 'taking an impartial stand' is not a contradiction in terms, and the issue is further confused by the statement that impartiality is based on an unexplained concept of justice and an unquestioned 'veneration for the great'. The Spens Report of 1938 similarly seeks but fails to avoid this problem by arguing that history should

> be taught so as to induce a balanced attitude which recognizes differing points of view and sees the good on both sides. As we have said elsewhere it is in this way, by precept or still more by the breadth of their own sympathies, that teachers can best educate pupils to become citizens of a modern democratic country.[27]

The statement says nothing about just how 'the good' is to be identified, where the 'balance' is seen to lie, or how these are related to a particular political system.

The clouding of the moral purpose is further illustrated in the government pamphlet *Teaching History*,[28] where it is acknowledged that history provides moral example, but the issue is barely discussed. The problem continues. In the more recent HMI discussion document,[29] history is said to contribute to ethical/moral development by providing skills of judgment and relevant knowledge. But while accepting that history inevitably involves moral judgment, the document suggests we treat these as irresolvably subjective (a not uncommon moral relativism), and yet reference to moral 'obligations'[30] contradicts a complete subjectivism without clarification.

In the last decade official and academic discussion has most often focused on the importance of skills as the prime outcome of school history. Partly in response to the difficulties of content selection, and to avoid the controversy of the moral purpose, and partly in answer to demands for more lasting results applicable to other aspects of life, history educators have looked to the skills of analytical thinking and the use of evidence as the subject's greatest potential contribution. This has diverted attention from the knowledge and civic purposes, especially the latter, though both continue to be cited.

In tracing these three aspects of history teaching, the aim has been to show at one level the variety and fluctuation complemented at another level by a persistence of the three types of purpose. Care must be taken, however, for the developments have been traced through statements *about* history teaching, and it cannot be assumed that they have made a great impact on practice. Commentators have long noted and sometimes lamented the persistence of a traditional type of history teaching; surveys of teachers suggest that the skills emphasis is by no means universally accepted,[31] and that citizenship goals have been the least of the concerns of history teachers.[32] Given the official commitment in the recent past to, say, moral and civic goals and the weakness of apparent efforts to clarify and realize them, one might suspect that these stated intentions were not genuine, or that the problem was too difficult to solve in practice. On the other hand, it might be thought unlikely that so many people could believe in an element of history teaching which did not exist. This suggests a closer look at the content of much current history to identify through the images presented just what moral and political message might be there.

Social Images and History

Any attempt to identify theoretical assumptions in history and their implicit or explicit images of the individual and society, is complicated by the relatively amorphous and diffuse role served by explanatory models in historical explanation. While distinct approaches and theories can readily be identified in the more systematic and nomothetic disciplines of geography and economics, the concern for particular events has limited such developments in history. Debates over the role of covering laws and generalization[33] have done little to convince historians that this should be their aim. But they have highlighted that the historian, in explaining, colligating, narrating or interpreting (however what historians do might best be labelled), must resort to generalizations about how actions are related to each other and to social, technical or natural conditions at the time.[34]

Historians have acknowledged the selectivity involved in identifying problems and evidence thought relevant to them,[35] and that the selection will be based on usually implicit assumptions about what is likely to be the case. Hexter has described this background of knowledge and beliefs as the historian's 'second record':

> It is everything he can bring to bear on the record of the past in order to elicit from that record the best account he can render of what he believes actually happened in the past. Potentially, therefore, it embraces his skills, the range of his knowledge, the set of his mind, the substance, quality, and character of his experience – his total consciousness.[36]

In decribing a similar idea, other historians have suggested that the second record contains principles and ideas:

> Principles may be defined as referents of analysis which historians will recognize as valid in themselves and which they regularly have occasion to employ. Ideas may be defined as referents of suggestion which historians entertain for the insights they afford into historical situations . . . however far historians may believe in the inductive nature of their studies, all historical interpretation – as distinct from undisciplined accumulation of isolated facts – involves the use of such referents.[37]

Historians are, in this, not unique, for it has been shown that no investigation can be merely inductive (Chapter 2), but in trying to retain the complexity of the events they address, and in their consequent reluctance to accept specific theories which may narrow the focus, they risk using theories or assumptions which may not be made explicit nor critically examined. Any explanation of human action involves assumptions about human nature, and any attempt to link or 'place in context' individual action with social conditions will similarly involve theoretical judgments. As Nisbet notes, 'If there is to be a theory of social change, must it not be drawn from the same elements, though perhaps in different patterns of interaction, which comprise our theory of social organization, of order?'[38] The following analysis focuses on those aspects of the discourse of history text books which contribute most directly to the images of human nature and society which the texts present.

Progress and Moral Judgment

A perspective relevant to the present argument is the idea of progress, that history is best, even necessarily seen as a process of development, a sequence of continuous elements traceable to the present.[39] In the formative years of the modern concepts of history, the idea of progress, of society as a developing organism offered an alternative for those disenchanted with utilitarianism. It gained support from the popularity of evolutionary ideas at the time, and provided an explanatory model to historians, anthropologists and students of law and social science.[40] An early exponent whose influence on the teaching of history is often remarked on, was Thomas Arnold,[41] and it was essential to Acton's philosophy of history.[42] For both men progress was revealed through a scientific study of history, but the nature of this progress was spiritual, and fitted the Christian idealism which attracted them.

It is this combination of moral precept and scientific explanation which seemed to excite educators, for discussions of school history in the inter-war period provide some of the strongest of more recent statements of the idea. A prominent headmaster and text author, Worts, believed successful history teaching would show 'that Man, *homo sapiens*, has been successful in his long and gigantic struggle with life's adversities, and, having emerged triumphantly so far, is justified in his conscious dignity and self-pride'.[43] Others referred to progress as 'the great truth which history alone can teach',[44] and 'the grand human development' of civilization:

The development of habits of order, co-operation, and mutual respect; the development of humanity through nature-conquest, industry, art, literature, science, politics and ideals, and through gradual release from slavery, poverty, disease, ignorance and war.[45]

Jeffreys attracted much attention in his writings and experimental work in schools on history as 'lines of development'. Though aware of dangers in the approach, Jeffreys argued that

> in an organic process, which human history presumably is, 'causes' are to be understood teleologically rather than mechanically – not as pushes which set objects in motion but as meanings which become apparent only when we survey the growth process as a whole.[46]

While the technical flaws of progress, teleology and historicism are well appreciated,[47] it has also been persuasively argued that it is difficult to see how any meaningful history could be conceived without some idea of progress.[48] While the technical difficulties are important, present interest focuses on the implications of the idea for the social images which it might present. There are numerous manifestations of the idea of progress in current history textbooks.

Given the widespread view that history should help explain the present, it is not surprising that syllabuses and texts give most importance to tracing the origins and development of modern institutions and problems. Parliament, trade unions, trade and industry, franchise and living standards are the stuff of general school history – more so in social and economic history. While some authors are obviously aware of the dangers of presenting British history 'as a triumphant and uninterrupted march towards political democracy and social reform, both sponsored by a liberal-minded governing class',[49] none can fully escape them, since the idea of development, unless presented as decline, will connote maturity, fulfilment, progress.

The first element is simply that of change, but a unilinear, one-dimensional, directional change most often brought home by comparison with the present.

> The main developments since 1700 are outlined and particular attention has been paid to those features of the contemporary social scene which we take for granted but which are the end point of a period of rapid change.[50]

> We only need to compare our country today with what it was just over a hundred years ago to see how tremendous these changes have been in every possible way.[51]

> The Industrial Revolution was the greatest change that had ever taken place in British history.... The explosion shook

the nation to its very foundations and turned its whole way of life upside down.[52]

It is not so much that change is exaggerated, but that to focus so clearly on change is necessarily to detract from elements of continuity and persistence. And when such radical change is presented as progress, as it most frequently is, the result is a clear approbation of the conditions of the present:

> We have only to compare our own everyday lives with the lives of people who lived only fifty or sixty years ago to see how far we have progressed, at least in the direction of material comfort and physical well-being.[53]

The welfare state has 'virtually eliminated poverty'.[54] Of Victorian England: 'never, I think, has so much progress been compressed into so short a time'.[55] Few are as extravagant as one recommended text:

> Just as a child grows up to maturity, learning by experience and teaching, so a country must develop its own institutions and ideas, growing through its history into a responsible nation. Some of the lessons are hard, some of the experiences are shattering, like the Civil War in the reign of Charles I, but all play their part. We in Britain have developed gradually towards a country where the law protects our liberties and Parliament represents the majority of our wishes.[56]

This is the perfect example of teleological explanation, where continuous progress leads to the present as the ultimate stage of development, and all that has happened in the past is a contribution to it. But this most extreme example is implicit in the organization of many texts. The analogy of organic growth, of maturity and progress, has obvious pedagogical appeal, but uncritical use of it carries clear favourable judgments about the citizen's present lot.[57]

Also clear are its implications for political socialization, for if change is inevitable, and almost certainly beneficial, is there not ground for compecency, faith that the system and its progressive dynamic will do the best for all in the end? The air of inevitability is a part of the idea of progress. Everything happens in good time, when conditions are ready, or time is ripe.

> Education and housing are two matters which have produced special difficulties, but these should be overcome with time and patience.[58]

In fact, government control of railways had been steadily increasing throughout the twentieth century, and in this case nationalization was only a logical final step.[59]

(Charles Edward's '45) had been a foolhardy attempt to turn back a page of history which had closed with his father's defeat in 1715.[60]

It is greatly to the credit of the English people that the distress of the early industrial age did not bring more disturbance. . . . Their patience was justified by the fact that, in time, practically all their demands were met. Possibly, looking back, one can see wisdom in the refusal of the middle and upper classes to grant political equality to the mass of people. If they had it is possible that the institutions of government would have been destroyed in the process of change, and England, in chaos, could well have found itself ruled not by a democratically controlled House of Commons but by a dictator.[61]

Chartist aims were 'ahead of their times',[62] and the greatest statesmen were those who were able to see the necessary course of progress and become its agents. Peel was 'progressive' and 'ahead of his time'; 'enlightened' industrialists provided conditions which were 'exceptionally good for their time'.[63] Among factory owners 'there were a few farsighted men who realised that the working class were not a different race of human beings'.[64] 'Progressive' Tories were those who followed the dictates of the passage of time rather than the distribution of power, opportunity for advancement, or humanitarian ideals. This view of progress combines the moral approbation of change characteristic of Whiggism, with the air of inevitability of the Tory interpretation.

Hart has criticized the 'Tory interpretation of history', and in debating the explanation of nineteenth-century social reform argues:

In explaining progress in nineteenth-century England, they belittle the role of men and ideas, especially the role of the Benthamites; they consider that opinion, often moved by a Christian conscience, was generally humanitarian; that social evils were therefore attacked and dealt with when people felt them to be intolerable; that many changes were not premeditated or in some sense planned, but were the result of 'the historical process' or of 'blind forces'.[65]

The image of society presented is that of a self motivating system whose future is somehow determined, waiting only the natural working out of the process in time. People do not create but rather predict and support this natural development. Clairvoyance becomes the motive in politics. While this description exaggerates by concentration, the idea is pervasive in the texts. The ideological significance of this aspect of text book explanation lies in its view of the origin of social change. As Hart observes, 'The implication is that social progress will in the future, as in the past, take place without human effort; all will turn out for the best if we just drift in an Oakeshottian boat'.[66]

Pragmatism and Common Sense

If progress is inevitable, gradual, steady, there is little point in a commitment to radical change. It will be safer to conduct affairs moderately, so that conflict or sudden change are avoided, and the inexorable march forward is not disturbed. This may explain the striking tendency of some text book authors to laud the pragmatic and the expedient in men and women. The figures of the past most beloved of these historians are those who show 'common sense', a term of universal praise.

Common sense is being 'practical' and is essentially the antithesis of idealism. It is conservative, moderate, cautious rather than radical or fervent or volatile. When the last Chartist demonstration on Kennington Common broke down, we are told 'Either O'Connor's nerve failed, or common sense prevailed'.[67] James, the Old Pretender, 'was surrounded by those whose enthusiasm for the Stuart cause outran their common sense. Like many sincere people, who believe so much in their cause that they will not listen to anyone else's point of view, they had become fanatical'.[68] Peel 'disapproved of changes in the Constitution ... he bitterly opposed making changes which attempted to create a new kind of government or a new kind of system of organising the country. He was essentially a sensible, practical man who was completely sincere'.[69]

Queen Anne 'possessed a sturdy common sense';[70] Walpole's was 'profound'.[71] Keir Hardie was 'a kindly, common sense Scotsman'.[72] Wellington was not only brilliant, but had 'sound common sense'.[73]

Common sense actions are those which avoid confrontation, as may have been the case on Kennington Common, but was clearly so in other notable moments in history. In the Suez crisis: 'Fortunately, common-sense prevailed. The troops were withdrawn and the matter was handed over to the United Nations'.[74] On the 1832 Reform Bill and the King's agreement to the creation of peers: 'In the face of this threat the Tories in the Lords withdrew their opposition, led by the Duke of Wellington who displayed his usual common sense in ordering an about turn'.[75] On the revolution of 1688: 'So the Tories gave way, and the Convention named William and Mary as joint King and Queen. It was the common-sense solution, giving effective power to William'.[76] Numerous other references to common sense, revealed in moderate, expedient actions which avoid conflict, give the clear message that this is the best way to solve a problem. It should be noted however, that this is not a simple vote for peace, since none of the authors wishes to depict Chamberlain's 'peace with honour' as a manifestation of common sense.

Associated with the reference to common sense is the use of pragmatism as a criterion for judging actions and policies. If it works, and especially if it works financially, it is successful, and good. Practical policies are the ideal. Bribery and corruption in early nineteenth-century elections might seem 'quite scandalous', but they 'worked in practice remarkably well'.[77] 'By present day standards the system was anything but representative, yet in practice, it did not work out quite so badly....'.[78] 'The new "Poor Law Bastilles" ... were hated by the poor.... But the system did work.... The cost of poor relief was halved, and employers after 1834 were forced to pay at least a minimum living wage...'.[79] Conservative success in the 1950's 'was largely because they had continued in the steps of Disraeli, combining an appeal to Nationalist emotion with a practical approach to government'.[80] And the present electoral system

> is a rough and ready way of representing people's views because the M.P.'s are usually told which way to vote by the party leaders and do not vote as they think fit; still less do they vote the way the people whom they represent may wish. However, the great merit of the system is that it works.[81]

If any moral were to be drawn from these aspects of text book history, it would be that moderation, pragmatism, and expediency were the first requirements of political action, and that policies are successful if they seem to 'work', a feature held in common by Poor Law Bastilles and the modern Parliament. This is history as the great mistress of prudence, but we might wonder about its effects on Clio's acolytes in schools.

Pragmatism serves as an alternative to moral judgments, but in avoiding comment from criteria of good and evil, text authors have established a new form of good, and are mainly moral relativists on criteria other than pragmatism. For instance, while an increasing number of history texts openly condemn the Peterloo Massacre as at the very least a blunder, the pragmatic view is that the government's action was understandable:

> The government officially congratulated the magistrates on their resolute action in breaking up the meeting. We may wonder at such a commendation by the government, but this is only because we cannot put ourselves in the minds of the rulers of the times. Undoubtedly they acted in good faith, believing as they did that meetings of this nature were the beginnings of revolution.[82]

Similarly, while more critical histories are ready to attribute much of the suffering in the industrial revolution to exploitation or culpable neglect, the pragmatic view is that 'before you think that the hardship and squalor must have been somebody's fault, remember that nobody planned the changes'.[83] But while the morality of pragmatism is inadequate, it is not the only kind, for other text authors refer to fairness, justice and similar moral conventions in discussing historical actions. Unfortunately the treatment of these issues is so uncertain that it raises as many problems as it solves.

This seems to result from a belief that historical events and therefore explanations have an essential moral component, but a parallel reluctance to specify the nature of that morality. In discussing beliefs and values, and social policies reflecting them, very rarely is any attempt made to identify a principle which might explain or give a rational basis to them. Take as an example the following discussion.

> It is now generally recognized that no one should be allowed to suffer unreasonably because of poverty or misfortune, and that money should be taken from the better-off sections of the community by means of taxation, in order to finance a wide range of social services.[84]

While it is shown that this would have been thought 'revolutionary' a hundred and fifty years ago, and is still questioned in the United States, there is no attempt in the text to analyze the principles underlying the beliefs. There are then no grounds for choosing among the conflicting values or even for thinking that such things are open to rational discussion. In the absence of principles of justice or rights, there seems no way of deciding what constitutes 'reasonable' as opposed to 'unreasonable' suffering, or what should count as misfortune.

Other texts decry the lack of social justice in Victorian society,[85] or express surprise at Wilberforce's humanitarian stance on slavery and indifference to the conditions of child labour in England.[86] But in the absence of any attempt to show the ethical bases of these problems and judgments the bland humanitarian sympathy which provokes the comments does nothing to help explain them, nor to enlighten the reader as to what problems might be involved in such decisions. If the study of history has a moral purpose, as curriculum discussion recommends; if it includes the making of moral judgments, as it manifestly does in the texts; then there are grounds to expect some direct treatment of moral issues and their role in historical explanation. The argument that history is not ethics does nothing to solve the problem so long as the moral element of history remains, as it must. The following examiner's report on British Economic History candidates suggests the result of this neglect of morality:

> The basic moral and political issue was rarely faced, though it arises in connection with most economic changes; how much benefit to how many justifies great damage to a few?[87]

If neither pragmatic nor moralist text authors offer principled grounds for discussing the morality of human action: if efficiency, expediency and caution are the keys to successful decision making: then the political message is a conservative one. Compromise, consensus, gradualism and quietism are the elements of political behaviour most frequently promoted by the texts. This has already been seen in the role of common sense as an epithet of praise, but it surfaces elsewhere, as in the discussion of trade unions, which must 'change the attitude of their members, many of whom remember the days of very difficult labour relations before the war, from one of antagonism to the "bosses" to one of cooperation with management and industry for the good of the country'.[88] Elsewhere, trade union leaders are praised for being 'more moderate and statesmanlike in their conduct; Bevin and Citrine dealt firmly with employers, but sought compromise solutions rather than outright victory'.[89]

The explanation of events as a sequence of progress brought about by practical men of common sense is a fundamental part of a potential image of how society does and should operate, since it presents a view of how the present society came to be. If this can be called the dynamic element of a diachronic perspective, other elements describe the nature of people and society in a more static way, telling the reader not how things came to be but what they are. Descriptions of what British people and British society are like are obvious vehicles for establishing particular images of the social world.

Human Nature

Historians could well object to the claim that they use an amateur and outmoded psychology in discussing human action, arguing rather that psychologists have wrongly abstracted human nature from the complex reality of human action.[90] Nevertheless, it is clear that historians do require a concept of human nature and its connection with action, and that this has ranged from emphasis on the role of irrational self interest,[91] through accounts of principled action to deterministic explanations based on economic or other forces. The perspective taken will vary with the style of history, and the texts which display the most overt images of people are the traditional 'general' histories, where political events are seen as the actions of influential individuals.

In 1969, an 'O' level examiner's report complained

it is somewhat daunting to find that old-fashioned text-book assessments (many of them almost '1066 and All That' in approach!) evidently die hard. To many candidates John thus remains a 'bad' king, and James I is still 'stupid'. But just as examiners expect candidates in History to show an informed and sympathetic grasp of period problems and standards, so too they can surely expect to find some appreciation of the complex characters of prominent statesmen.[92]

The longevity of this aspect of school history continues, and the assessments, while perhaps old-fashioned, are nonetheless current in texts still published and recommended for schools. Descriptions of people are in many cases crudely judgmental. Monarchs are frequently 'stupid', especially James I and George III, while successful statesmen like Wellington, Pitt and Disraeli are 'brilliant'. Queen Victoria 'showed a strength of character and a power of endurance which surprised many of those around her. Her will of iron was more than a match for many experienced statesmen and politicians'.[93] Florence Nightingale's 'clear brain sized up the deficiencies of the hospital administration, and her iron will gradually imposed order'.[94]

Observations on human nature provide quite unsupported generalizations. Workers in 1815 had an 'inbred habit of respect for social superiors'.[95] We learn that 'people as a whole are not very logical when what they regard as their interests are involved'.[96] 'Arkwright was ambitious . . . and a good businessman, qualities rarely found in an inventor'.[97]

These are the marks of an outdated history, but the shibboleths of the 'great men' approach live on. Their failing lies not only in the distortion of the relative contributions to events made by the various participants, but also in the quite fantastic images of people which they present. Take the following examples of character sketches of Pitt:

> His tall figure, his great hooked nose and his eye that, as it was said, 'could cut a diamond': his withering sarcasm and superb gift of phrase: his power of tearing an opponent's arguments to shreds, and his sustained eloquence – all combined to overwhelm the Commons. . . . In some way that is hard to explain . . . he managed to communicate to the country a sense of his greatness, winning popularity and confidence among every class in the community.[98]

> A good administrator, William Pitt could still rise in Olympian majesty above the details of organization to view the needs of Britain with distant but acute perception.[99]

At other times, images of political figures can be crudely expressed: 'To fill in time before the next chance for a fight came up, Churchill wrote his first and last novel'.[100] Or simply funny: 'Home's lordly background was a target for socialist criticism and witticism; yet he did have experience of canvassing (at best of times an arduous job) in working-class areas, and of meeting the unemployed'.[101] Cynicism is an easy reaction, and might best be tempered by the thought that history would be failing if it did not try to explain the acts of individuals; but there is a strong tradition of inadequate conceptions of human nature which, while pretending to uphold the importance of the individual in history, in fact distorts it. Again the examiner's comment, while evidence of the continued existence of this approach to history, advises concern over its effects:

one had the impression that many candidates had no understanding of the great men of the age whose names they conscientiously recited in a wide variety of spellings.[102]

The exaggerated accounts in the traditional emphasis on great political figures have given way in more recent histories to a new line of heroes.

For social and economic history has become the dominant style, and has recently been called 'the nearest thing we now have to common core syllabus'.[103] Its nature is indicated in a study of English examination papers in social and economic history for 1968–72 which concluded:

it seems that Social and Economic history are defined in the manner which Professor Hobsbawm has recently identified as typical of the twenties and thirties, that is to view the two types of history as largely the study of the development of agriculture and industry.[104]

The inventors and industrialists, the humanitarians and union leaders are becoming the great men (if more modestly so) of the age. Now the names which many pupils may conscientiously recite are likely to be Bakewell, Telford, Watt, Wedgwood, Tillett. But some of the old exaggeration remains, the emphasis changing from brilliance in public affairs to genius in invention and commerce. James Watt is most extravagantly praised for his 'genius' and 'natural ability'; too few of the authors are careful to point out that the inventions were not sudden creations of ineffable genius, but more often parts of a long process of solving particular problems, each building on earlier ideas.

Explaining past success in business covers the range that might be expected, from the conclusive notion that 'Arkwright was a born man of business',[105] to the non-committal attribution of Robert Owen's success to 'enterprise, intelligence, work and luck'.[106] What these qualities mean and how they can be separated in human experience are not clear; only one of the books analyzed called on evidence relevant to this issue by analyzing the extent to which prominent industrialists were products of family background.[107]

Inventors, in being rescued from the neglect of 'drums and trumpet' history, must be inflated beyond life size in order to compete. They become, in all seriousness, 'a strange collection of geniuses and frauds, dazzling successes and abject failures, attractive personalities competing with some men of quite outstanding nastiness'.[108]

If a peremptory treatment of human nature is forced on text book writers, if thumb nail sketches are all that space will allow, in searching for interest, character becomes caricature, and the value of seeing men and women achieving in the face of life's problems is lost. Readers must be forgiven for feeling that success in the past is due as much to supernatural powers as to human agents, and that such people can only be deferred to, not emulated. Again a political conclusion can be drawn from the image of human nature presented in many of the texts.

It has been argued that

> Historians who deny that greatness in politics can exist, who refuse to find overwhelming personalities in history and cannot ever admire greatness in affairs, ought to look into their own hearts. Men who do not recognize and respect greatness have no business to write history ... impersonal forces are the refuge of the feeble.[109]

There seems little cause to fear that many text authors will deserve criticism of this sort, but the *ad hominem* of the argument should not discourage a healthy scepticism at accounts of history which give a decisive role, not to individual human beings, but to extraordinary figures who seem to exist only in the pages of fiction and history text books.

But if the images of human nature carry implications for socialization, how much more important might be the image of British people, the characteristics which are said to be best and distinctive in them. Text authors seem keen to generalize about the nature of the British people revealed in history, and typical references tell us that in 1926 'compromise was still a part of the British way of life',[110] and refer to 'the pride in independence that is so typical of most of our people',[111] or 'the British tradition of individual freedom and enterprise'.[112] Occasionally individuals epitomize characteristics of the nation:

> Wellington may be said to have created the pattern of the tight-lipped Englishman with his emotions sternly under control, ready at whatever cost to obey the call of duty.[113]

Johnson ... captured the spirit of the London in which he lived. He had many characteristics that might be called 'national' – courage, a sense of humour, honesty, quiet religious conviction, common sense, a love of the established order, a prejudice against foreigners and a cheerful acceptance of his lot.[114]

Baldwin's bowler hat and pipe came to typify the popular conception of the sane, balanced, common-sense Englishman, averse to extremes of both Right and Left.[115]

Of particular interest to text authors seems to be the nature of the British working class, described in generally favourable tones for its patience and moderate character. William Lovett was 'one of the best types of Englishman. He was self-educated, well read and possessed great moral courage.... Lovett hoped that the aims of the charter would be achieved peacefully'.[116] 'Hardie was a very British type of revolutionary; he was a kindly, common sense Scotsman, believing firmly in the need for a separate Labour Party, and seeing socialism not as a system of economics but as a humanitarian necessity...'.[117] In the nineteen twenties, 'the essential insularity, conservatism and patience of the English worker was never fully recognized'.[118] When mass political action was taken, moral was always better than physical force: Lovett was 'one of the best types of Englishmen'; O'Connor was mad. Certainly the image is not one to encourage radical political activists.

Images of Society

Given the concept of social change as a progressive development towards a state of freedom and rights, and a concept of human nature which highlights common sense and moderation, the image of society is the complementary one where opportunities for advancement are guaranteed to those with ability, and a democratic Parliament acknowledges the right and provides the means for each to influence his or her destiny.

First, social structure is said to be open, and mobility the outstanding feature of the social process. In contrast to the nineteenth century picture with its frequent juxtaposition of squalor and luxury, and the more recent disparity of the dole queues and the bright young things of the nineteen twenties, the constant reference to the present is in terms of greater equality and opportuntiy. 'Society today is much more closely integrated than ever before. Sociologists call the easy movement between classes, *social mobility*, and this has become so much a feature of twentieth century life that it is sometimes difficult nowadays to distinguish between social classes'.[119] 'In the second half of the twentieth century the lives of the factory worker or the shop assistant and the managing director of the firm for which he works are really very similar: fifty years ago they would have been completely different'.[120] 'Greater economic equality than in the past and the disappearance of old social distinctions have produced a situation in which people can claim that all are roughly speaking on the same level'.[121] The welfare state has 'virtually eliminated poverty' and 'one of the most significant developments in this century has been the massive redistribution of wealth which has taken place'.[122] Occasionally the most generous comment on the texts, that brevity calls for a forced simplicity, is strained by the treatment of some complex issues: 'there are opportunities for everyone, but poorer children, in the main, do not take them. They go into jobs much the same as those of their parents, and there is little the schools can do about it'.[123]

The effects of such assumptions can be less obvious, as when, for instance, social conflict is almost universally discussed in terms of classes only up to the first world war, occasionally in the twenties. Since then the struggle for power is seen as being between governments or business and the unions.

In describing, if exaggerating the real gains made in these areas, the tendency to emphasize change leads to a picture which is quite unrecognizable beside the evidence of continuing marked inequality of wealth and mobility. Combined with the necessity of simplifying complex issues, the result can hardly be described as a balanced description of social mobility and the distribution of wealth.

The typical picture of the British political system is simple enough:

> Britain today is a Parliamentary Democracy. This means that it is ruled by people called *Members of Parliament*. These M.P's are chosen by everyone over the age of eighteen. They are supposed to run the country in the way that most of the people want. Every five years at the most they must put their ideas or policies to the voters and ask to be re-elected. In this way Britain is ruled by its people.[124]

You may believe that the right to vote is nothing very special. You may even believe that voting is a nuisance and a waste of time. If you do believe that, then you are wasting one of the most precious things that you have – the right to say what YOU want the government to do for you and for people like you. For today, governments are chosen by the people and to stay in power, they have to try to do what they think is best for the people.[125]

The heritage of political history naturally gives rise to a conception of political power in exclusively parliamentary terms. Unions are the marked exception to this, increasingly presented as challengers to the government as the wielders of power. Other possible candidates, the State bureaucracy and Civil Service, multi-national companies and big business, are not mentioned. A small number of texts acknowledges problems in the system, such as the debate on proportional representation, or party line voting,[126] but more fundamental questioning of the system is not seen as relevant to the history of British politics.

Thus political problems are viewed from the perspective of the present system.

the great merit of the present system is that it works. It is successful largely because we have only two big political parties which are sufficiently evenly balanced for each to have a chance of forming the government.[127]

Problems are presented as having only two sides, and authors make a point of showing both. The alternatives then are reduced to more or less of the same thing: a bit more or less nationalization or private enterprise; higher or lower levels of state welfare provision; more or less social mobility. By defining problems in this way in the past and the present, radical alternatives are ignored: syndicalism, market welfare or economic equality do not fall within the spectrum of political possibilities of the system, nor then of the historian's definition or discussion of the problem.

By conceiving of problems from the perspective of a given political context, there is the danger of presenting them narrowly, of seeing them always as solvable within the system, when in fact they may require a fundamentally different social order. What implications lie in the following superficial review of a major social problem:

> Is it right in a time of acute housing shortage that houses, whether council or privately owned, should stand empty? Or that one person's house should have so many rooms while another person is homeless through no fault of his own? As in other problems facing the community as a whole, e.g., traffic restrictions, population direction and control, and pollution, the housing shortage could be solved sooner if we could all agree on a solution and carry it out, regardless of personal inconvenience.[128]

Apart from the difficulties of deciding who is and is not homeless 'through no fault of his own', or the tautology that the problem would be sooner solved if we could all agree on a solution, the real question of what to do when there is no such agreement is avoided by this quite unhelpful ploy. If consensus politics cannot provide an answer, the author sees no other way out.

A similar superficiality can be seen in the notion of political rights, which in aggregate is a quite confused concept. The most common view is that 'Today we regard the freedom to vote as a natural right. It is, however, a right that should be prized for it is the most important liberty in our democratic system'.[129] In describing the development of the franchise as a long but natural process, historians tend to neglect the questions of principle and rights underlying the idea. Take the following explanation of the extension of the franchise in 1867, and the implication that 'respectability' and 'comprehension' are the requirements of franchise:

> For a generation, accordingly, the middle class, in so far as its members chose to study political questions and used their right to vote, decided the results of every General Election. But the skilled artisans and other urban workers in regular employment were gradually drawing closer to the middle class, both in their standard of respectability and in their comprehension of public affairs.[130]

Similarly, in discussing the winning of the vote for women, the 1918 reform is unanimously attributed to the economic contribution of women to the economy and the war effort. If respectability, comprehension, productivity and power struggles won the right to vote, it is not clear what is meant by describing it as a natural right. Are there other natural rights which are not yet allowed? If political equality is a natural right, to what extent can social and economic equality be demanded on the same grounds? The quagmire of political philosophy and the theory of rights is avoided, the expedient but not the intellectually honest way of dealing with the problem. When such evasion becomes overt distortion, the fault is simply mischievous:

> Greater economic equality than in the past and the disappearance of old social distinctions have produced a situation in which people can claim that all are roughly speaking on the same level. In this case, political equality is a natural consequence of social and economic equality.[131]

Inevitably the images of society in history texts are less obvious and more varied than in other more systematic social disciplines. Nevertheless, social theories, political models and values permeate the texts. Generally imprecise, but sometimes quite explicit, they present or assume images which have clear descriptive and evaluative implications for the interpretation of the present society and its problems. Further, when we consider the effects of omission as well as commission, and the lack of deliberate analysis of important issues, the picture is of an unsystematic but neither random nor comprehensive selection of social images in history.

Opinion and Bias in History Books

It has been a tenet of this discussion that descriptions of social phenomena, and assumptions underlying explanations of social events, will carry with them evaluative implications of varying directness and certainty, this being the point of the idea of an image, with its combination of descriptive, explanatory and evaluative elements. So far, the analysis has sought to identify how such images are implied by assumptions about historical process, human nature and society which are built into the selection and interpretation of events. But other means exist whereby evaluative aspects of images will be presented, ranging from overt to less obvious expressions of opinion quite apart from the connotations mentioned above, and from intentional to unavoidable value judgments.

Gratuitous value judgments are not common, but when they occur they reiterate the underlying judgments already discussed. For instance, in the 'traditional' texts, support can be found for conservative, nationalistic and rather puritan values. Syndicalism is an 'essentially selfish doctrine'.[132] Elsewhere:

Irresponsible and selfish use of wealth in this style and the great ostentation of the rich were among the key-notes of the Edwardian period, and the huge fortunes derived from the South African gold mines made matters worse.[133]

The difficulty of avoiding judgments is nicely shown in the following contradictory comment on early nineteenth century elections:

To us all this sounds wrong but we must not judge by the standards of the twentieth century and we must remember that whatever its faults, and they were many, the eighteenth century parliament was incomparably better than anything which existed elsewhere.[134]

More recent texts can be equally open in their support for what might be termed more modern goods:

Better conditions for the urban worker is a nineteenth and twentieth century cry: it should have been that of the previous five hundred years.[135]

So when you start work and notice on your pay slip each week the words 'Deduct National Insurance contributions' just think of all that you have had, and are going to get, for this. It is perhaps the best value in the world.[136]

Less obvious judgments can lie in descriptive language. This can result from the use of terms which have developed wider political connotations, as when the difference between Labour and Conservative policies is described in the jargon of the right:

But the idea of rigidly planned growth targets and close, prescriptive controls over crops and techniques was relaxed. Instead, farmers and consumers were to have greater freedom of choice, and the market was to find its own level.[137]

Or when imperialism is explained in terms which its victims might find highly selective if not wholly inappropriate:

No one can dispute that Britain became a Great Power in the eighteenth century and that Britannia ruled the waves in the nineteenth primarily through the skill, resourcefulness, and energy of her industrialists, shipowners, bankers, and craftsmen.[138]

More difficult still are cases where the inevitable distortion of meaning through everyday use unfortunately turns essentially descriptive or representational words into pejorative terms. This may be exploited, as when one author comments that 'like most Marxist ideas this one was based on theory rather than fact';[139] but an examiner's comment shows that it can result from simple misunderstanding: 'Beveridge's own terms were not understood; "idleness" was interpreted as "laziness" and "want" and "greed".'[140]

The intricacies of language will always create problems of this kind, whatever the subject; in presenting disguised images, intentional or unpredictable, they complicate further the inherent evaluative and ideological elements of historical discourse.

Historical Images and Social Philosophy: A Review

The 1923 Board of Education pamphlet *The Teaching of History* held that the 'growth of the human spirit' through its struggle with the environment 'rises to greater power and fuller consciousness of itself', and that this evolution deserved prominence in the study and teaching of history.[141] This idealism and its connection with the idea of progress were strongly argued in educational debate around that time,[142] but became increasingly difficult to sustain as the discipline of history developed more materialist and empirical emphases.

Today such idealism has a very tenuous place in the discussion of history teaching, having been usurped even in the civic and moral aspects of school history by the emphasis on realist explanation and skills. While the idea of progress lives on, it is translated into the materialist terms of economic history, or the undifferentiated notion of political rights developed in the history of Parliament and the franchise. The decline of idealism has left the field open to emphases on method addressed to historical problems, and to a selection of content determined largely by the desire to explain the origins of present institutions and their problems. In some cases it has prompted spurious claims of a detached empiricism:

> The art of studying History is, first of all, to search for facts within a period or topic; then to sort out the facts; and finally to try to see the significance of the facts or to understand their meaning.[143]

More typically it has led to the historicist views of history as progress or as the development of present social problems, usually both. But there is a fundamental lack of an explicit social philosophy within which these can be seen as problems. A problem becomes anything which causes unrest, or which obstructs material progress. Conflict in history is in the more determinist texts an automatic indicator of prosperity:

> Since disorder was fed by distress, it was also natural that the levels of both should vary directly, and it is this relationship between disorder and economic fluctuation which explains the irregularity of outbreaks.[144]

Elsewhere, and more commonly, it is a result of group demands for 'social justice', but since this concept is not explored, it is an inadequate explanatory device. Tied as it is to a progressive view of development, with contemporary society as the final stage, 'social justice' becomes defined as what presently applies – universal franchise within a Parliamentary system of government, a limited and variable set of personal opportunities and freedoms, a minimal level of economic security, and an unspecified degree of social mobility. Beyond this, the commitment to harmony and moderation is the major principle offered. Questions of freedom and equality which do not fall within these parameters are not seen as problems of 'social justice'. Thus increasing industrial conflict is a power struggle between government and unions, threatening the principle of harmony, but not solvable or even conceivable in terms of a fundamental principle of social justice. Discrimination on grounds of race or sex, when mentioned, poverty, inequalities of opportunity, are seen as isolated problems, mentioned or ignored depending on the authors' predilections. Intellectual history is rarely a part of the history syllabus in the lower secondary school, effectively ruling out even an historical approach to concepts of morality or justice;[145] yet there is frequent reference to justice as a motivating force in history and as a ground for moral judgment, as if the nature of the concept and its applications were known and uncontroversial. It may be thought that the history of ideas, or discussion of moral philosophy, are not appropriate for the thirteen to sixteen year age group, being perhaps too abstract or complex. But this is an unacceptable view, since text authors do use moral argument in their explanations, and developments in moral education have demonstrated the feasibility of treating such issues with these pupils.[146]

Vagueness may be in part a means of avoiding commitment on

contemporary issues, an increasing problem for authors as history courses continually edge towards the present as their finishing point. It is now the common practice for history syllabuses and texts to take seriously the limit of courses 'to the present day', some texts containing material on the year before publication. This quite radical practice follows a lengthy debate on contemporary history and the possibilities of a proper perspective on recent events, and seems to signal victory for the view that history should provide an understanding of the present by tracing past events to present ones.

During the inter-war discussion of civic education in history, a history master gave the following warning:

> I should like to plead that it is the business of us teachers to keep ourselves more strictly to the cold and ascertained facts of the past. We draw up our own syllabuses and choose our own books. That difference between our country and others is due to the fact that it used to be the custom of English teachers to keep away from present-day and controversial topics; we did not draw attention to the immediate past. Did we not get that freedom because we respected that convention?[147]

The trend to contemporary history would seem to put this independence at risk,[148] but there are compensating factors which reduce the danger. Some already mentioned are the support for moderation in politics, the tendency to define problems in terms of present political machinery, the lack of fundamental critiques of notions of justice and freedom, the idea of progress. But combined with these emollients is the tendency to treat recent events with a reserve which avoids even the moderate controversy and judgment which is applied to earlier periods. Consisting often of little more than a chronology of government policies, technological change and economic problems, there is little attempt to place developments in a broader context, or to view them critically.[149] The texts' treatment of the recent past is even less likely to develop a productive social understanding than their flawed versions of the past.

Some Illustrative Issues

So far the analysis has focussed on separate aspects of the approach to history in the texts, showing recurring patterns of explanation or comment which can apply to many contexts. To balance this artificial analytical structure, it is useful to consider how these various means of image building actually combine in the treatment of particular issues, how the synthesis of elements of description, explanation and evaluation occurs in particular explanations. Of interest are two issues relevant to questions of social and political values, and sufficiently significant in historical terms to be widely treated by the texts: female suffrage and trade unions.

The suffrage movement and the events leading to the franchise of 1918 have received increasing attention as social history has grown in importance, and as a feminist consciousness gradually invades the male stronghold of history texts. Most often, however, the issue is seen in the context of the development of the franchise in general rather than as a part of the struggle for women's rights. Of the fourteen texts which dealt with the issue, ten saw female suffrage in this restricted fashion. One of the remaining texts points to the significance of this tendency.

> Some books suggest that the demand for Votes for Women was the only, or at least the main, demand by women looking for emancipation (or freedom). In fact, women wanted freedom to have the same sort of education as their brothers had. They wanted freedom to get the same sorts of jobs and the same wages as the men got. They wanted to be really free, not only to vote.[150]

Along with so many complex issues treated briefly in the general texts reviewed here, the most instructive aspect of the presentation is the selection of items which the texts see fit to include. The striking feature of this selection is the emphasis given to and the judgments made about the political tactics of the suffragette movement. In keeping with the tendency to condemn violence and to support the parliamentary process, the texts present the view that the feminist cause overreacted in its impatience to gain the vote, and actually delayed the granting of their demands. Because texts ignore the fact that female suffrage had been called for over a hundred years earlier, and that active associations of women had been campaigning for the right to vote for over fifty years, the militancy of the suffragettes appears precipitate.

One text remarks that in 1800, 'no women possessed the franchise, for a start, nor did anyone dream that they should'.[151] This is an unfortunate statement, since Mary Wollstonecraft's *Vindication of the Rights of Women*, advocating that women be allowed 'to share the advantages of education and government with man',[152] was published in 1792. Bentham had considered the question four years earlier, and Tomalin quotes a discussion of the issue at a local government meeting in 1765.[153]

There is also the viewpoint that women's participation in civil society actually declined in the eighteenth and nineteenth centuries; certainly the 1832 Reform Act was the first to qualify 'persons' with the word 'male' in such legislation, an exclusion then instituted in later legislation on local government suffrage and inheritance. This view and evidence were current in the suffragette campaign, and are cited in Helen Blackburn's 1902 contribution to the movement.[154] Also, a women's suffrage bill had passed the second reading stage in 1870, yet forty years later the parliamentary prospects of such a measure were as dim as ever. But Whiggism and the idea of progress blind many historians to these possibilities of negative change and stagnation, with the result that suffragette discontent, and especially their militant tactics, are more difficult to understand and justify.

In some cases, authors seem to belittle the motives of the suffragettes. Miller calls the suffrage campaign an 'onslaught on the liberal system which was essentially irrational'.[155] Jones explains the energy of the women's rights campaign in terms of boredom and the general climate of opinion:

> In part this was a reaction to the narrow and empty life of social entertainment to which middle-class women were condemned. . . . In part it was due to a rising tide of opinion demanding more equality of the sexes.[156]

Gill claims that 'the vote was not really being sought for any practical object but more as a symbol of equality'.[157]

Further, the texts' judgment is that the tactics and militancy of the suffragettes were unwarranted when parliamentary means were available. The intrigue of party politics, Asquith's opposition, the class interest involved in the cases for and against are totally ignored, and parliament is presented as a benign patron whose failure to act was due more to neglect than to conscious opposition. In the face of such an innocent patron, suffragette militancy seems impossible to understand, much less condone. Similarly, the interests of moderation are best served by showing that militant actions are not successful in politics but are more likely to be counter-productive.

All this was, however, in vain, and did more harm than good. More thoughtful suffragists began to turn back to the less spectacular but painstaking societies that preferred to use constitutional means.[158]

Although the suffragettes started off as a serious and high minded body, they were affected by the current unrest and irresponsibility, indeed, they began to attack the very foundations of the democratic system which they were claiming the right to join.[159]

The agitation probably delayed reform, if anything....[160]

On the whole, however, the resort to violence seems to have alienated male opinion, for none of the series of measures for female enfranchisement, which were brought before Parliament in various forms every year from 1908 to 1914, succeeded in reaching the statute book.[161]

Violence of this kind, however, only offended the majority of opinion and made it impossible for Asquith to yield without betraying weakness.[162]

These views are doubtful on a number of counts. First, the evidence is that at no time did the majority of public opinion even approach a position favouring women's suffrage.[163] More importantly, there is a consensus in recent research that, while militancy hindered the possibility of suffrage legislation, other factors were crucial in denying it passage; the absence of militancy would not have reversed the result.[164]

The nature of the question meant, in Parliamentary terms, that the real obstacles lay elsewhere – in the Lords, among Liberals and the Irish, if not some Labour M.P.'s.... It seemed reasonably clear that Asquith had no intention of including Suffrage in the Franchise Bill and, if the question had come to a vote, Tories, Liberal dissidents, and the Irish would have killed it for reasons other than the behaviour of militants.[165]

The texts fail completely to mention the important role of Asquith's opposition,[166] or what have been called 'the vicissitudes of party politics' which prevented the consideration of the principle divorced from personal and party intrigue.[167]

Instead, in keeping with the tendencies identified earlier, the texts claim that moderation, patience and service had their reward when the franchise was granted in recognition of women's war service.

> But neither the violent suffragettes, nor those (like the Pethwick-Lawrences) who sought the vote by peaceful means, were successful. Women got the vote because the nation recognized their importance in the community as a result of their war work.... [168]

> Even so, when women finally gained the vote in 1918, it was more as a result of their contribution to the war effort from 1914 onwards, than as a direct result of pressure, militant or constitutional, before the First World War. [169]

> This belated concession to women was largely a recognition of the prominent part they were playing in the war effort, and of the fact that they had abandoned militant suffragette tactics. [170]

> In 1918, partly as a reward for their good work and partly because they had shown themselves responsible citizens, women over 30 were given the right to vote. [171]

> ... the majority of the people in the country sympathised with their aspirations, though not with the violence of their methods. The suffragettes' aims were to be achieved not by violence but by work of all types done by women during the 1914–18 war. [172]

Again this is a doubtful interpretation. While the argument of war service was important in the rhetoric of the time, if only in allowing some earlier anti-suffragists to succumb without losing face, at the level of application it was clearly not a major factor, for the thirty year age limit still excluded the majority of women who had done the war work. What finally made the measure possible was the changed political environment of the war, especially the change of Prime Minister and the resolution of related Irish questions, two factors which had prevented success in a parliament which was in other respects favourable to the idea of female suffrage. As the Lords could not refuse female suffrage without denying its extension to servicemen, their hands were tied. There was also some fear of a return to pre-war militancy. [173] Rather than a failure of militant action, the events of the suffrage campaign suggest the foibles of parliamentary and cabinet government and a party system based on expedient interest groups.

But this judgment is never made; only militancy falls foul of the history texts' political values, committed more to moderation than principle.[174] Criticism of the government manifests itself only in the suspiciously ingenuous comment that 'It is difficult to see why women were refused the vote for so long....'.[175] Finally, episodes like the suffrage campaign are the events which have led to the present, and the contrast with those times, inevitably favourable, masks the deficiencies which still exist:

> Today women have equality with men in most ways. Many opportunities are open to them in everyday life. If they wish to pursue a career in industry, business or a profession, they have the chance. In education, they have the same opportunities as those existing for boys.[176]

The case of militant action for female suffrage finds an interesting parallel in the treatment of trade unions and strikes. On few other specific issues are the texts in greater agreement. Nineteenth century unionism is seen as a desirable development in the growth of political liberty and greater fairness in material prosperity. Owen, the Tolpuddle Martyrs, Ben Tillett and Aneurin Bevan are the typical agents of this cause, which, until universal franchise, was always just. Thereafter, the judgment becomes ambivalent, often supporting the cause but condemning the methods.

For instance the 1926 strike is generally seen as 'the last stirring of the revolutionary feelings generated by the First World War'.[177] As such, it becomes a typical case of a valid cause gone wrong, and is generally interpreted as the last instance in British history where extreme action might have been justified. Ultimately, however, its failure and its claimed lack of popular support are proof that direct confrontation with the government is beyond the pale of British politics.

> The strike caused severe disruption but it was called off after nine days without any gains for the unions. It failed because the government stood firm and was supported by the major part of the general public who not only supplied volunteers to keep vital services going but were not in favour of revolution.[178]

The failure of the General Strike was a great humiliation for the Trade Union Movement. It failed because the government was better prepared and stood firm; because probably a majority of the population opposed; above all, because the English political tradition discouraged this form of direct action.[179]

Trade Union leaders learnt the bitter lesson that direct action which involved challenging the government could not be effective unless one was prepared to go on to revolution. . . .[180]

But the General Strike also had some more constructive results. The Labour Party dissociated itself more firmly from the doctrine of the class war. . . .[181]

Most people, however, would still agree with Baldwin that in a democracy a general strike is unconstitutional. Major issues must be settled by Parliament and not by industrial action aimed at the government.[182]

Clearly the many thousands of volunteers showed that, though they sympathised with the miners, a National Strike was not acceptable.[183]

The General Strike signals a turning point in the text book version of British industrial relations. Before the strike unions were representing their class in a struggle for justice in which the ends generally justified the means. Since that time, because the general view is that classes no longer exist in any real sense, texts show unions seeking better rewards and conditions for their members, but advocate submission to the established procedures for the good of the country, presumably because progress is thought to have eradicated the grounds for earlier militancy. Social justice and matters of principle have given way to demands for more money and comfortable working conditions. The proper course lies in moderation, patience and co-operation.

The recent story of trade unions has shown that perhaps the time has come for them to think of the good of the country as much as the good of their own members. In the past nobody took much notice of them, and they had real hardships to fight. Today the unions have more power, and the government is asking them to take part in the whole country's efforts to fight inflation. This is how the role of the union has changed since their beginnings many years ago.[184]

The movement entered the 1970's with undiminished power, though its willingness to exercise this too freely was tending to accelerate the inflationary process and incite governments to curb it.[185]

Today, the Unions ... are under strain because they are having to reorganise their movement ... and to change the attitude of their members, many of whom remember the days of very difficult labour relations before the war, from one of antagonism to the 'bosses' to one of co-operation with management and industry for the good of the country.[186]

Texts are unanimous in the view that, if the country is to overcome its economic difficulties, unions must cooperate with government and employers, and that this is sufficient reason for such cooperation. Support for the proper channels will smooth this progress; this means support for parliament and especially 'responsible' union leadership. Shop stewards, unofficial strikes, any action which contravenes the rulings of union leadership threaten the proper procedure and the harmony it is designed to maintain. Such events are, in keeping with the text authors' general position on harmony, to be avoided.

Many unionists did not accept that responsible behaviour would lead in the long run to a much better standard of living all round. . . .

The T.U.C. did what it could to stop the Unions from going too far along this dangerous path and to exercise a greater control over them.[187]

Whatever the organisation, the problem of size is a serious one. Many of the important decisions are made at factory level with the shop stewards playing a prominent part, rather than by the leadership. The unofficial or 'wild cat' strike is one consequence of this. Another is that irresponsible members may block the wishes of the leadership, though it would be a mistake to assume that the leadership always knows best.[188]

So the problem remains, and perhaps will remain until the local leadership and the rank and file of the trade union movement gain the same patience and insight into economic problems as the national leadership has developed, though the latter must in turn always be sensitive to the reality of local issues.[189]

Trade unions are granted their important place in the political and economic system, and are supported in the valid pursuit of their members' interests. Occasionally the support can reach potentially controversial levels:

> Normally you will not be pressed to join a union immediately, although in some cases you will have to join – this is called a closed shop policy. You can take it as an honour if you are asked to become a member, and you should accept.[190]

But this support is not free of political intent:

> A union can go badly astray if the members do not take a proper interest in what is going on.

> There are many people, particularly communists, who are only too ready to take advantage of the apathy of the ordinary trade unionist and win control of the whole union.[191]

In none of the texts was trade union activity seen as a fundamental questioning of the system. Rather, unions through their leadership are seen as a part of the institutional fabric of the political process, with accepted procedures offering the means of attainment of union goals. To step outside these procedures is irresponsible and damaging to all. Again the wisdom of this lies in its demonstrated success in producing the present which, with perhaps minor qualifications, provides a satisfactory way of life, the outcome, as one text would have it, of moderate and careful progress:

> This rather unhappy period of Trade Union history, however, ought not to make us forget the real success story of the wider labour movement.. Using all the means described in this chapter, working men and women have brought about tremendous social change. They have made sure that the benefits and rewards of a prosperous Britain have been shared among the majority of those who have worked so hard to make it so. This has been achieved without the violence and destruction which has taken place in some other countries – a great tribute to the determination and good

sense of all those who have worked for this goal for so long.[192]

Whether the issue is women's suffrage or union demands, a common pattern appears. The texts emphasize the means of achieving the goals, and ignore the principles underlying them; a clear line divides acceptable from unacceptable campaign methods; while texts sympathize with the cause of the Suffragettes and the miners in 1926, criticism and even questioning of the system which frustrated them is avoided. Correct procedures, if followed, are the best guarantee of success; the evidence of this lies in the improved conditions of the present. The selective emphases and condemnations, the definitions of what are and are not to be considered problems, conceptions of 'responsible' behaviour, and the favourable judgments of modern society, combined with overt value judgments, provide an image of society and its origins which is clearly not politically neutral.

Conclusion: The Composite Image

Images in history are relatively diffuse. At no time do text writers state a systematic theory of action or social structure as found in economics texts. The degree of explicitness and frequency of judgments on these issues varies from text to text, and even in more overtly judgmental texts images of human nature and society are often embodied in copious descriptions and narrative only indirectly related to the images analyzed in this study. Similarly, studies of this kind, in focussing on textual messages related to pre-selected issues like human nature and society, may disguise the variety of text positions on other matters. Images identified in this way must be treated cautiously.

Nonetheless, the reported events of history must be colligated by some set of principles, revealed in the selection and ordering of statements, the judgments made, the language used, and there is sufficient reference to aspects of human nature and society to provide a composite picture. Figure 3 attempts to combine the elements discussed in the texts, and to relate them according to their roles in explaining social change.

In geography the over-arching problem which generated and was generated by the image was progress in living standards and production. In economics, ideas of the abstract individual and the

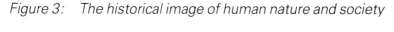

Figure 3: The historical image of human nature and society

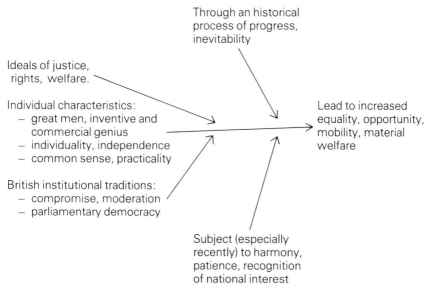

Through an historical process of progress, inevitability

Ideals of justice, rights, welfare.

Individual characteristics:
- great men, inventive and commercial genius
- individuality, independence
- common sense, practicality

British institutional traditions:
- compromise, moderation
- parliamentary democracy

Lead to increased equality, opportunity, mobility, material welfare

Subject (especially recently) to harmony, patience, recognition of national interest

market comprised a way of articulating and solving the problem of satisfying group needs in an orderly fashion. In history texts, the common goal is to explain the process by which individual agents and social change have addressed and largely solved the problems of equality, opportunity, mobility and material welfare. This has been achieved by the working out of general ideas of justice and welfare by historic groups and individuals through traditional institutions and procedures. The individual characteristics which have most favoured this development have been, separately or in concert, common sense, practicality, genius and the will of the great. The interaction of these elements of change has occurred within or produced a continuous and apparently inevitable process of improvement, which will continue as long as the need for harmony and a concern for national interest are observed.

At an abstract level, some features of the textbook version of history are universal – the idea of progress, the emphasis on favourable judgments of the present, the influence of currently dominant institutions and ideas in the formulation of problems, the advocacy of harmony and accepted procedure in seeking social goals. But fundamental criticism, alternative possibilities, analysis of moral, social or political ideals and principles are omitted, denying a basis on which the former commitments might be identified and questioned. In the images of history, what is not said is of central importance.

Historians have been wary of speculation, of counterfactual conditional arguments and of utopian considerations. Associating such practices with bias and inferior scholarship, many take pride in the fact that 'Political history is likely to attract the sceptics, the particularizers, the conservatives ... it repels the generalizers, the radicals, and the believers',[193] and that '*most* historians, if sceptical, are also inclined to be pragmatic and to judge by results rather than to argue on abstract grounds of methodological principle'.[194] But if this explains the features of the texts reviewed (it does only in part) it is misguided, for in eschewing radical belief and abstract principles, the ground is left to unchallenged assumptions and thinly disguised value judgment.

This is poor history, but it is even poorer school history, for to the extent that it applies it sacrifices the values by which the teaching of history is justified. Its narrow approach to the past, especially its neglect or inadequate treatment of concepts of morality or justice are disappointing given the potential of history as a critical humanistic discipline. While history need not be seen as 'philosophy teaching by example',[195] to realize its full potential as an educational experience would require some answers to the criticisms here proposed.

Such an analysis cannot predict how these features of the text content will be treated by teachers or received by pupils, nor will any class come into contact with the total composite picture presented here. But in light of the general deficiencies outlined and the examples cited, there is cause for considerable scepticism of the claim with which the chapter opened. While it may be true that 'No subject tears away the scales of prejudice and shortness of sight so readily and completely ...', this is not necessarily a comforting thought.

Notes and References

1 MACADAM, R. (1975) 'Fundamental study for all', in *The Times Educational Supplement*, 14 February, pp. 59, 60.
2 GREAT BRITAIN BOARD OF EDUCATION (1943) *Curriculum and Examinations in Secondary Schools,* Report of the Committee of the Secondary Schools Examination Council appointed by the President of the Board of Education in 1941, HMSO, p. 98.
3 HARRIES, E. (1975) 'Teachers' conceptions of history teaching', in *Teaching History*, 4, 14, pp. 151–3.

4 HASLUCK, E. (1920) *The Teaching of History*, Cambridge, Cambridge University Press, p. 2.

5 JONES, R. (1970) 'Towards a theory of history teaching', in *History*, 55, pp. 54–64.

6 BOOTH, M. (1969) *History Betrayed?* London, Longmans, pp. 73, 148; STEELE, I. (1976) *Developments in History Teaching*, London, Open Books, p. 3.

7 LONDON COUNTY COUNCIL EDUCATION COMMITTEE (1911) *Report of a Conference on the Teaching of History in London Elementary Schools*, London, London County Council Education Office, p. 33.

8 In many nineteenth century schools history was learned but not taught, since it was thought, and no doubt was, the kind of subject that could be 'got up' in pupils' spare time.

9 BOOTH, M. (1969) *op. cit.* p. 29.

10 LAMONT, W. (1969) 'Teaching history: a Black Paper reconsidered', in *Teaching History*, 1, pp. 109–113.

11 SPEED, P. (1977) *A Course Book in British Social and Economic History from 1760*, London, Arnold, preface.

12 In a survey of history teachers, the most frequently cited purpose of teaching history was 'to develop understanding of how the present evolved'. HARRIES, E. (1975) *op. cit.* p. 151.

13 GREAT BRITAIN MINISTRY OF EDUCATION (1952) *Pamphlett No. 23 Teaching History*, London, HMSO.

14 KEATINGE, M. (1910) *Studies in the Teaching of History*, London, Black, p. 7.

15 GREAT BRITAIN MINISTRY OF EDUCATION (1952) *op. cit.* p. 18.

16 HURSTFIELD, J. (1968) 'The historian's community', in *The Times Educational Supplement*, 26 April, p. 1383.

17 WAKE, R. (1970) 'History as a separate discipline: the case' in *Teaching History*, 1. pp. 153–7.

18 JONES, R. (1970) 'Towards a new history syllabus', in *History*, 55, p. 387.

19 LANE, P. (1979) *British Social and Economic History from 1760 to the Present Day*, Oxford, Oxford University Press, p. 1.

20 GREAT BRITAIN BOARD OF EDUCATION (1943) *op. cit.* p. 100.

21 LONDON COUNTY COUNCIL EDUCATION COMMITTEE (1911) *op. cit.* p. 34.

22 WALKER, E. (1935) *History Teaching for Today*, London, Nisbet, p. 159.

23 FIRTH, C. (1929) *The Learning of History in Elementary Schools*, London, Kegan Paul Trench, p. 4.

24 DRUMMOND, H. (1929) *History in School: A Study of Some of its Problems*, London, Harrap, p. 77.

25 GREAT BRITAIN BOARD OF EDUCATION (1923) *Education Pamphlet No. 37. The Teaching of History*, London, HMSO, p. 23.

26 *Ibid.*, p. 52.

27 GREAT BRITAIN BOARD OF EDUCATION (1938) *Report of the Consultative Committee on Secondary Education with Special Reference to Grammar Schools and Technical High Schools*, London, HMSO, p. 174.

28 GREAT BRITAIN MINISTRY OF EDUCATION (1952) *op. cit.*

29 GREAT BRITAIN DEPARTMENT OF EDUCATION AND SCIENCE (1977) *Curriculum 11–16. Working Papers by H.M. Inspectorate: A Contribution to Current Debate*, London, HMSO.
30 *Ibid.* p. 51.
31 HARRIES, E. (1975) *op. cit.*
32 HEATER, D. (1972) 'History teaching and political education', in *History*, 57, pp. 56–62.
33 GARDNER, P. (Ed.) (1974) *The Philosophy of History*, Oxford, Oxford University Press.
34 MANDLEBAUM, M. (1977) *The Anatomy of Historical Knowledge*, Baltimore, John Hopkins University Press, pp. 5, 6.
35 STRETTON, H. (1969) *The Political Sciences: General Principles of Selection in Social Science and History*, New York, Basic Books.
36 HEXTER, J. (1972) *The History Primer*, London, Allen Lane, The Penguin Press, p. 104.
37 CONNELL-SMITH, G. and LLOYD, H. (1972) *The Relevance of History*, London, Heinemann Educational, p. 106.
38 NISBET R. (1969) *Social Change and History: Aspects of the Western Theory of Development*, New York, Oxford University Press, p. 238.
39 While development can be distinguished from, in that it lacks the judgmental tone of progress, the two have always been closely associated, and in most writings of this kind it is difficult to separate them.
40 BURROW, J. (1966) *Evolution and Society: A Study in Victorian Social Theory*, Cambridge, Cambridge University Press.
41 FORBES, D. (1952) *The Liberal Anglican Idea of History*, Cambridge, Cambridge University Press.
42 FASNACHT, G. (1952) *Acton's Political Philosophy*, London, Hollis and Carter.
43 WORTS, F. (1935) *The Teaching of History in School: A New Approach*, London, Heinemann, p. 22.
44 JARVIS, C. (1917) *The Teaching of History*, Oxford, Clarendon.
45 GOULD, F. (1928) 'Transformations in history teaching', in *History*, 13, p. 235.
46 JEFFREYS, M. (1939) *History in Schools: The Study of Development*, London, Pitman, p. 22.
47 BUTTERFIELD, H. (1931) *The Whig Interpretation of History*, London, Bell; BERLIN, I. (1954) *Historical Inevitability*, London, Oxford University Press; POPPER, K. (1957) *The Poverty of Historicism*, London, Routledge and Kegan Paul. In this discussion, the term 'historicism' is used throughout in the Popperian sense.
48 POLLARD, S. (1968) *The Idea of Progress: History and Society*, London, Watts, p. 155.
49 HUSSEY, W. (1971) *British History 1815–1939*, Cambridge, Cambridge University Press, p. xi.
50 CASE, S. and HALL, D. (1977) *A Social and Economic History of Britain 1700–1976*, London, Edward Arnold, preface.
51 GILL, W. (1971) *British History for Secondary Schools – Book V: 1815 to the Present Day,* London, Edward Arnold, p. 15.
52 MOSS, P. (1976) *History Alive. Book 3. 1789–1914,* London, Hart-

Davis, p. 6.
53 CASE, S. and HALL, D. (1977) *op. cit.* p. 115.
54 *Ibid.* p. 119.
55 GILL, W. (1971) *op. cit.* p. 75.
56 STEWART, L. (1966) *A Course in British History. 1688 to the Present Day.* Book 1: 1688–1870, London, Arnold, p. 17.
57 A 1965 study of 147 secondary pupils' understanding of history noted a similar '"meliorist" view of history; most saw history as the story of things getting better and better'. BOOTH, M. (1969) *op. cit.* p. 70.
58 PARKER, M. and REID, D. (1972) *The British Revolution 1750–1970: A Social and Economic History*, London, Blandford, p. 24.
59 CASE, S. and HALL, D. (1977) *op. cit.* p. 107.
60 COLGATE, H. (1969) *British History for Secondary Schools. Book 4. 1688–1815*, London, Edward Arnold, p. 42.
61 GILL, W. (1971) *op. cit.* p. 34.
62 SPEED, P. (1977) *op. cit.* p. 213.
63 HUDSON, K. (1971) *Towards the Welfare State*, London, Ginn, pp. 37 and 40.
64 MOSS, P. (1976) *op. cit.* p. 59.
65 HART, J. (1965) 'Nineteenth-century social reform: a Tory interpretation of history', in *Past and Present*, 31, p. 39.
66 *Ibid.*
67 CASE, S. and HALL, D. (1977) *op. cit.* p. 57.
68 COLGATE, H. (1969) *op. cit.* p. 36.
69 GILL, W. (1971) *op. cit.* p. 38.
70 BRANDON, L., HILL, G. and SELLMANN, R. (1951) *A Survey of British History: From the Earliest Times to 1939. Book III. 1688–1815,* London, Arnold, p. 29.
71 *Ibid.* p. 82.
72 HILL, C. (1977) *British Economic and Social History*, London, Arnold, p. 170.
73 STEWART, L. (1966) *op. cit.* p. 137.
74 UNSTEAD, R. (1963) *A Century of Change. 1837 – Today*, London, A. and C. Black, p. 223.
75 TITLEY, D. (1973) *Machines, Money and Men: An Economic and Social History of Great Britain from 1700 to the 1970s,* Leicester, Bland Educational, p. 204.
76 BRANDON, L. *et al.* (1951) *op. cit.* p. 14.
77 *Ibid.* p. 136.
78 COLGATE, H. (1969) *op. cit.* p. 64.
79 CASE, S. and HALL, D. (1977) *op. cit.* p. 49.
80 ARNOLD, D. (1973) *Britain, Europe and the World 1871–1971*, London, Edward Arnold, p. 386.
81 COLGATE, H. (1969) *op. cit.* p. 44.
82 GILL, W. (1971) *op. cit.* p. 8.
83 PITT, H. (1969) *A New English History. Book 3. The Age of Wealth and Power*, London, Evans, p. 22.
84 HUDSON, K. (1971) *op. cit.* p. 7.
85 HUSSEY, W. (1971) *op. cit.* Chapter 20.

86 JONES, R. (1979) *Economic and Social History of England 1770–1977*, London, Longman, p. 19.

87 UNIVERSITY OF LONDON (1975) *General Certificate of Education Examination. Subject Reports*, p. 177.

88 JONES, R. (1979) *op. cit.* p. 253.

89 ROBSON, W. (1973) *Twentieth-Century Britain*, Oxford, Oxford University Press, p. 146.

90 Collingwood argued that irrational elements of mind were the stuff of psychology, rational elements those of history. COLLINGWOOD, R. (1946) *The Idea of History*, Oxford, Clarendon.

91 This view is found in Namier's work. NAMIER, L. (1970) 'Human nature in politics' in STERN, F. (Ed.) *The Varieties of History*, London, Macmillan. It is illustrated in the following school text. '. . . unofficial strikes cannot always be blamed on the unions alone – human nature comes into it as well. Most production line jobs are intensely boring, as well as demanding that the worker gears his efforts to the pace of the machine. Many wildcat strikes are therefore a result of the tensions caused by modern mass-production techniques? ROBERTS, J. and ROWE, A. (1975) *Making the Present. A Social and Economic History of Britain 1918–72*, London, Heinemann Educational, p. 87.

92 UNIVERSITY OF LONDON (1969) *General Certificate of Education Examination. Subject Reports*, p. 110.

93 RAY, J. and RAY, M. (1969) *The Victorian Age*, London, Heinemann Educational, p. 3.

94 RICHARDS, D. and QUICK, A. (1967) *Britain 1851–1945*, London, Longman, p. 30.

95 GILL, W. (1971) *op. cit.* p. 5.

96 HILL, C. (1977) *op. cit.* p. 88.

97 RUNDLE, R. (1973) *Britain's Economic and Social Development from 1700 to 1975*, London, Hodder and Stoughton, p. 69.

98 BRANDON, L. *et al.* (1951) *op. cit.* p. 90.

99 STEWART, L. (1966) *op. cit.* p. 69.

100 RODDIE, T. (1970) *Making the Modern World: Winston Churchill*, London, Longman, p. 6.

101 METHVEN, J. (1967) *A Course in British History: 1688 to the Present Day*, London, Edward Arnold, p. 33.

102 JOINT MATRICULATION BOARD (1976) *General Certificate of Education. Examiners' Reports*, Manchester, p. 16.

103 ROBOTTOM, J. (1980) 'Starting point for a new debate', *The Times Educational Supplement*, 11 April, p. 29.

104 INGLIS, W. (1979) 'A content analysis of GCE and SCE papers on social and economic history', in *History Teaching Review*, 11, p. 27.

105 CASE, S. and HALL, D. (1977) *op. cit.* p. 11.

106 CAIRNS, T. (1978) *Power for the People*, Cambridge, Cambridge University Pess, p. 42.

107 JONES, R. (1979) *op. cit.* p. 78.

108 PARKER, M. and REID, D. (1972) *op. cit.* p. 88.

109 ELTON, G. (1970) *Political History: Principles and Practice*, London, Allen Lane, p. 71.

110 DERRY, T. and JARMAN, T. (1979) *Modern Britain: Life and Work through Two Centuries of Change*, London, John Murray, p. 227.
111 GILL, W. (1971) *op. cit.* p. 22.
112 PARKER, M. and REID, D. (1972) *op. cit.* p. 292.
113 LINDSAY, D. and WASHINGTON, E. (1954) *A Portrait of Britain 1688–1851*, Oxford, Clarendon, p. 228.
114 COLGATE, H. (1969) *op. cit.* p. 81.
115 PEACOCK, H. (1976) *A History of Modern Britain. 1815–1975*, London, Heinemann Education, p. 213.
116 CASE, S. and HALL, D. (1977) *op. cit.* p. 55.
117 HILL, C. (1977) *op. cit.* p. 170.
118 GILL, W. (1971) *op. cit.* p. 182.
119 JONES, R. (1979) *op. cit.* p. 179.
120 MOSS, P. (1971) *op. cit.* p. 5.
121 PARKER, M. and REID, D. (1972) *op. cit.* p. 381.
122 CASE, S. and HALL, D. (1977) *op. cit.* p. 119.
123 SPEED, P. (1977) *op. cit.* p. 310.
124 O'CALLAGHAN, B. (1974) *Making the Modern World: The Chartists*, London, Longman, p. 4.
125 COCHLIN, R. (1978) *Life and Work from 1700 to the Present*, London, Hutchinson, p. 214.
126 COLGATE, H. (1969) *op. cit.*; MILLER, S. (1977) *British Political History 1784–1939*, Plymouth, MacDonald and Evans.
127 COLGATE, H. (1969) *op. cit.* p. 44.
128 ROBERTS, J. and ROWE, A. (1975) *op. cit.* p. 108.
129 TITLEY, D. (1973) *op. cit.* p. 60.
130 DERRY, T. and JARMAN, T. (1979) *op. cit.* p. 163.
131 PARKER, M. and REID, D. (1972) *op. cit.* p. 108.
132 ARNOLD, D. (1973) *op. cit.* p. 182.
133 RICHARDS, D. and QUICK, A. (1967) *op. cit.* p. 241.
134 COLGATE, H. (1969) *op. cit.* p. 54.
135 JONES, R. (1979) *op. cit.* p. 101.
136 MOSS, P. (1977) *op. cit.* p. 119.
137 PARKER, M. and Reid, D. (1972) *op. cit.* p. 278.
138 ROBSON, W. (1973) *op. cit.* p. 114.
139 RICHARDS, D. and QUICK, A. (1967) *op. cit.* p. 1151.
140 JOINT MATRICULATION BOARD (1971) *General Certificate of Education. Examiners' Reports*, Manchester, p. 15.
141 GREAT BRITAIN BOARD OF EDUCATION (1923) *op. cit.* p. 47.
142 JARVIS, C. (1917) *The Teaching of History*, Oxford, Clarendon; WILLIAMS, A. (1931) 'The teaching of history in schools', in *History*, 16, pp. 115–27.
143 METHVEN, J. (1967) *op. cit.* p. iii.
144 *Ibid.* p. 24.
145 An exception is the common reference, usually critical, to the laissez-faire ideology which delayed social reforms in the early nineteenth century.
146 KOHLBERG, L. (1973) 'Moral development and the new social studies' in *Social Education*, 37, pp. 369–75; JONES, C. (1976) 'Contribution of

history and literature to moral education', in *Journal of Moral Education*, 5, 2, pp. 127–38.

147 HERBERT, J. (1934) 'History teaching in English secondary schools', in *History*, 18, p. 336.

148 The trend may be rather limited, for one recent observer of history has referred to it as 'a professional community which often insists that the way to avoid bias and hidden propaganda is not to confront them openly but to regard the recent past as unfit matter for study'. ROBOTTOM, J. (1980) *op. cit.* p. 29.

149 See for example PEACOCK, H. (1976) *op. cit.*; RUNDLE, R. (1973) *op. cit.*; TITLEY, D. (1973) *op. cit.*

150 LANE, P. (1979) *op. cit.* p. 183.

151 PARKER, M. and REID, D. (1972) *op. cit.* p. 383.

152 WOLLSTONECRAFT, M. (1967) *A Vindication of the Rights of Women*, New York, Norton, p. 250.

153 TOMALIN, C. (1974) *The Life and Death of Mary Wollstonecraft*, London, Weidenfeld and Nicolson, pp. 104, 274.

154 BLACKBURN, H. (1902, 1971) *Women's Suffrage*, New York, Kraus.

155 MILLER, S. (1977) *British Political History 1784–1939*, Plymouth, MacDonald and Evans, p. 136.

156 JONES, R. (1979) *op. cit.* p. 180.

157 GILL, W. (1971) *op. cit.* p. 131.

158 CASE, S. and HALL, D. (1977) *A Social and Economic History of Britain 1700–1976*, London, Edward Arnold, p. 91.

159 PARKER, M. and REID, D. (1972) *op. cit.* p. 395.

160 MILLER, S. (1977) *op. cit.* p. 137.

161 DERRY, T. and JARMAN, T. (1979) *op. cit.* p. 211.

162 RICHARDS, D. and QUICK, A. (1967) *op. cit.* p. 195.

163 ROVER, C. (1967) *Women's Suffrage and Party Politics in Britain 1866–1914*, London, Routledge and Kegan Paul, p. 47; MORGAN, D. (1975) *Suffragists and Liberals: The Politics of Woman Suffrage in Britain*, Oxford, Blackwell, pp. 53, 91; HARRISON, B. (1978) *Separate Spheres: The Opposition to Women's Suffrage in Britain*, London, Croom Helm, pp. 157–8.

164 MORGAN, D. (1975) *op. cit.* p. 160; HARRISON, B. (1978) *op. cit.* p. 170.

165 MORGAN, D. (1975) *op. cit.* p. 160.

166 ROVER, C. (1967) *op. cit.* p. 97; MORGAN, D. (1975) *op. cit.* p. 157.

167 ROVER, C. (1967) *op. cit.* p. 180.

168 JONES, R. (1979) *op. cit.* p. 183.

169 CASE, S. and HALL, D. (1977) *op. cit.* p. 91.

170 RICHARDS, D. and QUICK, A. (1967) *op. cit.* p. 305.

171 MOSS, P. (1977) *op. cit.* p. 33.

172 OCKELTON, D. (1974) *G.C.E. Model Answers: English and European History*, Harsham, Artemis, p. 74.

173 HARRISON, B. (1978) *op. cit.* pp. 204, 216.

174 The British Schools Council History 13–16 Project is relevant here, in illustrating how the historical method approach also ignores the question of principle. A useful set of exercises engages pupils in

technical problems of the interpretation of evidence, such as photo-graph and documentary analysis to identify facts, bias and the use of language. The problem with this approach is its lack of comprehensiveness, for the exercises are addressed exclusively to the death of Emily Davison on Derby Day 1913, hardly an adequate perspective on the significance of the time and its events. SCHOOLS COUNCIL HISTORY 13–16 PROJECT (1976) *What Is History? 4. Problems of Evidence*, Edinburgh, Oliver and Boyd.

175 JONES, R. (1979) *op. cit.* p. 182.
176 RAY, J. and RAY, M. (1969) *op. cit.* p. 23.
177 RICHARDS, D. and Quick, A. (1967) *op. cit.* p. 327.
178 LARKIN, P. (1979) *Living and Working in Britain 1750–1950. An Illustrated Social History,* Amersham, Hulton, p. 105.
179 PARKER, M. and REID, D. (1972) *op. cit.* p. 192.
180 ARNOLD, D. (1973) *op. cit.* p. 185.
181 DERRY, T. and JARMAN, T. (1979) *op. cit.* p. 228.
182 RICHARDS, D. and QUICK, A. (1967) *op. cit.* p. 330.
183 GILL, W. (1971) *op. cit.* p. 191.
184 COCHLIN, R. (1978) *Life and Work from 1700 to the Present*, London, Hutchinson, p. 213.
185 FLINN, M. (1975) *An Economic and Social History of Britain since 1700,* Basingstoke, Macmillan, p. 224.
186 JONES, R. (1979) *op. cit.* p. 253.
187 PARKER, M. and Reid, D. (1972) *op. cit.* p. 197.
188 ROBERTS, J. and ROWE, A. (1975) *op. cit.* p. 86.
189 SMITH, A. (1969) *The Trade Unions*, Edinburgh, Oliver and Boyd, p. 103.
190 *Ibid.* p. 99.
191 *Ibid.* p. 100.
192 PARKER, M. and REID, D. (1972) *op. cit.* p. 197.
193 ELTON, G. (1970) *op. cit.* p. 69.
194 BULLOCK, A. (1977) *Is History Becoming a Social Science? The Case of Contemporary History,* Cambridge, Cambridge University Press, p. 4.
195 The term is Henry Bolingbroke's (1678–1751) and is quoted in STERN, F. (1970) *op. cit.* p. 27.

6   Learning the System: The Individual and Society in Social Science

Histories of the social studies curriculum are rare, perhaps because as an idea and even more as a set of curricular practices its development has been diverse, discontinuous, and lacking in logical or institutional unity. While it is possible to speak of a series of orthodox conceptions of economics and geography, and to identify central aspects of history which have alternately dominated approaches to history curricula, no comparable precision can be applied to the range of elements of the social studies.

Cannon[1] and Lawton and Dufour[2] see the 1930s as the origins of widespread moves to include in the social subjects a broad study of society whose main explicit purpose was to prepare pupils for citizenship through direct teaching. The Association for Education in Citizenship produced in 1935 what has been described as 'the first well-reasoned case for the teaching of social sciences in British secondary schools'.[3]

The Association's case may have been well reasoned, but it did not offer any unified concept of what was being advocated. Its publications argued the need for a wide knowledge of, among other things, politics, economics, geography, history and literature; people of 'independent judgment' who are 'indoctrinated' in certain notions of liberty, the role of law and reformist politics; a moral stance based on either religious or humanist principles;[4] and practical activities ranging across community service, military drill, athletics and wood carving.[5]

This apparently chaotic vision was not much improved by the aspirations of the post war advocates of social studies, and commentators have pointed to similar problems of unrealistic specifications of content and vague and grandiose aims.[6]

The last two decades have seen a reaction to this problem in the form of a more modest assessment of the potential of the social subjects, and a concentration on more specific and circumscribed courses. Encouraged by the 'project' method of curricular innovation, the result has been a proliferation of separate approaches to social studies: some focussing on particular content, such as moral education or political education; some emphasizing a particular pedagogical approach to issues, such as neutrally led discussion or values clarification; others attempting integration of concepts and methods from established disciplines.

But the mainstream of the social studies can still be identified in courses dealing comprehensively with social relationships and structures from a largely sociological and anthropological perspective. Usually labelled 'social science' these courses can be seen as archetypes of 'the new social studies' movement described by Lawton and Dufour;[7] frequently the logical conclusion of this trend to more specialized, concept based and scientific courses is the teaching of sociology. For this reason the following analysis concentrates on what is held to be the mainsteam of general social science courses and sociology, and discusses illustrative central themes within typical textbook presentations.

Social Studies and Citizenship

It is instructive to see social studies courses in the light of varying interpretations of the idea of citizenship. As argued in chapter 2, an investigation into how curricula sustain ideologies will find much of interest in specifications of the role of the citizen in the political process and the kind of knowledge which the role is thought to require. This connection can be traced in most documents relating to the aims of teaching the social subjects.

A useful first example is the concept of citizenship revealed in the 1911 London County Council conference on history teaching in elementary schools, where there is, to the modern reader, a striking emphasis on 'civic duty',[8] and a conspicuous neglect of rights. The conference Chairman, historian A.F. Pollard, illustrates the priority in his observation that, 'Every child in an elementary school has to be educated to fulfil two functions in life. He will have to earn a livelihood, and he will have to perform some of the duties of a citizen....'[9] On the other hand, the Association for Education in Citizenship emphasized the idea of service to the community. A founder, Ernest Simon, exalted the type of person with 'the will to sink his own immediate interests and the interests of his class in the common good: to do his full share in working for the community. . . .' For the rest, the educated voter in a democracy would have 'the power to select men of wisdom, integrity and courage as public representatives, and such knowledge of his own limitations as will dispose him to trust and follow his chosen leaders'.[10] The Spens report supported 'the unformulated but very real demand of the community that the young shall grow up in conformity with the national *ethos*'.[11]

In contrast, present educational discussion generally gives greater emphasis than in the past to the rights of the individual to expect and even demand satisfactions from society. The discussion retains ideas of service and duty to the community, but acknowledges also that civic education is a service to individuals, providing knowledge of how they might best promote their interests in dealing with other people and institutions. This idea is nonetheless quite compatible with the continued strengthening in main stream social science courses of the commitment to objectivity and detachment, for if knowledge of how society works is useful to the individual, then the more accurate the knowledge the more valuable it will be. The best service the school can provide is thought to be knowledge and skills, rather than the direct inculcation of civil virtues. The potential tension is obvious between the continuing tradition of encouraging civic duty and conformity, and the claim to serve the interests of the individual.

A review of social science syllabuses (see table 5) shows the most frequent aims to be an understanding of individual-society relationships, and the development of a critical approach to the environment. Sociology courses reveal even greater concentration on the mastery of a given body of knowledge and skills. In general, notions of service, duty and responsibility are rare, and never attain the prominence recommended in the past. The following foreword of a school text might fairly represent the intentions of most curricula in social science.

The purpose of this book is to describe some of the basic features of the British working world so that you can better understand the economy and the society of which we are all a part.

Information brings understanding which, in turn, allows us to use our rights to the best advantage and makes us aware of our responsibilities. We are then in a better position to

Table 5: Aims of eleven social science syllabuses at 16+ level, 1979–80

Aims stated	East Midlands CSE Social Studies 1980	Middlesex REB CSE Social Studies 1979–80	Metropolitan REB CSE Social Studies 1979–80	East Anglian EB CSE Social Studies 1979	Ass Lanc SEB CSE Social Studies 1979	Sth Western EB CSE Citizenship 1979	Joint Matric Bd O Level Social Science 1980	East Anglian EB CSE Sociology 1979	South East REB CSE Sociology 1979–80	AEB O Level Sociology 1979	Oxford Local Exams O Level Sociology 1979	TOTAL
To develop responsibility	✓				✓							2
Increase self respect	✓											1
Encourage service to community	✓											1
Develop a critical approach to environment	✓		✓		✓							3
Understand societies in a cross cultural way			✓				✓					2
Understand self and one's place in society			✓	✓		✓	✓	✓				5
Become aware of/sensitive to social problems			✓		✓							2
Develop international awareness					✓							1
Understand environment					✓							1
Understand political issues						✓						1
Gain experience through participation												1
Master social science concepts, methods							✓		✓			2
Understand social processes, influences of group on individual								✓	✓			2

Middlesex REB CSE Social Studies 1979–80: None stated
AEB O Level Sociology 1979: None stated
Oxford Local Exams O Level Sociology 1979: None stated

change those things with which we are not satisfied – and put up with those things we cannot change with, perhaps, less resentment.

It is hoped that the book will help you to gain sufficient knowledge of the world of work so that you can develop into a full citizen of your country, taking a lively interest and active part in what goes on around you rather than simply become a subject of the state with little awareness of the opportunities and problems existing in Britain today.[12]

Good citizens then have a more active role than in past interpretations, for they have rights to press and demands to be satisfied. Rather than Ernest Simon's followers of leaders there is here greater emphasis on participation, but the whole is moderated by notions of responsibility and acceptance of the inevitable, and development into a 'full citizen' of the country. Knowledge is the key to this role, and is what the school can contribute to the growing citizen. This is far from a radical proposal, but its modest terms do allow rights and criticism, balanced by responsibilities and acceptance of what cannot be changed.

This notion of citizenship requires that the social subjects provide accurate knowledge. For if citizens are not fully informed of their rights, if they are given a false picture of what can and cannot be changed, or of what avenues for change do exist, if they are led to be satisfied with conditions which may be seen as acting against their interests, the laudable aims become hypocritical and unjust.

The chief significance of the social studies for the idea of citizenship lies in the subject's attempt to explain in a comprehensive theoretical fashion the relations between individuals and groups, and how these create and are influenced by social patterns and structure. To complete this ambitious brief, social science must confront the central problem of social theory – how can the relationship between the individual and society be understood in all its variety and complexity? Since no unified theory exists which can satisfactorily cope with this problem, it seems pointless to show that social science in secondary school deals with it in an incomplete or contradictory fashion. What is interesting is not that school courses cannot solve the problem, but rather what they take to be satisfactory approximations to its solution, which of the competing perspectives they adopt, what inaccuracies they are willing to accept for their purposes.

The Social System

The typical design of these courses presents society as a system whose parts are the major institutions which organize the activities of its members. The table of syllabus content (table 6) shows the most frequent topics to be work and industry, government, law, education, leisure, the family, mass media and social stratification. These elements are described as activities necessary to the operation of the system, and their relation, to the extent that it is described, is a functional one. In fact, the connections are seldom drawn, for in the topic approach to the institutions, industry, law, government, mass media are treated separately, and relationships among them seldom referred to, much less analyzed or illustrated.

The explanatory model is structural-functionalism (the ideal form being that of Talcott Parsons), implicit in general social studies texts, but explicitly chosen in most sociology books at this level. The difficulties of structural-functionalism are well known and some aspects of it have been severely criticized. Among its major deficiencies (though they are not exclusive to it) are its denigration of human agency,[13] a failure to resolve internal contradictions of voluntaristic individuals and deterministic structures,[14] and a view of social dynamics which inflates equilibrium and harmony above conflict, and consensual norms above power as explanatory concepts.[15]

A revealing example is provided by one O-level sociology text:

The social system consists of a vast structure of social institutions and social organisations which interact with one another to make it possible for us to live and carry on our everyday activities.

We talk about the *social structure* to indicate the complex ways in which the social system is organised. This structure is rather like the human body. If it is to be healthy it must *function* properly. That means that all the social organisations must interact with one another for the benefit of the community. But sometimes a part may become out of gear as, for example, when people in a state resort to violence. Then the whole system suffers.

We have to study our own social structure and see how it is composed. This means looking at the different parts like the family, the educational organisations and the government.

We need to look at each part and see what functions it has. But we also have to observe the whole system functioning as a whole, and see what happens when it does not function satisfactorily.[16]

Of the many problems in this approach, perhaps the most conspicuous is its normative component. Since the social system is organized 'to make it possible for us to live and carry on our everyday activities', the student's task is to see how contemporary institutions achieve this. But such a study provides no basis for criticizing present society, for institutional functions are studied only for their contributions to it. Is this perhaps a desirable objectivity, scientific neutrality? No. For the passage contains a clear reference to the structure functioning 'properly' and 'satisfactorily' as does a 'healthy body'. Thus a desirable society is part of the explanatory scheme, since interaction must be 'for the benefit of the community'. The only criterion provided for such a judgment is that parts should not come 'out of gear', as occurs in violent upheaval. The system of explanation is value laden, and its evaluation falls favourably on the continuation of the present arrangements which 'make it possible for us to live'. The passage nicely illustrates the tendency noted by Bernard Crick: 'Only a lunatic would attack order as such, or could possibly adjust to a complete breakdown of expectations; but those who justify "order" as such, rather than simply point to its minimal necessity, are usually smuggling into the concept their own particular ideas of the best form that "order" should take.'[17]

The reference to the human body is a popular metaphor, and is echoed, with similar normative effect, in another text which uses the structural-functionalist model:

A good example of the structural-functionalist approach is to take the human body as a total unit made up of various parts – arms, legs, heart, lungs etc. These parts can themselves be further divided up into substructures – the arm is made up of fingers, hand, wrist, bones, muscles, etc., and the heart is made up of valves and compartments. If we ask what these various parts of the body should do we are concerned with their function: in order for the total human body to perform the many tasks required of it, the arms, legs, heart, and lungs each have to perform *their* own particular task. When they are performing these tasks well, they are said to be functioning; they are doing the job they are intended to do, and so

Table 6: Topic content of eleven social science syllabuses at 16+ level, 1979–80

Topic content	East Midlands CSE Social Studies 1980	Middlesex REB Social Studies 1979–80	Metropolitan REB Social Studies 1979–80	East Anglian EB CSE Social Studies 1979	Ass Lanc SEB CSE Social Studies 1979	Sth Western EB CSE Citizenship 1979	Joint Matric Bd. O Level Social Science 1980	East Anglian EB CSE Sociology 1979	South East REB CSE Sociology 1979–80	AEB GCE Sociology 1979	Oxford Local Exams O Level Sociology 1979	TOTAL
Local government	✓	✓	✓	✓	✓	✓						6
Central government, political parties	✓	✓	✓	✓	✓	✓	✓	✓	✓	✓	✓	11
Justice and law	✓		✓	✓		✓	✓	✓	✓	✓	✓	8
Responsibilities of the citizen as a person, householder, and voter etc.	✓	✓										2
Industrial organization and industrial relations	✓	✓		✓	✓	✓				✓	✓	8
Economic knowledge, personal economics	✓			✓								2
World problems	✓			✓	✓							3
Mass media	✓	✓		✓	✓	✓	✓		✓	✓		9
Rights of the citizen			✓									1
Family		✓	✓	✓		✓	✓	✓	✓	✓	✓	10
Education		✓		✓		✓	✓	✓	✓	✓	✓	8
Religion		✓		✓				✓	✓	✓		5
Leisure		✓		✓	✓			✓	✓	✓		6
Welfare services		✓	✓	✓		✓			✓			5
Social stratification, class, status	✓	✓	✓				✓		✓	✓	✓	6
International affairs		✓	✓	✓	✓		✓					5

Topic	Count
The individual, personality, heredity	4
Types and nature of groups	3
Development of ideas and attitudes, beliefs	1
Work-types, aspects, conditions	9
Housing and the urban environment	5
Women's role in society	4
Social problems, deviance, poverty, drugs etc.	5
World government, world politics	5
Socialization, development	4
Roles	2
Culture, norms, values	3
Conflict	1
Power, authority	3
Research methods	4
Population	2
Race Relations	1

enabling the body to carry out the many tasks required of it. If any one part fails to perform its task correctly then it is said to be not functioning or to have a malfunction.[18]

Here again we find the evaluative ideas of what the parts 'should do', of their performing tasks 'well' or 'correctly'. The biological metaphor highlights the determinism of the functionalist approach, aggravated in this case by the idea that the parts of the body (read social institutions) have jobs they are 'intended to do', and that the body (read society) has tasks 'required of it'. We need ask only how such intentions and tasks are determined, and by whom, to see that the biological metaphor, and its simple common element of survival, has minimal usefulness as an explanatory model of society. Its effective denial of morality, rational action, sectional interest and power is an instance of a common omission which will be further discussed later.

Determinism occurs in other aspects of functionalist explanation. In the following passage, social order is produced by the existence of norms which are self adjusting, and whose relations can be machine-like. The abstraction of characteristics of human belief into self-motivating systems is clear in this extreme example, in which norms are said to be

> the standards that are expected to be followed. Such norms are of great importance in society for it is through their adjustment with one another that social order is maintained. In a well-organized society the norms fit in with one another like the parts of a machine. It is this dovetailing of norms that produces the equilibrium in society which we call social order.[19]

The Concept of Role

Human agents fit into the functionalist model by adopting the roles which the social system constructs. According to Parsons, role is 'the primary point of direct articulation between the personality of the individual and the structure of the social system'.[20] Giddens[21] points out the tendency for role theory to emphasize the 'given' nature of roles, as if there is no conflict of expectations or interpretations of what a particular role should or might be. This again is a case of functionalist theory tending to determinism, and ignoring the fact that role definitions, as with norms and system goals, are achieved by the use of power.[22]

These features of role theory are easily identified in text presentations:

> A person's behaviour is governed largely by his *role* in the community at any particular moment. Such a role is the customary way of doing things which he is actually doing at that time. . . . He is like a chameleon – he has to be constantly changing himself to fit the particular role that he occupies at the moment.[23]

So behaviour is 'governed largely' by role, and the process is as automatic as a chameleon's colour change. The overdetermined presentation of role and role behaviour robs actors of the need to interpret role definitions for themselves, and the chameleon simile is not uncommon:

> Although they remain basically the same, people can show different sides of their personalities according to the company they are in. Like a chameleon, which changes the colour of the skin to match its surroundings, some adapt themselves to those they are with.[24]

Another explanation of role illustrates a related problem:

> As Jane gets older she will assume various 'status' positions: she may have the status of a mother or the status of an employee; she will have the status of a teenager and the status of an old age pensioner. Each status will demand a particular cultural pattern, and it is this cultural pattern which will be Jane's 'role' in that situation.[25]

Here roles are fixed to 'status positions', which 'demand' certain patterns of behaviour. In suggesting automatic and inevitable connections between such things as aging, status and role, there is an implicit denial of the need for individual interpretation of role expectations, of conflicting role definitions, of the effect of beliefs and ideology on conceptions of roles, and of the part played by power of some people over others in deciding how these problems are resolved in everyday life.

One metaphor often used in preference to automatic processes like the chameleon's skin is the dramaturgical notion, which, after all, was the origin of the concept role. Its advantage is that it seems to allow for the individual's contribution to the role, in the way that a theatrical actor will interpret a part. A typical explanation calls on us to

> imagine society as a playwright which (*sic*) writes the particular parts its members (the actors) play. In order to portray the part accurately the individual actor must conform to an expected pattern of behaviour. Only if he does this is it possible for the other actors to play their parts. . . . Roles are not so rigid that they do not allow for individual interpretation. In the theatre many great actors have interpreted the role of Hamlet in Shakespeare's play in different ways. This is referred to as their role style; they recognize that there is a broad framework within which they must remain but they can still express individuality.[26]

This is an improvement on total determinism, but it still glosses over the question of who or what 'society' is, how it writes the 'parts', and who decides when the parts are portrayed 'correctly'. An even more realistic version of the drama metaphor is provided in another definition of role:

> We come to know roughly what part we are supposed to play in a particular situation, and then we make up the 'script' as we go along.[27]

But again two elements of the process are glossed over. How do we 'come to know' our parts, and how are the parts themselves produced? To ignore such questions is to become party to the normative impact of functionalist explanation. For if structures and functions are derived from the need for society to survive, and if roles are dictated by these structures and functions, then to question the roles is to question the need to survive. Central to this sequence is the assumption that the society being referred to is the present one, and that to 'survive' means to persist in its present form. Any change in the structure of present society would destroy it: it would no longer survive. In this way the functionalist explanation can conflate survival with conservation of present institutions.

Only by questioning why the roles are created, how and by whom they are defined and sustained, in whose interest, and in the face of what alternatives, can structural-functionalist explanation avoid this pitfall. In failing to do this, in presenting consensual notions of society whose structure and roles are given, and in ignoring the distinction between biological survival and the persistence of a social system in a particular historical form, it denies pupils insights into the workings of society which would increase their power in it.

The Individual, Groups, and Society

Between the simplicity of the idea of free will and the neatness of social determinism, there lies the problem of conceiving of individual and group relations in a way which will replace the duality of most social theory. Individualists have used phenomenological theories of action in history and sociology in seeing human behaviour as rational, purposive, and initiating, limited by material conditions and the actions of other individuals. Determinists have tended to see human action as the product of material conditions or cultural systems involved in the task of survival of the group. The solution lies in a theory which shows the role of language, belief and power in an historical process in which social structure and human action constitute each other. Neither individual action nor human nature can be satisfactorily conceived outside of a social context. The development of the qualities which distinguish human beings as rational, purposive and reflexive actors can take place only in a social setting with other similar actors. But forms of rationality, purpose and reflexivity will vary in time and place, giving rise to different institutional arrangements, and in turn being affected by them. In other words, social structures provide the means for human belief and action, but are manifested only through such beliefs and action. Any attempt to see the two as separate, to see one as the outcome of or as existentially or logically prior to the other will destroy the necessary identity of the two terms.

At an abstract theoretical level such ideas appear rather obscure, but in their concrete instances they are in fact quite obvious. To speak of unskilled workers and social class as if the two entities had some independent existence is to create a false dichotomy. The meaning of 'unskilled worker' depends on understanding 'worker' as a term in relation to 'employer', and 'unskilled' in relation to 'skilled' or 'professional'. The existence of an unskilled worker as a type requires a hierarchical organization of human activity, just as the label requires some system of stratification to give it meaning. Equally, social class is a relation between people of different occupations, resources and power, and can be manifest only in the activities of these people. To separate the terms as if 'unskilled worker' described the activities of an individual and social class was a feature of the social system destroys the significance and validity of the terms, suggesting that a person is a manual worker because of the activities engaged in or the qualities displayed by the individual, and that social class is a division within the system into which people must somehow fit.

The syllabuses and texts analyzed are forced into such a position by the choice of structural-functionalism as the major explanatory model. For structural-functionalism, as has been pointed out, does not solve the dilemma, but rather retains the dichotomy, switching from an individualist theory of action to a determinist theory of social organization as the problem demands.[28] Given criticisms that structural-functionalism errs on the side of determinism,[29] and the tendency until recently for social deterministic explanations of a hypothetico-deductive kind, it could be expected that the texts would reveal, even exaggerate, this disposition. However, while deterministic explanation from reified social structures is evident, there is also an irreducible element of simple individualism which in some ways is equally strong. The dichotomy remains intact, but the particular forms it takes are worth analyzing.

The first instance of this individualism is the common practice of starting the explanatory sequence with the individual, usually by encouraging introspection in the pupil. A common argument asks the pupil first to consider the individual and how society influences or serves him or her. Some texts introduce the idea of the unique individual by calling on pupils to record their attitudes, opinions and values on issues.[30] In the words of one author

> This book ... starts with the individual as a person and the immediate world with which he or she is ultimately involved; by studies of self, friends, family, school and community, a network of social relationships is investigated.[31]

This immediate focus on individual characteristics gives them an air of being fixed and removed from a social context, despite the fact that attitudes and beliefs are products of and known to vary with context. An example is the following separation of personality and values from the contexts of knowledge and personal influence in which they are formed:

You could say '*my* abilities', '*my* personality', '*my* needs' and '*my* values'. But you would have to say '*availability in the place where I live*', '*pressure from the people with whom I mix*', '*information from books and people I come into contact with*' and '*other people's* advice'. So influences are partly self-directed, or 'internal', and partly directed by others, or 'external'.[32]

The concept of personality which results from this individualism is a rather static version of trait psychology, in which the individual's qualities, though influenced by past upbringing, are nonetheless said to be stable characteristics which a person must accommodate to rather than change:

> a person who gets excited and emotional very easily is not likely to fit into a job where it is essential to remain cool and calm. Again, someone who is very shy in dealing with other people will be at a great disadvantage in work which involves close and regular contact with strangers.[33]

The traits typically mentioned are the labels of everyday evaluations rather than psychological descriptions, a strange submission to uncritical common-sense in a self proclaimed social science. For instance, in answer to the question 'What sort of person do you think you are?' one text provides as possible descriptions a list including thrifty, mean, carefree, greedy, lazy, cunning, generous, hard working, modest, conceited, unpopular, serious, and quiet.[34] Elsewhere, pupils are asked to

> Take a good look at yourself: What makes you tick? What kind of person are you – friendly? bad-tempered? super-intelligent? light-hearted? cheeky? ambitious? modest?[35]

And similarly:

> Consider your best friend and your worst enemy. What are they really like? Jot down words which help to describe them, *as people*. For instance, cheerful or miserable, cruel or kind, brave or cowardly, a 'sticker' or gives up easily. The words you have chosen describe someone's *personality*.[36]

Apparently innocent of interactionist social psychology, and especially of attribution theory, the authors treat as equally stable and inherent traits qualities as disparate as intelligence, generosity and cheerfulness, and as obscure as cunning, light-heartedness and seriousness. Such terms do not describe 'what a person is like', but rather how a person behaves in given situations, which will vary as much as will the accuracy of the person interpreting the meaning of the behaviour.[37] Static trait theory of such an evaluative kind reveals a crude concept of individuals, divorced from social context and judged in naive terms.

From considering individuals, at which the texts frequently show themselves to be less than adept, the focus moves to groups, how they are constituted and how they operate. Here the sociological perspective of the authors is on firmer ground, but still subject to the difficulties of their chosen theory and its perpetuation of the duality of individual and society. The general position is that groups are aggregates of individuals sharing some common characteristics, but by extension there is the implication that there is nothing common to everybody across group boundaries, or at least if there is, it is not treated with the attention given to group membership. The notion of universal human qualities held in common seems less important than differences which determine group allegiance. Some typical descriptions illustrate the approach:

> Groups are the basic unit of organisation in society, and they are formed for a variety of purposes. They occur when individuals come together for some purpose, with some relationships between them, and some kind of social interaction.[38]

> When people in a group act in a similar way we say that they adopt *group norms*. . . . When people from different groups meet, conflict may arise because of a lack of understanding. This conflict can be lessened if people get together and accept each other's customs. But it is often difficult to reach agreement.[39]

If groups are regarded as the basic organizing unit gathering together people having different purposes, then the model for coordinating their interaction must be a pluralistic one, rather than a libertarian individualist or a socialist one. The emphasis of the level of analysis carries with it implications for political organization.

The combined image so far is of independent individuals coming together for particular purposes to form groups, which are the major focus of analysis. A common description of this process is that individuals willingly sacrifice some freedom and independence for the sake of group membership and the furtherance of its aims.

> When people live together, however, there have to be adjustments: some personal independence has to be given up for the greater good of the group.[40]

> But individuals must give up some of their freedom when they join a group.[41]

> As it is, you give up a bit of your freedom and other people give up a bit of theirs.[42]

This idea of independent individuals trading off freedoms for group membership is inadequate when both the individual freedoms and the groups' operation are inconceivable outside more widespread social processes. Voluntarism is the basis of individualism in this most 'social' of subjects. In presenting individuals as given entities, rather than showing how they derive from social origins; in claiming that people somehow choose to come together to cooperate for their mutual interest, the texts create an impossible notion. People live in groups. They do not choose to join them. And yet there is a voluntaristic strain in much of the text material as further examples illustrate.

> Sociology is the scientific study of all forms of human groupings that come about as a result of human beings attempting to solve problems by organizing themselves into recognizable and regular patterns.[43]

> Members of a school come together for a *common purpose* – that of education – and one of the ways in which this is achieved is by fostering *loyalty* to the school, i.e. *loyalty to the group*.[44]

> The term *society* covers the whole network of human relationships resulting from individuals coming together in response to a basic urge towards self-preservation.[45]

Exaggerated voluntarism of this kind helps to create the dilemma mentioned earlier, for it presents a view of people and society which cannot adequately integrate the two concepts. While independent individuals and a detached external society are the elements of the interaction, the two cannot be joined. We can sympathize with attempts to overcome this problem, as in the following passage, but

we must conclude that the attempt fails in its inadequate dichotomous concepts and its static view of personality.

> Socialisation helps the development of the personality, and
> vice versa. This is because a person has a dual role to play in
> life. He has to be both an individual and a member of society.
> As an individual he cannot grow up separated from his social
> group. He becomes the kind of person he is at each stage of
> his development through the interaction between himself as a
> person and his social and physical environment. Yet he is still
> an individual with his own unique gifts and qualities, and the
> effect that the school has upon him depends partly upon his
> individual make-up and party upon the school context.[46]

Contrast this with one text and its rare acknowledgement of the
social origins of individual consciousness:

> Animals live in herds, birds live in flocks, and people live in
> GROUPS. From the second we are born, and throughout
> our lives, we are claimed by a number of different groups –
> our family and relations, school friends and work-mates,
> members of the same club or team, our trade union or our
> neighbours. All of them help to look after us, bring us up,
> influence us or control us at different times in our life.. . .
> People don't have different ATTITUDES and behave in
> different ways because of 'human nature' – or at least, not
> very much. Their attitudes and BEHAVIOUR depend much
> more on the kind of society they are brought up in.[47]

There is no need in this approach to sustain the fiction of independent
individuals coming together to form groups. People are born and
live in groups, and could not develop as people if they did not. While
the passage does focus on groups, it acknowledges that these are
subsidiary to the context of the total society. This approach avoids
the unrealistic voluntarism of the predominant individual-group
analysis.

A static conception of human nature makes impossible a satisfactory idea of individual-society relations, but in many cases the
idea of society is equally questionable. For there is a frequent image
of society as either a reified entity or a harmonious consensus of
members, which becomes an active agent wielding people like
puppets. In some cases, the effect probably results from ambiguous
wording of otherwise acceptable explanations, but in others it is
clearly an unrealistic image of a reified society.

In the first case society becomes an objective agent capable of organizing its members:

A society may have a particular way of organising its members in order to ensure law and order, for instance it may be totalitarian or democratic.[48]

When we speak of social stratification we refer to the way in which society has arranged status positions in order of greater or lesser importance.[49]

Certain groups of people are regarded as above or below other groups of people because they possess characteristics which their society regards as desirable or less desirable. Society becomes a hierarchy, that is a society which is organised in successful grades.[50]

This reification of society is really an extreme form of presenting society as a consensus of its members, rather than as consisting of structures which people sustain in their activities through abiding by rules and exerting or submitting to power. The idea that the activities and rules are reached through some universal agreement is surprisingly strong.

As people became civilized they felt the need for somebody in *power*, a chief, or king (or sheriff) who would protect their lives and property. They felt the need for *rules* which all members of the society could live by. So each group or nation set up an *authority* to *make* and *enforce laws*.[51]

As we have seen, social laws are agreed rules of behaviour set out for the good of the community and of the people in it.[52]

Society can be described as a grouping of human-beings who agree on what is or is not permissible, what is harmful and what is beneficial for their group. In short, men in a group hold common values and agree on the manner in which they should be complied with.[53]

A law is a rule agreed upon by a society.[54]

Like teenagers, other members of the community form groups. We may think of some of these groups as being *for society*; they are made up of people who conform to the rules and customs of present-day society. Others are *against society* because their members do not accept many of the standards and values of the society in which they live.[55]

This last passage raises the interesting spectacle of a society whose rules and customs are somehow distinguishable from the people who support them, so that some people, presumably the majority, can be seen as being 'for society'. The earlier selections are less odd but no less conscientious in omitting any reference to the fact that some groups can and do impose their wills on others, and that active consensus in society of the kind presented is rare indeed.

A Powerless Society

It is not necessary to deny in principle any examples of positive consensus in society in order to criticize the consensual image presented in many texts. For even if acquiescence is interpreted (wrongly) as positive agreement, there is still a large area of conflict in social relations which this image glosses over. The society described is not one where politics and power play an important part.

Notions of consensual society, of roles as given rather than negotiated have already been cited. This pattern is carried over into the concept of socialization which is most often seen as a process whereby children learn the norms and values either of a monolithic culture or of the self contained groups in which they mix. In ignoring the fact that social norms and values are themselves matters of dispute, the texts do little to explain how conflicts are resolved either in the social environment or the developing individual. Typical examples illustrate the mystery surrounding peremptory treatments of this process and the false simplicity of conflict free presentations:

> Where a number of people act together, they *interact* (mix, communicate and affect each other by their actions). As a result, all sorts of group customs develop and ideas of what is the 'right way' to do things.[56]

> Through socialization then, we learn those physical and mental skills that society expects of us at any stage in life. It also makes us aware of the ways of behaving that are accepted as proper in our society. We also learn the demands and expectations of the roles that we play, and the goals and values of the groups to which we belong....

Briefly socialization is the way society builds its values and rules into the individual and the way the biological animal becomes the social animal.[57]

The powerless society image is sustained by separating out from many social processes elements of conflict and power. Part of this fragmentation, as mentioned earlier, results from the rather static analysis of social structure characteristic of structural-functionalism, and is aggravated by the topic approach to social science courses and texts which organizes content along traditional institutional lines (see table 6, page 194). The result is that law, government and the economy are treated in isolation. It might be expected that at least in the discussion of politics there would be due recognition of power and conflict, but the treatment of democracy as a form of government presents a picture of a system which works for the benefit of all because it provides equal power to all through the ballot box.

As could be expected, the meaning of democracy is articulated by describing the present system of representative Parliamentary government. Not only are alternative forms not entertained, but the descriptions of the present system take the form of a defence.

Democracy means the sharing of power and influence by methods of delegation and consultation.[58]

The scale and complexity of our society makes it impossible that we, the electorate, should make final decisions on political issues. . . . It is far better, then, that we should see democracy as meaning that we should have the chance to choose between competing teams of experts, the politicians, who are committed only to following broad principles of policy. The teams have different long-term aims, and basically different ways of achieving them. The most the electorate can hope to do is to make up its mind on the basis of these broad differences, and, once the team has been elected, to leave to it the more detailed policy-making. After all, if the team does not come up to scratch, the electorate can give the other lot a chance next time.[59]

In this partisan discussion, such moderate practices as referenda and pressure group activity are rejected, and more radical levels of participation or devolution of power to local groups seem unthinkable. The principle on which the position is usually justified is the equal power which voters wield in the electoral system, ignoring the discrepancies which exist in access to other forms of power, and even in the access to electoral influence through the media.

> When you reflect you will realize what great power lies in the hands of us all by virtue of the fact that we have a vote after we reach the age of eighteen. The vote gives us a voice equal to that of any other person in the land, and with it we can say what kind of government we shall have.[60]

> For on the final question of who is to have ultimate law-making power in our land, the right to vote gives every man the same voice. At the ballot box, difference of birth, wealth and advantage is irrelevant.[61]

That people can be satisfied with such indirect influence over government decisions is partly understandable given what some texts see as the benign motives of the decision makers who work in the community interest. The elusiveness of the concept of community interest, and its different interpretations across political doctrines seem no hindrance to this process, as evidenced in the following explanations of democracy.

> A democratic political system is one which attempts to bring these pressure groups into some sort of agreement – to reconcile many differing viewpoints in the general interest of the whole community, and provide a government that will serve the country to the best advantage.[62]

> Each person has an equal right to live as he wants, to say and think what he likes and to do what he pleases provided he keeps within the rules which are laid down by law for the good of the community and the protection of the individual.[63]

One way in which this sanguine view of the political process is sustained is to avoid close attention to problems it seems unable to handle. In dealing with social problems, authors generally conclude that the passage of time or a conscientious citizenry or more money will provide an answer, and that the present political system is adequate to the task if these other requirements are fulfilled. One text suggests a novel solution to a range of problems ranging from unemployment and poverty to racial intolerance and crime:

> Naturally, the problems we have looked at will not be solved overnight. But only by education will they be tackled: starting in schools and continuing in the home and at work.[64]

This extreme example is nonetheless symptomatic of the unwillingness of authors to contemplate radical change as a response to deep rooted social problems. Accordingly, discussion of the problems themselves is seldom taken to their fundamental structural basis, and controversial conclusions which might question the system are avoided. Most often this occurs where the solutions or explanations of social problems are left at a superficial level, and what might be unpleasant truths are replaced by trivial substitutes.

> It doesn't matter so much if you end up in a job you really don't like; you can always look for another.[65]

> Most people who fail in work or school or college do so because they have been unable to find good enough reasons for working hard.[66]

> If you are starting your working life in a factory you may feel unimportant at first, and you may feel confused.

> Well, the first thing to remember is that what you do is important (no matter what your job be) for these reasons: firstly the firm is giving you money for your work so you must be worth something to them, and secondly, you have your own place in the scheme of things.

> Every firm has its own plan of work and you will be part of your firm's plan, even if no one goes out of his way to make you feel needed.[67]

It may be that authors wish to avoid painting a depressing picture of a society where some people will be forced to accept jobs they dislike, where examination systems are designed to produce a proportion of failures irrespective of effort, and where some workers may well be regarded as unimportant by firms. But if truth hurts, pain is not avoided by disguising the cause of injury. Similar comments can be made of explanations of homelessness solely in terms of cost of housing,[68] and recommended solutions to poverty which limit themselves to welfare payments.[69] Refusal to expose basic causes of such problems conceal the political, economic and ideological structures which produce and sustain them.

In fact, avoidance of embarrassing weaknesses in the system is often accompanied by overt support for it, and texts reflect various ways of encouraging acceptance of the existing system. Necessity of present arrangements for survival, consensus views of society and claimed equality of political power are some already cited. Another is

the unmitigated benefits for all which are said to result from
obedience to the law.

> Laws regulate the rights and duties that are important for the
> life of the whole group; that is, those which affect the
> COMMON GOOD. They also protect the rights and decide
> the duties of the individual; this can be called the PRIVATE
> GOOD. Laws limit what an individual can do that might
> harm others, and they also set limits on what society can do
> that might harm individuals.[70]

> ... we must know and believe that laws are not made by
> Members of Parliament (M.P.'s) for the benefit of them-
> selves or judges, but for *us*.[71]

A perennial problem of civic education is to sustain order and
promote ideals of cooperation, and at the same time resist the view
that the rule of law must prevail over any injustice. The most
common position in social science texts is that the rule of law is
inviolable but that citizens have a responsibility to use their power in
the system to ensure that laws are fair. Given the picture of equal
power for all citizens which texts often present, this seems a
reasonable conclusion for liberal democrats committed to the virtues
of majority rule, individual rights and equality of opportunity. But
the realities of modern two-party politics include lobbying, pressure
groups and sponsored members, media influence, secrecy in government and legal concepts rooted in liberal capitalist ideas of property
and rights. It can hardly be claimed that the law is free of ideology,
influence, and bias in its origins in a particular historical situation and
its operation in a context of conflicting interests and power. To
suggest otherwise is to be less than frank.

Knowledge and Explanation in Social Science

The difficulty in dealing with such issues is that once the notion of
opposing the law on superior moral grounds is raised, the question
arises of which grounds are acceptable, and the argument shifts to the
area of ethics and moral philosophy. Social science texts, like the
other social subjects reviewed, strongly resist making this shift. In
the first place the scientific aspiration leads to a search for objectivity
impossible in the kinds of subjects raised, given the goals of raising

them in school. The typical view is that while it is difficult to achieve the separation:

> Sociology is concerned not with what we think societies *ought* to be like but with how they actually *are*. Therefore anyone who attempts to study society sociologically must try to put aside his personal beliefs and principles.[72]

This statement, a valid description of the aims of much sociological method, conceals the values inherent in social science's selection and framing of problems, and the judgmental character of the images of human nature and society which underlie all concepts, theories and methods of social enquiry. This fallacy, as in other subjects, is sustained by the belief in naive empiricism, that people can observe, describe and theorize about social events uninfluenced by prior concepts and explanatory systems residing in the images already held.

> This way of looking at behaviour is frequently called 'the sociological perspective'. Quite simply the three elements in this perspective are:
>
> 1 Observing and recording systematically and without bias the ways in which groups act and react towards one another.
> 2 Constructing a theory of behaviour based on observations and previous research which attempts to explain the behaviour described.
> 3 Testing the accuracy of the theory against observable behaviour and if necessary modifying the theory in the light of further research.[73]

> Both kinds of scientist (natural and social) are always collecting information but one collects it about *people* whilst the other collects it about natural *things*. The next step after collecting information is to put it into some kind of order. Finally the social scientist has to try and describe the facts he has collected and to explain them.[74]

But social scientists observe and collect data to answer questions, and the questions must themselves be framed in terms of some set of concepts which will delimit the range of possible conclusions. These questions will to varying degrees reflect a programmatic interest in what has been defined as a social problem, requiring value judgments from the outset. These points make it impossible to exclude value considerations from social science, and especially from school courses which aim at significance for pupils' own lives. One result is that a spurious objectivity is claimed for explanations and descriptions which have clear evaluative content, as shown in many instances above. Further, authors are often placed in contradictory situations, as in the case of Scotson, who is cited above as advocating inductive empiricism as a method, but who seems to think that evidence so derived can be applied to social policy without an accompanying value position:

> It is not the task of the sociologist to advocate one system at the expense of the other unless he can produce objective evidence of the effects of the systems on human groups.[75]

The same problem occurs for another group of authors[76] who seem aware of the problems of values in a policy science, but whose neglect of moral issues leaves them open to similar criticism. In claiming special privileges for the sociologist's knowledge they neglect to mention that only values can determine its relevance to the solution of social problems, and that without values the information is useless in deciding policy:

> Just as doctors conduct a diagnosis of their patients, so too sociologists make a diagnosis of society. Not all doctors agree on their findings or the ways of approaching particular illnesses, and neither do all sociologists agree on their findings.... The difference between a qualified sociologist and the ordinary man in the street is that the sociologist will accumulate data in a systematic way about some of the problems of society, instead of pronouncing what should be done purely from his own personal observation.[77]

> The study of sociology should make us aware of the many changes that are taking place within society, and perhaps able to point out some of the least desirable aspects of change.[78]

Information itself cannot recommend action on a problem. It must be combined with some idea of a situation more desirable than the present one, just as the identification of the problem in the first place required some set of values which were not satisfied by events. Such ideas lie in the realm of moral judgments. But moral judgments and even the role of morality in action are avoided in the 'scientific' approach to society. In part this results from determinist explanations derived from functionalist views of social events, where individuals are motivated by group norms rather than rational purpose. Normative explanations reduce actors to puppets of an imaginary consensus.

> When a number of people act together, they *interact*. . . . As a result, all sorts of group customs develop and ideas of what is the 'right way' to do things. Members are expected to observe these social rules or NORMS. . . .[79]

This tendency to see norms as natural developments which are accepted by all for the purpose of group survival has been analyzed earlier. It shares with much sociological explanation the reduction of rational action to non-rational responses to social forces. But action is the work of thinking beings coping with problems as well as their resources of power, knowledge and skills allow. The fact that problems are perceived by a socially derived consciousness, and resources determined by one's location in the social structure does not make the action any less purposive and rational, and it can only be fully understood in this light. As mentioned earlier, functional explanation has generally rested on too simple and conflict-free an analysis of the nature of norms and institutions and how they operate. The following textbook example of deterministic explanation leaves little place for individual agency.

> We have seen how society is shaped on the small scale and large scale: the way in which our lives may be influenced by economic forces, by government decisions, or by changes in population; how the individual is moulded by the family, peer group, school and work. A human being undergoes a multitude of experiences which cause attitudes and opinions to be formed. Class position in society has a strong influence in determining behaviour and performance. Physical characteristics and environmental surroundings together play their part in making the individual what he or she is as a person.[80]

The rejection of direct consideration of moral issues leaves only pragmatic grounds for determining the acceptability of social arrangements. As functionalism implies harmony and consensus as the measure of a social system and its aims, there is no room for concepts of indoctrination, submission to power, false consciousness or objective interest. The following passage shows the consequences of such a position: if stability and persistence are the only criteria for judgment (itself a value judgment), then there is nothing to choose between totalitarianism, democracy, or any other system, so long as they exist.

> In the last resort, the success of a political system depends on how well it works. If the system is successful in welding people together in a society, in resolving conflicts and arguments, if it ensures that the necessary rules are made and kept, and if the people for whatever reason, are persuaded that the government can protect them from threats from another society, the system will continue.[81]

This minimal criterion of success gives individual citizens little insight into how to judge the success of the system for themselves, for as long as it produces stability, peace and order, it is judged to be working well.

Conclusion

The image of human nature and society constructed from this analysis is shown in figure 4. It reflects the individual-society dichotomy, the voluntarism of group formation, and the idea of individuals as prior to social formation. However, this is combined with a social determinism manifested in role theory and the structural-functionalist model of organization of groups. The outcome, and the main problem which the image constructs and tries to explain, is the survival of social order and its ideational concomitant of a consensus about community interest. In keeping with the nature of images, the goal of a consensual social order is a description of what is, as well as a judgment of what should ideally be. The significance of this combination of description and value judgment in much of the social science material can be seen in its implications for the idea of citizenship discussed earlier.

Modern versions of citizenship and education see knowledge as the means to better decisions in society, and an informed citizenry as the best guarantee that decisions will promote the community interest. But just how this interest is to be determined, how the claims of existing institutions and individual goals bear on it, are problems beyond simple solution, yet central in selecting and framing the types of knowledge thought to be most needed.

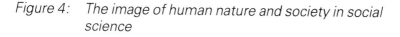

Figure 4: The image of human nature and society in social science

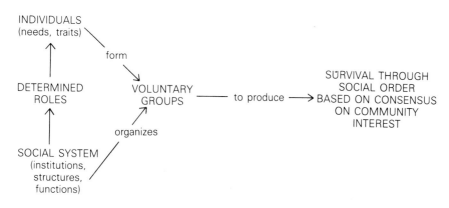

It was earlier argued that knowledge was crucial in interpreting individuals' interests and rights, in defining what can and cannot be changed, and what avenues exist for implementing change. The analysis of textbook explanations identified a number of ways in which these points were so resolved as to limit the power of people to understand and influence their dealings and destiny in society.

First, notions of individual interest are not often considered. Arising from the individualism inherent in the textual interpretations of society, interests at the individual level are treated as subjective, to be dealt with either as completely individualistic, or more often as pluralist, as evidenced in the emphasis on groups as the basis of society's operation. The idea of universal human characteristics which might give rise to objective interests[82] as a basis of resolving conflict is not considered. Rather the alternative to subjectivism is the idea of community interest or the benefit of society as a whole, an unexplored and unexplained concept which seems to be utilitarian and shallow. Crucial questions like the problem of distributive justice cannot be dealt with within such a vague and inconsistent framework of ideas.

The idea of community interest has to be seen in connection with the functionalist models of explanation, presented in the texts in ways suggesting that harmony and stability are the ultimate criteria for a healthy society. The implication is that community interest is best served when existing institutions are working smoothly, since this will indicate that conflict, and therefore individual dissatisfaction, are eradicated. This view is valid only if one denies the possibility that ideological forces can distract and power can prevent people from realizing or expressing their real interests. The neglect of power in the textbook explanations of social dynamics prevents this alternative interpretation being considered.

The second aspect which might inform how people see their position in society and their role with respect to its institutions is that of rights, a concept more often and favourably mentioned in the texts. It is clear that rights themselves are an uncertain guide for the individual's dealings with social institutions. Rights do not *exist*, but are won and maintained by people asserting values and establishing rules to implement them. Existing rights have been achieved in history. Given the lack of a philosophy of humanity, a concept of the person or ideas of objective interests, there is no basis in the texts for deriving rights *a priori*. Thus no basis exists for judging present rights in law against any desirable set of additional or alternative rights. The rights referred to in the texts are those which the present system of rules allows, and no other. Again the individual is faced with a set of ideas which are derived from existing political and economic structures, and the argument from rights provides no basis for criticizing present arrangements.

This situation is exacerbated in the texts by the avoidance of ethical issues, and by the attempt to explain values as norms thrown up by the necessity of group life. Norms are said to arise or emerge from group interaction in the course of survival, and are not seen to be subject to a rational morality. Values are more determined than determining in their relation with social structure. It then becomes difficult, given the neglect of power and the idea of the necessity of norms for survival, to entertain the possibility that social arrangements may be sustained by the values of dominant groups, rather than by a consensus of freely choosing members. If rights are conceived only as those which present conventions allow, and if the values on which they are based are produced by the need to survive, then there is little space for considering alternatives.

Definitions of what can and cannot be changed are probably the most important single impact on how individuals will interpret their options in dealing with society's institutions. It could also be seen as the most direct contribution of social science to the citizen's willingness to accept existing social arrangements. If alternatives are not considered, or, if considered, presented as impossible, then they are not alternatives. This problem has been shown to exist in aspects of functional explanation, such as the failure to distinguish sufficiently between the survival of society and the survival of society *in its present form*. The possibility of this conclusion exists also in the reification of society into an entity separate from its members who constitute and create it.

Abstract, detached and reified descriptions of social processes and institutions must discourage individuals' assessments of their power unless the descriptions show how these structures are produced and reproduced in and by the actions and consciousness of individual actors and groups. But equally, the power of the individual cannot be expanded if the image presented shows individual action and its success as being determined and limited by inherent qualities independent of the social structures which produce them and decide their relevance. The central problem of social theory, of explaining the relation between individual and society has been solved in most of the texts by adopting a dichotomous model which on balance is more likely to limit than encourage individuals in their promotion of their own and others' interests.

This limiting effect is manifest most specifically in treatments of politics and government, where the predominant view is supportive of present representative rather than a more participatory democratic ethos, where alternative operations of power in society are often ignored, and where the rule of law is sacrosanct. All this is aggravated by the treatment of power, government and law at very abstract levels, where the ideal might sound very reasonable, however much its practice in reality diverges from it. If the operation of power in society is depicted solely in terms of parliamentary practice, other avenues which the citizen might use are kept hidden, especially if parliamentary elections are described in glowing terms exaggerating the equality of access to power they provide.

Modern social science shows a shift from earlier times to a greater concern for the right of the individual to expect certain satisfactions from society. In this it can be seen to be correcting an earlier imbalance in favour of conformism and submission to tradition. The means by which curricula seek to do this is the presentation of images of people and society which, by developing more accurate understanding, might allow people to conduct their affairs with greater success and satisfaction. It has been argued here that in important respects the content of social science does not provide an adequate basis for achieving this goal.

Notes and References

1 CANNON, C. (1964) 'Social studies in the secondary schools', in *Educational Review*, 17, pp. 18–20.
2 LAWTON, D. and DUFOUR, B. (1973) *The New Social Studies*, London, Heinemann Educational.
3 *Ibid.* p. 5.
4 ASSOCIATION FOR EDUCATION IN CITIZENSHIP (1935) *Education for Citizenship in Secondary Schools*, Oxford, Oxford University Press, p. 7, chapters 3 and 4.
5 HAPPOLD, F. *et al. (1937) Experiments in Practical Training for Citizenship*, London, Association for Education in Citizenship.
6 LAWTON, D. and DUFOUR, B. (1973) *op. cit.* p. 9.
7 *Ibid.*
8 LONDON COUNTY COUNCIL EDUCATION COMMITTEE (1911) *Report of a Conference on the Teaching of History in London Elementary Schools*, London County Council Education Office, p. 33.
9 *Ibid.* p. 8.
10 SIMON, E. (1935) 'The aims of education for citizenship' in ASSOCIATION FOR EDUCATION IN CITIZENSHIP *op. cit.* pp. 7, 10.
11 GREAT BRITAIN BOARD OF EDUCATION (1938) *Report of the Consultative Committee on Secondary Education with Special Reference to Grammar Schools and Technical High Schools*, London, HMSO, p. 148.
12 MAY, J. (1978) *The World of Work*, Birmingham, Clearway, p. i.
13 GIDDENS, A. (1976) *New Rules of Sociological Method: A Positive Critique of Interpretative Sociologies*, London, Hutchinson, p. 21.
14 SKIDMORE, W. (1975) *Sociology's Models of Man*, New York, Gordon and Breach, chapters 13 and 14.
15 WESTERGAARD, J. 'Sociology: The Myth of Classlessness' in BLACKBURN, P. (Ed.) *Ideology in Social Science: Readings in Critical Social Theory*, London, Fontana.
16 HEASMAN, K. (1973) *The Study of Society*, London, Allen and Unwin, p. 17.
17 CRICK, B. (1978) 'Basic concepts for political education' in CRICK, B. and PORTER, A. (Eds.) *Political Education and Political Literacy*, London, Longman, p. 54.
18 JONES, O. and HILL, S. (1974) *Sociology for 'O' Level*, Leicester, Bland Educational, p. 15.
19 HEASMAN, K. (1973) *op. cit.* p. 138.
20 PARSONS, T. (1967) *Sociological Theory and Modern Society*, New York, Free Press, p. 11.
21 GIDDENS, A. (1979) *Central Problems in Social Theory: Action, Structure and Contradiction in Social Analysis*, London, Macmillan, pp. 116, 117.
22 These comments are elaborated in BRADBURY, M., HEADING, B. and HOLLIS, M. (1972) 'The man and the mask: a discussion of role theory' and COULSON, M. (1972) 'Role: a redundant concept in sociology? Some educational considerations' in JACKSON, J. (Ed.) *Role*, Cambridge, Cambridge University Press.

23 HEASMAN, K. (1973) *op. cit.* p. 18.

24 MATHIAS, P. (1974) *Groups and Communities*, London, Blandford, p. 9.

25 O'DONNELL, G. (1977) *The Human Web. An Introduction to 'O' Level Sociology*, London, Murray, p. 34.

26 JONES, O. and HILL, S. (1974) *op. cit.* p. 8.

27 COOTES, R. (1974) *The Family: An Introduction to Sociology*, London, Longman, p. 8.

28 SKIDMORE, W. (1975) *op. cit.*

29 WRONG, D. (1964) 'The oversocialized conception of man in modern sociology' in COSER, L. and ROSENBERG, B. (Eds.) *Sociological Theory*, London, Collier-Macmillan.

30 NIXON, B. (1977) *Focus on the Community 1: The Family and Housing*, London, University Tutorial Press; RANKIN, M. and RANKIN, J. (1972) *Choosing a Job*, London, Nelson.

31 NOBBS, J. (1979) *Introducing Social Studies*, London, Macmillan, p. 4.

32 LAW, W. (1977) *Decide for Yourself*, Cambridge, Hobsons, p. 3.

33 MAY, J. (1976) *Work, Jobs and Careers*, Birmingham, Clearway, p. 2.

34 DALGLEISH, N. (1973) *Living in a Changing World. Book 1*, London, Nelson, p. 6.

35 THOMPSON, J. (1978) *Studying Society*, London, Hutchinson, p. 7.

36 NOBBS, J. (1979) *op. cit.* p. 43.

37 Evidence on these points and other criticisms of trait psychology can be found in HUNT, J. (1971) 'Traditional personality theory in the light of recent evidence' in HOLLANDER, E. and HUNT, R. (Eds.) *Current Perspectives in Social Psychology*, New York, Oxford University Press; and HOLLANDER, E. (1976) *Principles and Methods of Social Psychology*, New York, Oxford University Press.

38 MATHIAS, P. (1974) *op. cit.* p. 7.

39 NOBBS, J. (1979) *op. cit.* p. 8.

40 DUNTHORN, J. (1974) *Heredity and Environment*, London, Blandford, p. 42.

41 NOBBS, J. (1976) *Modern Society. Social Studies for C.S.E.*, London, Allen and Unwin, p. 32.

42 THOMAS, M. (1971) *Law in Action*, London, Nelson, p. 3.

43 JONES, O. and HILL, S. (1974) *op. cit.* p. 5.

44 LAMBERT, K. (1974) *Life in Our Society*, London, Nelson, p. 27.

45 LEWIS, G. (1978) *'O' Level Revision Notes: Sociology*, Newcastle on Tyne, Felton, p. 3.

46 HEASMAN, K. (1973) *op. cit.* p. 59.

47 THOMPSON, J. (1978) *op. cit.* p. 9.

48 JONES, O. and HILL, S. (1974) *op. cit.* p. 2.

49 *Ibid.* p. 71.

50 HEASMAN, K. (1973) *op. cit.* p. 71.

51 KING, S. (1972) *Living in Society*, London, Cassell, p. 108.

52 BULMER, P. (1975) *Law and Society*, Poole, Blandford, p. 7.

53 DUNTHORN, J. (1974) *op. cit.* p. 42.

54 WELSH, J. and BRIDGER, V. (n.d.) *Do We Care?* Birmingham, Clearway, p. 59.

55 NOBBS, J. (1976) *op. cit.* p. 24.
56 COOTES, R. (1974) *op. cit.* p. 2.
57 JONES, O. and HILL, S. (1974) *op. cit.* p. 11.
58 HEASMAN, K. (1973) *op. cit.* p. 63.
59 HAMBLING, C. and MATTHEWS, P. (1974) *Human Society*, London, Macmillan, p. 101.
60 MURRAY, J. (1971) *State and People. A Handbook of Citizenship for Young People*, London, Harrap, p. 112.
61 PHILLIPS, A. (1976) *The Living Law*, Birmingham, Clearway, p. 41.
62 LAMBERT, K. (1974) *op. cit.* p. 60.
63 HEASMAN, K. (1973) *op. cit.* p. 152.
64 CHURCH, D. and FORD, B. (1975) *People in Towns*, London, Nelson, p. 45.
65 GREEN, B. (1976) *Facing Society*, Birmingham, Clearway, p. 6.
66 LAW, W. (1977) *op. cit.* p. 5.
67 GREEN, B. (1976) *op. cit.* p. 28.
68 CHURCH, D. and FORD, B. (1975) *op. cit.* p. 34.
69 CULLEN, M. (1978) *The Family and the Social Services*, London, Heinemann, p. 112.
70 BULMER, P. (1975) *op. cit.* p. 7.
71 PHILLIPS, A. (1976) *The Living Law*, Birmingham, Clearway, p. 5.
72 COOTES, R. (1974) *op. cit.* p. 8.
73 SCOTSON, J. (1975) *Introducing Society*, London, Routledge and Kegan Paul, p. 1.
74 HAMBLING, C. and MATTHEWS, P. (1974) *op. cit.* p. 1.
75 SCOTSON, J. (1975) *op. cit.* p. 93.
76 NOBBS, J. HINE, R. and FLEMMING, M. (1979) *Sociology*, London, Macmillan.
77 *Ibid.* p. 8.
78 *Ibid.* p. 380.
79 COOTES, R. (1974) *op. cit.* p. 2.
80 NOBBS, J. HINE, R. and FLEMMING, M. (1979) *op. cit.* p. 371.
81 HAMBLING, C. and MATTHEWS, P. (1974) *op. cit.* p. 86.
82 LUKES, S. (1974) *Power. A Radical View*, London, Macmillan.

7   Images and Reflections

If we accept that social knowledge is not simply a body of truth statements to be applied to experience, but rather the means by which social experience is given sense and direction; if we acknowledge that society consists of sets of rule governed practices conducted through common understandings, then social knowledge takes on a central role in social experience. Rather than describing actions, social knowledge constitutes them. When we tell people that 'Parliament passed a law' or 'The Company won the contract', we do not apply an objective language to an observed event; we characterize the event in the terms which constitute it, with all that they imply about authority, legitimacy, and the history of institutions. If enough people ceased to regard the events in this way, they would lose this legitimacy, and become different events. In describing social events we attribute grounds for action; in this sense social knowledge is 'essentially contestable'[1] or 'defeasible'[2].

Social education assumes a connection between knowledge and social practice, and tries to promote people's well being and control over their own destinies. It draws on a participatory and egalitarian ethos, but in the face of evidence that society is neither open in the access to power it provides, nor egalitarian in the way its economic and other practices operate. This dilemma is a likely clue to curricular problems of success and relevance.

Theories of knowledge have not long addressed this constituting and contestable aspect of social knowledge. Empiricism and objectivism have sought to describe and explain social events through universal truth statements, ignoring the problem oriented and theoretical frameworks in which all statements are rooted, and which are related in an ideological fashion to social practice. These frameworks, represented here as images, identify problems and how they are best conceived. In the process they define options, state or imply goals and in other ways structure how the event will be viewed, constraining the possible conclusions.

The Composite Image

In the texts, problems were largely material and consensual ones: efficient spatial organization and productive use of resources; increased production and the attack on scarcity; promoting the general welfare and harmony of all through existing institutions and community consensus. In assuming efficiency and harmony as goals of society and therefore of an appropriate social understanding, texts were accordingly influenced in their selection of issues. Strikes and unrest were problems primarily because they caused disturbances, or did not use the proper channels, rather than because they were the expression of genuine grievance. Problems that were controversial, potentially unpleasant, or radical in their implied criticism of the existing order were not addressed. Largely overlooked were the various aspects of inequality in wealth and power, and the conflict which this habitually generates in social interaction. Problems were viewed from the perspective of the present and its particular institutional arrangements, limiting the alternatives which could be considered, and disguising the relationship between the problems and the institutions themselves, as in the case of Parliament's handling of female suffrage. The origins of the problems addressed in the texts' discourse lie in the history of the disciplines and their connections with social movements of the past; in theories of knowledge in which they have developed; but no doubt also in the tacit search for safety, a way of avoiding controversy.

This corresponds with the procedural emphasis in the texts' ideology, the advocacy of moderation and the use of proper channels. Pragmatism and common sense in history, rational planning and technology in geography, efficiency, specialization and the division of labour in economics, the rule of law in social science – these are offered as the best and only appropriate means for social action. In all subjects the unquestioned and sometimes laudatory support for the present form of Parliamentary government established the framework in which politics and change were viewed. Such an approach was vindicated as a part of the British national character, but also by its claimed success in producing equality and progress.

Equality was seen to occur in economics, where the market

allowed every consumer to participate in decisions about prices and the allocation of resources. In the social science version of politics it inhered in representative Parliamentary government. History texts noted it in contrast with past inequality, sometimes stating its present existence, at others implying it in the comparison. More generally, however, the absence of inequality in the discourse created the assumption of its opposite – that equality exists, or is so near that inequality can be discounted for all practical purposes. For in discussing urban planning, the division of labour, the allocation of roles, socialization, the operation of the legal system, the spatial allocation of resources, at no time did the texts point to inequalities in power and resources which favour some over others. We could conclude only that such inequality is non-existent, or irrelevant to the social processes concerned.

This sanguine view was complemented by the optimism of the idea of progress. Patience and the passing of time were the chief requirements of solving social problems, so long as expert planning and proper procedures were followed. Housing provision, and regional and urban development were geographical problems in the course of solution by the even handed and rational application of expertise and models of spatial efficiency. Fine tuning and lubrication ensure that the smooth operation of the market will efficiently and satisfactorily deal with problems of scarcity. Moderation, proper channels of the representative Parliamentary process and the rule of law were, in history and social science, the means to a stable and harmonious social progress, free of the irrational and sectional self-interest of the past. Since social change is inevitable, and the selective comparisons of past and present demonstrate substantial social progress, there is no reason to believe that reasonable people of goodwill and the expertise of the State will not ensure the solution of those relatively minor social problems which might still exist.

This benign view of the social process is feasible because at no time do the prevailing images acknowledge the use of overriding power by those who would advance their own welfare over others. Class divisions no longer exist as a fundamental source of conflict. The plurality of groups in social science, and the uniqueness and sovereignty of the economic individual suggest that competition is open, and not distorted by large scale inequality in access to influence. Rather, community consensus decides the allocation of rewards and the distribution of roles, in conjunction with a set of natural forces where decisions are not made at all.

Various forms of determinism are the strategies of explanation which, with the notion of consensus, rule out the need for power in the image. In geography the environment and spatial 'forces' remove matters from human influence. Marginal productivity and the market determine wages, and natural ability the division of labour. Brilliance and iron will are the psychological determinants of the 'great men' of history (even when they are women), and the social system is determined by functional imperatives which produce current institutions and roles.

All this makes the consideration of values largely irrelevant, since there is little point in questioning the morality of a determining environment or natural market forces. If entrepreneurship, greatness and ability are natural qualities, why should we question the morality of the circumstances which allow such people to prosper over others? If social arrangements are arrived at by consensus in a position of equal power among groups or individuals, who can doubt their propriety? Economic individuals are unique, their wants subjective: comparisons of utility or ideas of justice are irrelevant to the market interactions which flow from them. Pragmatism, efficiency, rationality are valued in social relations; moral considerations are of minor importance, if any.

Through all of these elements of the social theories of the texts run the basic problems of social explanation. How can individual experience and intention be integrated with ideas of social structure, in both a diachronic and synchronic perspective? What images of the individual and society will most successfully represent the kinds of explanations sought?

The predominant image of the individual was that of abstract individualism. In trait theory, the state of nature argument, the atomistic economic concept, and voluntarism as the basis of social formation, human nature was seen to derive from and reside in discrete centres of consciousness capable of study detached from context. The concept was most important in economics and history in explaining how ability, genius or will are the means to success; it justified the hierarchy of reward. But such qualities can be developed in experience only with opportunity, and the definition and rewarding of them is a matter of cultural values and economic systems. They cannot be understood outside a social context.

Society operated as an element of text images only fitfully. The image of society joined the mechanistic and biological metaphors to present a view of an abstract collection of functions and forces operating beyond the influence of people. Most often an aggregate of individuals, sometimes of groups, social interaction was driven by the dynamic of the market, functionalism or progress. Society was at times a reified entity with a will of its own, allocating resources and making decisions. While abstract individualism provided a deterministic base for some explanation, the reified social model of the market of functionalism was another source. The two could never be integrated.

The analysis has demonstrated the connections between the images and the political order which has produced them, for if the problematic of the text images is traced in the ideology of liberal democracy, the networks of ideas are strongly paralleled. The central concepts, the most frequent connections, the gaps and unasked questions, the guiding conceptions of problems are strongly reflected in the two levels of discourse.

Pluralism and the diffusion of power are the justification of liberal non-intervention, and match the texts' neglect of unequal power and their focus on disparate groups and individuals. Elitism is the corollary of the texts' belief in expertise: their advocacy of technocratic planning and the proper representative channels restricts the range of legitimate participants in decisions; their claims on behalf of the great, the talented, the able further advise submission to the elite. The ideology of liberal democracy was seen to advance equilibrium as the guiding force underlying social interaction, and as the measure of a successful political system: equilibrium and harmony were correspondingly viewed in the texts as signs of rational and healthy social relations, and the guarantee that the forces of progress would continue to solve social problems. Empiricism and pragmatism in the texts parallel the concern for means rather than ends in the liberal democratic emphasis. Abstract individualism in explanation supports its use as a political philosophy.

The inadequacies of the prevailing form of liberal democracy lie chiefly in its inability to provide equal access to welfare for all its members. Plagued from the start by unequal resources, thrust into a competitive system of reward, and confronted by an ethos in which esteem results from individual success, an inevitable proportion of the population must be denied access to normal levels of welfare. The typical liberal democratic system can promise only a minimum level of support, and some vague hope of individual success in the long run. But this hope can never be universally achieved, and in any one generation (the only meaningful time scale for any person), the individual prospects are far from equally distributed.

For people caught in the lower levels of the present distribution of wealth and power, their interests cannot lie in such a system. To instil in them the view that it is the most or only desirable form of social relations is to prevent the expression of their genuine grievance, and the exploration of alternatives. If social education is to claim to act for a participatory and egalitarian ethos, it must confront this political reality, and provide means by which people are able to assess and improve their situation.

An Approach to Explanation in the Social Subjects

A knowledge which people can apply to action must in the first instance assume an action theory of social explanation. As in Friedman's example of the billiard player (see page 131), to teach people how to do something is impossible through abstract empiricism. Determinist explanations like the factors of location or market forces similarly remove action from any decision making context. Action knowledge requires at least a study of how decisions are made, with what goals in mind, in the fact of what problems and conflicts, with what resources and options. Whether of town planners locating a road, entrepreneurs opening a business or James Watt struggling with a machine, the learning experience will be productive and useful to the extent that learners share the problem and its possible solutions, and critically examine the course taken. Deterministic explanation removes the matter from human influence and adds nothing to the learner's resources for taking similar decisions.

This is not to argue that events can be explained simply through individual intentions, or that people are all powerful, but that such a strategy is a necessary starting point given the goals of social education. The constraints on individual action must also be addressed. If we wish to increase people's welfare and control over their destinies, we would need to show them how present social arrangements limit these aspects of their lives, and to consider if and how the arrangements might be changed. To understand this requires an appreciation of how life chances and resources are distributed, how they are not universally or randomly available, and the historical origins of this structured system of opportunity.

Arrangements can be changed to the extent that they are rules of social practice generated in history from the application of power. New forms of power applied to new goals can create new rules. If people are to be made aware of this (and thereby given the increased power that comes from knowledge), the curriculum cannot avoid a questioning approach to the rules which underlie current social structures and practice; it must acknowledge the role of interested power in historical conflict in the origins of the present system; it cannot shy away from controversy. This should not simply be a pathological concentration on current social problems, for much is to be learned from past struggles, successes and failures, if only the focus on these past events is as advocated here.

The crucial need is for a form of explanation that can synthesize individual action with social process. The idea of historically produced structures sustaining relations through rules is the first requirement. The role in action of expectation and presupposition advises a study of the beliefs people wield in making sense of and deciding on action, again an aspect of conduct that must be understood historically. An integration of action, structure and practice is needed to replace the determinism, voluntarism and simple mechanical aggregate model of society which plagues the texts.

The text critique showed the weakness of the approach to values. Values analysis was never seen to be part of the subject, and yet values were always evident in the selection and treatment of problems, and even overt judgments. Values and morality are unavoidable in social study, more so in one which claims to be conducted in its students' interests. Concepts of welfare, the participatory and egalitarian ethos of the curriculum, notions of reasonable conduct in explanation are interpretations derived from value positions. To act in pupils' interests, subjects need to acknowledge this moral element and increase pupils' ability to identify and deal with values. Social education must also be based on a clearly worked out and explicit value position itself, if it is to fulfil its self chosen brief of increasing people's power to influence their lives.

These general exhortations must be capable of concrete implementation, and some demonstration of this in the social subjects is in order. In most cases, the recommendations have existing exemplars in the social disciplines, and do not require the creation of new forms of knowledge. A shift in emphasis is the chief need.

In geography, the determinist emphasis should be replaced by an approach through decision making. Location decisions, the spatial allocation of goods and services and the distribution of welfare are social events and processes, and require the kind of study that implies. Conflict, power, values must be elements of the study, and the eradication of social deprivation an important part of the problem. The approach should be concrete, critical and oriented to solving problems in ways advocated in the discipline by Stretton and Olsson.[3] This would involve increasing the historical and political elements of the subject at the expense of its current environmental and economistic determinism. Actual case studies within theoretical frameworks from welfare and political geography would lend the required concreteness and human relevance.

Economics' greatest need is for the translation of reified mechanisms into their manifestations in the beliefs, rules and laws which guide human action. Only then are economic events amenable to influence. Again this requires a more concrete historical and political study of problems of welfare and institutions. Two particular needs are for a more critical approach to the abstract model of human nature, and an acknowledgment of the dynamics of power and social structure in the operation of the economic system. The embarrassing existence of poverty, unemployment, and inequality of wealth, welfare and opportunity must be more squarely faced. Without this economics is little more than an uncritical rationalization of a system of inequality, to the detriment of the system's losers. Comparative and case studies of welfare and how decisions in economic institutions affect it are also needed. Concrete and institutional approaches to problems of welfare must supplant the abstract analytical theory of positive economics.

If history is to fulfil its potential as a comprehensive synthesis of social understanding, it must take more seriously its base in action theory, for much of it is an ill-formed combination of psychological and social determinism. Organized as a narrative survey, it draws explanatory statements at will from a range of covering laws without critical examination. Similarly, the narrative structure disguises the selection of problems, emphases and interpretations of events according to identifiable but unexamined values. More thematic line of development studies of explicit problems, combined with patch studies of how people made decisions about these problems in contexts of beliefs, goals and resources – this is how history can best inform people about the nature of their own historical context and how they might operate effectively in it. Historians choose problems according to criteria of importance. In school history problems should similarly be chosen by such criteria, in this case to reflect those problems the pupils themselves will confront.

Of all the subjects, social science addressed the problem of the individual-society relation most directly in the study of socialization, social relations and citizenship. Its neglect of power in all these areas of life, and the pluralism which its focus on groups implies, deny the possibility of a comprehensive view of the structure of power relations in society, and limit the value of its political knowledge. Social science would do well to reduce its reliance on such restricted versions of psychological and sociological theory, and again take a more problem oriented and comparative approach, focusing on case studies for their concreteness and authenticity.

Ultimately the problems will not be solved by revisions of individual subjects. The separation of political, economic and other social structures is a deficiency in the images reflected in the separation of the subjects themselves. A comprehensive synthesis will be best developed in an interdisciplinary approach. The need for a more explicit acknowledgement of pupil problems in selecting curricular content also makes the disciplines an inadequate base for curricular organization.

Images in the present subjects are remnants of the past, related to social structures of the time. In geography the commercial and environmental emphases derive from an imperial and Darwinist milieu. The abstract models of location analysis, the market and functionalism are associated with positivism and the 'end of ideology' faith in technocratic planning. Market analogies and functionalism gloss over the role of power in social relations, as does the pluralist democratic ideology from which they arose. Whiggish ideas of progress and harmony are upheld by neglecting the persistence of injustice. The dominant images parallel in important respects the principles of the political culture of the liberal pluralist democratic state: the emphasis on harmony and proper procedure; the technocratic faith in objectivist empiricism and planning; the subjective approach to values and the rejection of objective interest; and the acceptance of representative parliamentary government. The problems around which the images of the present social subjects are composed are not drawn from traditions of strong egalitarian or participatory ideals. Their theories and concepts are not likely therefore to support individuals in a quest to make society rewarding and responsive for all its members.

Curriculum planners must take a more positive role in identifying the problems their subjects will address. Present practice consigns this responsibility too freely to the traditions of the disciplines, with the results claimed above. To call for such an instrumental approach to knowledge is to invite accusations of sacrilege, of fouling the discipline with a banausic taint. It is true that programmes of life skills or citizenship often tend to uncritical trivia. The approach implied and outlined throughout this study rejects such accusations, for life skills and citizenship as here conceived cannot be adequately understood or successfully exercised without wide ranging and critical study. In fact the accusation here is that, in their selections from the disciplines, the social subjects themselves have been parochial, philosophically naive and uncritical of the historical relationship between their origins and forms of social practice.

One major gap in the argument has been the nature of the problems which should guide the selection and presentation of images in the social subjects. Such a task is beyond the scope of the present study, but certain major problems can be identified. Pupils will need to understand how power operates at the personal and institutional level; the concepts of the legal system and their ideological roles; the nature of ownership and control over economic activity at the micro- and macro-economic levels; the application of justice and integrity for persons in face to face interactions and their institutional embodiment in law. The implications of current social practices for a general humanitarian interest should be the guiding criterion of choice.

An important issue is whether such a project is not too ambitious for the intended age group. Is it beyond their cognitive capacities? For the most part the answer can be a confident negative. The concrete approach to problem oriented studies should more easily engage pupils in the tasks at hand. Notions of social structure can be made concrete in the rules and laws which sustain them. There seems no reason why such ideas should be any more difficult than the abstract models of geography, economics or social science, or the sweeping complexity of the historical survey. Ultimately however the extent of the connections pupils can make between their own experience and historical social structures can only be worked out in practice. Its importance warrants extensive and concerted attempts to devise appropriate curricular strategies.

Conclusion

The study began with the problem of the egalitarian and participatory aspirations of social education. These were accepted as valid grounds for schooling and an interpretation and implications of this position have been argued throughout.

Critics and clients of the social subjects have asserted a lack of relevance and genuine commitment. The critique of text images demonstrated good grounds for many of these accusations, for images did not address important problems facing society and adolescents in particular. When such problems were addressed, inappropriate epistemological and theoretical perspectives reduced the value of the exercise. The images presented were not so constructed as to provide support for people making decisions about life's problems.

It may well be true that these deficiencies are due to a lack of genuine commitment to the espoused egalitarian and participatory ideals. It is also, perhaps more likely that it reflects the inevitable power and conflict of interest in the selection of curricular content; text authors, in running the gauntlet of potential critics, avoid controversy and seek solace in objectivity. But the claim of value free knowledge is spurious. Text authors and the traditions in which they work assume values in their selections and interpretations. The escape to objectivity is not an option.

This may be the most productive course to press. The dominant epistemology in the social subjects is still that social events can be described and explained objectively, that is, from outside the event, and free of any particular interest. It has been argued here that this is mistaken, that text content is selected and organized to present perspectives on selected problems, that how the problems are conceived implies positions on the issues they raise, and that the constituting role of social knowledge sustains the practices associated with these positions. The positions taken have not been those of individuals in an unequal society striving for access to its normal rewards. The images they present will therefore be largely irrelevant to the needs of people facing such problems. If this point is pressed, curriculum planners, text authors and teachers may be forced to forsake the spurious solace of objectivity, and direct the social subjects to helping people solve their problems, a highly relevant and genuinely committed task.

Over a century ago John Stuart Mill called for

> ... the proper distinction between the laws of Production of Wealth, which are real laws of nature, dependent on the properties of objects, and the modes of its Distribution,

which, subject to certain conditions, depend on human will. The common run of political economists confuse these together, under the designation of economic laws, which they deem incapable of being defeated or modified by human effort; ascribing the same necessity to things dependent on the unchangeable conditions of our earthly existence, and to those which, being but the necessary consequences of particular social arrangements, are merely coextensive with these.[4]

While no licence for utopianism, Mill's distinction is still a salutary admonition for the planners of images in the social subjects. Without constant criticism the rules of society become enslaving; the lack of this criticism in the interests of an egalitarian and participatory society is the greatest single gap in the materials analyzed here. For as Hayek (interestingly a Mill scholar) notes:

The important point is that every man (*sic*) growing up in a given culture will find in himself rules, or may discover that he acts in accordance with rules – and will similarly recognize the actions of others as conforming or not conforming to various rules. This is, of course, not proof that they are a permanent or unalterable part of 'human nature', or that they are innate, but proof only that they are part of a cultural heritage which is likely to be fairly constant, especially so long as they are not articulated in words and therefore also are not discussed or consciously examined.[5]

It is the task of social education to articulate and critically examine these rules, and how they do and might operate to hinder or promote people's welfare. This requires a focus on the problems and theories on which curricular content is based, a neglected issue which this study has sought to highlight in its use of the image as a device for representing the problematic of school texts.

The study has also tried to acknowledge the complexity of curricular problems – their roots in history, social theory and epistemology. Discussions of social education, especially within the traditions of the social subjects, have not confronted arguments of the unique relationship between social knowledge, social practice and the individual. If these developments continue to give fresh insights, they promise important implications for the curriculum similar to those drawn here.

Much remains. This survey of the social subjects needs supplementing with more detailed analyses and developmental studies seeking the means of implementing the advocated reforms. More specific task oriented studies of pupils engaging with these ideas will help in building the path to a critical but constructive social education. The potential of social knowledge for enhancing people's ability to decide and act is the warrant for this, and a more just society its ultimate and urgent goal.

Notes and References

1 MACINTYRE, A. (1973–4) 'The essential contestability of some social concepts', *Ethics*, 84, pp. 1–9.
2 COULTER, J. (1979) *The Social Construction of Mind*, London, Macmillan.
3 See pages 84, 93–95.
4 MILL, J. (1971) *Autobiography*, London, Oxford University Press, p. 148.
5 HAYEK, F. (1973) *Law, Legislation and Liberty. Volume 1: Rules and Order*, London, Routledge and Kegan Paul, p. 19.

Author Index

Subject Index

Asquith, H., 169–71
Association for Education in
  Citizenship, 15, 23, 187, 188–9
autonomous model
  of human nature, 50–1

Birkbeck Schools, 102, 103
Britain, *passim*
British and foreign School Society
  (BFSS), 12, 13
Brougham, Lord, 102
bureaucracy, 29, 33

citizenship, 188–92
  see also civic education
civic education, 9, 14, 15, 16, 105,
  106, 140–5, 166–7, 187, 188–92,
  210, 214–17
community
  idea of, 52–4, 92–3, 116–17, 118,
  133, 208–10, 214–17
Crusoe, Robinson, 126, 137
curriculum, *passim*
  content of, 5–20, 44–59, 65–99,
  101–38, 139–85, 187–220,
  226–33
  economics in the, 101–38
  geography in the, 65–99
  history in the, 139–85
  and ideology, *passim*
  and politics, 6, 10–19, 27–34,
  221–33
  and school autonomy, 5
  social content of, 1, 5–19, 25–7,

44–59, 187–220, 221–33
  and social control, 10–19, 59
  and social education, 1–3, 5,
  6–19, 25–59, 221–33
  and social inequality, 2, 10–13,
  25–59, 80, 102–6, 116, 160,
  222–30
  and social participation, 2–3,
  8–10, 13–19, 25, 27–34, 50,
  58, 127–33, 191, 221, 226,
  230–3
  and social policy, 33–4
  social studies in the, 187–220
  and social subjects, *passim*
  and social system, 2, 5–19,
  25–59, 94–5, 159–60, 191,
  192–210, 213, 217, 224–33
cybernetics, 55

Darwinism, 57, 66, 91, 229
democracy, 27–34, 58–9, 207–8,
  214, 225, 229
  see also liberal tradition
division of labour
  see labour, division of

economic determinism, 78–86, 93–
  5, 228
economic geography, 40, 76
  see also geography
economics
  assumptions in, 127–33
  in the curriculum, 101–38
  images in, 106–12, 127–33,
  176–7